THE LITTLE BOOK OF
HISTORY

DK LONDON
Senior Art Editor Gillian Andrews
Project Art Editor Katie Cavanagh
Designer Vanessa Hamilton
Design Assistant Renata Latipova
Project Editors Alexandra Beeden, Sam Kennedy
Senior Editor Victoria Heyworth-Dunne
US Editor Christy Lusiak, Megan Douglass
Editorial Assistant Kate Taylor
Senior Managing Art Editor Lee Griffiths
Managing Editor Gareth Jones
Illustrations James Graham, Vanessa Hamilton
Senior Jacket Designer Surabhi Wadhwa
Jacket Editor Claire Gell
Jacket Design Development Manager Sophia MTT
Senior Production Controller Rachel Ng
Senior Production Editor Andy Hillard
Art Director Karen Self
Publisher Liz Wheeler
Publishing Director Jonathan Metcalf

DK DELHI
Senior Art Editor Mahua Mandal
Project Editor Antara Moitra
Art Editor Sonali Rawat Sharma
Assistant Art Editor Anurag Trivedi
Assistant Editor Antara Raghavan
Pre-production Manager Balwant Singh
DTP Designer Umesh Yadav
Production Manager Pankaj Sharma
Picture Researchers Aditya Katyla, Deepak Negi
Picture Research Manager Taiyaba Khatoon
Senior Jacket Designer Suhita Dharamjit
Jackets Editorial Coordinator Priyanka Sharma
Managing Jackets Editor Saloni Singh
Managing Art Editors Sudakshina Basu, Govind Mittal
Senior Managing Editor Rohan Sinha

Coproduced with
SANDS PUBLISHING SOLUTIONS
4 Jenner Way, Eccles, Aylesford, Kent ME20 7SQ
Editorial Partners David And Sylvia Tombesi-Walton
Design Partner Simon Murrell

original styling by
studio8 design

Content previously published in *The History Book*.
This abridged edition first published in United States in
2021 by DK Publishing, 1450 Broadway, Suite 801,
New York, NY 10018

For the curious
www.dk.com

CONTRIBUTORS

REG GRANT, CONSULTANT EDITOR

R G Grant has written extensively in the fields of
military history, general history, current affairs, and
biography. His publications have included the DK
books *Flight: 100 Years of Aviation*, *Battle at Sea*,
and *World War I: The Definitive Visual Guide*.

THOMAS CUSSANS

Thomas Cussans, writer and historian, has
contributed to numerous historical works. They
include DK's *Timelines of World History*, *History Year
by Year*, and *History: The Ultimate Visual Guide*. He
was previously the publisher of *The Times History of
the World* and *The Times Atlas of European History*.
His most recent published work is *The Holocaust*.

JOEL LEVY

Joel Levy is a writer specializing in history and
the history of science. He is the author of more
than 20 books, including *Lost Cities*, *History's
Greatest Discoveries*, and *50 Weapons That
Changed the World*.

PHILIP PARKER

Philip Parker is a historian specializing in the
classical and medieval world. He is the author of the
DK Companion Guide to World History, *The Empire
Stops Here: A Journey Around the Frontiers of the
Roman Empire*, *The Northmen's Fury: A History of
the Viking World*, and general editor of *The Great
Trade Routes: A History of Cargoes and Commerce
Over Land and Sea*. He was a contributor to *DK
History Year by Year* and *DK History of the World in
1000 Objects*. He previously worked as a diplomat
and a publisher of historical atlases.

SALLY REGAN

Sally Regan has contributed to over a dozen DK titles
including *History*, *World War II*, and *Science*. She is
also an award-winning documentary maker for
Channel Four and the BBC in the UK.

PHILIP WILKINSON

Philip Wilkinson has written many books on
historical subjects, heritage, architectural history,
and the arts. As well as bestsellers such as *What
The Romans Did For Us* and widely-praised titles
such as *The Shock of the Old* and *Great Buildings*,
he has contributed to numerous encyclopedias
and popular reference books.

CONTENTS

THE MEDIEVAL WORLD
500–1492

THE EARLY MODERN ERA
1420–1795

CHANGING SOCIETIES
1776–1914

THE MODERN WORLD
1914–PRESENT

The ultimate aim of history is human self-knowledge. In the words of 20th-century historian R. G. Collingwood: "The value of history is that it teaches us what man has done and thus what man is." We cannot hope to understand our lives without it.

History itself has a history. From earliest times, all societies—literate or preliterate—told stories about their origins or their past, usually imaginative tales centering around the acts of gods and heroes. The first literate civilizations also kept records of the actions of their rulers, inscribed on clay tablets or on the walls of palaces and temples. But at first these ancient societies made no attempt at a systematic inquiry into the truth of the past; they did not differentiate between what had really happened and the events manifest in myth and legend.

Ancient historical narrative

In the 5th century BCE, the Greek writers Herodotus and Thucydides were the first to explore questions about the past through the collection and interpretation of evidence—the word "history," first used by Herodotus, means "inquiry" in Greek. Herodotus's work still contained a considerable mixture of myth, but Thucydides' account of the Peloponnesian War satisfies most criteria of modern historical study. It was based on interviews with eyewitnesses of the conflict and attributed events to human agency rather than the intervention and actions of the gods.

Thucydides had invented one of the most durable forms of history: the detailed narrative of war and political conflict, diplomacy, and decision-making. The subsequent rise of Rome to dominance of the Mediterranean world encouraged historians to develop another genre of broader scope: the account of "how we got to where we are today." The Hellenic historian Polybius (200–118 BCE) and the Roman historian Livy (59 BCE–17 CE) both sought to create a narrative of the rise of Rome—a "big picture" that would help make sense of events on a large timescale. Although restricted to the Roman world, this was the beginning of what is sometimes called "universal history," which attempts to describe progress from earliest origins to the present as a story with a goal, giving the past apparent purpose and direction.

At the same period in China, historian Sima Qian (c. 145–86 BCE) was similarly tracing Chinese history over thousands of years, from the legendary Yellow Emperor (c. 2697 BCE) to the Han dynasty under Emperor Wu (c. 109 BCE).

Moral lessons

As well as making sense of events through narratives, historians in the ancient world established the tradition of history as a source of moral lessons and reflections. The history writing of Livy or Tacitus (56–117 CE), for instance, was in part designed to examine the behavior of heroes and villains, meditating on the strengths and weaknesses in the characters of emperors and generals, providing exemplars for the virtuous to imitate or shun. This continues to be one of the functions of history. French chronicler Jean Froissart (1337–1405) said he had written his accounts of chivalrous knights fighting in the Hundred Years' War "so that brave men should be inspired thereby to follow such examples." Today, historical studies of Lincoln, Churchill, Gandhi, or Martin Luther King, Jr., perform the same function.

The "Dark Ages"

The rise of Christianity in the late Roman Empire changed the concept of history in Europe. Historical events came to be viewed by Christians as divine providence, or the working out of God's will. Skeptical inquiry into what actually happened was usually neglected, and accounts of miracles and martyrdoms were generally accepted as true without question. The Muslim world, in this as in other ways, was frequently more sophisticated than Christendom in Medieval times, with the Arab historian Ibn Khaldun (1332–1406) railing against the blind, uncritical acceptance of fanciful accounts of events that could not be verified.

Neither Christian nor Muslim historians produced a work on the scale of the chronicle of Chinese history published under the Song dynasty in 1085, which recorded Chinese history spanning almost 1,400 years and filled 294 volumes.

Renaissance Humanism

Whatever the undoubted merits of other civilizations' traditions of history writing, it was in Western Europe that modern historiography evolved. The Renaissance—which began in Italy in the 15th century, then spread throughout Europe lasting until the

end of the 16th century in some areas—centered upon the rediscovery of the past. Renaissance thinkers found a fertile source of inspiration in classical antiquity, in areas as diverse as architecture, philosophy, politics, and military tactics. The humanist scholars of the Renaissance period declared history one of the principal subjects in their new educational curriculum, and the antiquary became a familiar figure in elite circles, rummaging among ancient ruins and building up collections of old coins and inscriptions. At the same time, the spread of printing made history available to a much wider audience than ever before.

The Enlightenment

By the 18th century in Europe, the methodology of history—which consisted of ascertaining facts by criticizing and comparing historical sources—had reached a fair level of sophistication. European thinkers had reached general agreement on the division of the past into three main periods: Ancient, Medieval, and Modern. This periodization was at root a value judgment, with the Medieval period, dominated by the Church, viewed as a time of irrationality and barbarism and separating the dignified world of the ancient civilizations from the newly emerging, rational universe of modern Europe. Enlightenment philosophers wrote histories that ridiculed the follies of the past.

The Romantic spirit

In stark contrast, the Romantic movement that swept across Europe from the late »

18th century found an intrinsic value in the difference between the past and the present. The Romantics drew inspiration from the Middle Ages, and instead of seeing the past as a preparation for the modern world, Romantic historians tried the imaginative exercise of entering into the spirit of past ages. Much of this was associated with nationalism. The German Romantic thinker Johann Gottfried Herder (1774–1803) burrowed into the past in search of roots of national identity and an authentic "German spirit." As nationalism triumphed in Europe in the 19th century, much of history became a celebration of national characteristics and national heroes. Every country wanted to have its sacred heroic history, just as it had its flag and its national anthem.

The "Grand Narrative"
In the 19th century, history became increasingly important and took on the quality of destiny. Arrogantly, European civilization saw itself as the goal to which all history had been progressing and constructed narratives that made sense of the past in those terms. The German philosopher Georg Wilhelm Friedrich Hegel (1770–1831) articulated a grand scheme of history as a logical development, which culminated in the end point of the Prussian state. Philosopher and social revolutionary Karl Marx (1818–1883) later adapted Hegel's scheme into his own theory ("historical materialism"), in which he claimed that economic progress, which caused conflict between the social classes, would inevitably

one day result in the proletariat seizing power from the bourgeoisie, while the capitalist world order collapsed under its own inner contradictions. Arguably, Marxism was to prove the most influential and durable of all historical "grand narratives."

Like other areas of knowledge, in the 19th century history underwent professionalization and became an academic discipline. Academic history aspired to the status of a science, and the accumulation of "facts" was its avowed purpose. A gap opened up between "serious" history—often heavy on economic statistics—and the colorful literary works of popular historians, such as Jules Michelet (1798–1874) and Thomas Macaulay (1800–1859).

The rise of social history
In the 20th century, the subject matter of history—which had always focused on kings, queens, prime ministers, presidents, and generals—increasingly expanded to embrace the common people, whose role in historical events became accessible through more in-depth research. Some historians chose to disregard the "history of events" altogether, preferring instead to study social structures and the patterns of everyday life, beliefs, and ways of thinking ("mentalités") of ordinary people in different historical periods.

A Eurocentric approach
Until the second half of the 20th century, most world history was written as the story of the triumph of Western civilization. This approach was as implicit in Marxist versions

of history as in those histories that celebrated the progress of technology, enterprise, and liberal democracy. It did not necessarily imply optimism—there were numerous prophets of decline and doom. But it did suggest that essentially history had been made, and was still being made, by Europe. For instance, it was deemed acceptable for respected European historians to maintain that Africa had no significant history at all, having failed to contribute to the onward march of humanity.

Post-colonial revisionism

In the second half of the 20th century, the notion of a single, historical "grand narrative" collapsed, taking Eurocentrism with it. The postcolonial, postmodernist world was seen as requiring a multiplicity of histories told from the points of view of many different social identities. There was a surge of interest in the study of black history, women's history, and gay history, as well as histories narrated from an Asian, African, or American Indian standpoint. The marginal and oppressed in society were reassessed as "agents" of history rather than passive victims.

A riot of revisionism upturned much of the history of the world as commonly known to educated people in the West, although often without putting any satisfactory alternative version in place of the old. For example, the puzzlement that resulted can be seen in the response to the 500th anniversary in 1992 of Christopher Columbus's first voyage to the Americas. It would once have been expected to excite widespread celebration in the United States, but was in practice acknowledged with some embarrassment, if at all. People are no longer sure what to think about traditional history, its Great Men, and its epoch-making events.

A 21st-century perspective

The Little Book of History reflects this abandonment of "grand narratives" of human progress. It aims to present a general reader with an overview of world history through specific events, which can act as windows upon selected areas of the past. In line with contemporary concerns, this book also reflects the long-term importance of key factors such as population growth, climate, and the environment throughout history. At the same time, it gives an account of matters of popular historical interest, such as the Magna Carta and the American Civil War.

The book begins with the origins of humans and "prehistory" and progresses through different historical ages to the present day. In reality, of course, there were no such clear breaks between epochs, and where there is an overlap on dates, entries are included in the appropriate ideological era.

As this book illustrates, history is a process rather than a series of unconnected events. We can only speculate on how the events we experience today will shape the history of tomorrow. No one in the early 21st century can possibly claim to make sense of history, but it remains the fundamental discipline for anyone who believes, as the poet Alexander Pope did, that "the proper study of Mankind is Man." ■

ANCIENT CIVILIZATI

6000 BCE–500 CE

About 5,000 years ago, humans began to form societies of unprecedented complexity. These civilizations typically had state structures and social hierarchies; they built cities and monuments such as temples, palaces, and pyramids; and used some form of writing. The basis for the development of civilizations was progress in agriculture. When only part of the population was required to work in the fields to produce food, the rest could inhabit towns and palaces, performing a range of specialty functions such as bureaucrats, traders, scribes, and priests. The invention of civilization undoubtedly raised human life to a new level in many ways—in technology, the arts, astronomy, the measurement of time, literature, and philosophy—but also established inequality and exploitation as the basis of society, leading to larger-scale warfare as states expanded into empires.

Emerging civilizations

The earliest civilizations developed in areas where it was possible to practice intensive agriculture, usually involving use of irrigation systems—for instance, along the rivers of the Tigris and Euphrates in Mesopotamia (modern Iraq), the Nile in Egypt, the Indus in northern India and Pakistan, and the Yangtze and Yellow in China. Although these civilizations of Eurasia and North Africa seem to have been founded independently of one another, they developed multiple contacts over time, sharing ideas, technology, and even diseases. All followed a pattern in which stone tools (the Stone Age) were replaced by bronze (the Bronze Age) and then predominantly iron (the Iron Age). In the Americas, where the Olmec and Maya developed the civilizations of Mesoamerica, the use of stone tools persisted and most of the epidemic diseases that plagued Eurasia were unknown.

Writing and philosophy

From around 1000 BCE, Eurasian civilizations found an innovative momentum. The use of writing evolved from practical record-keeping to the creation of sacred books and classic literary texts that embodied the founding myths and beliefs of different societies, from the Homeric tales in Greece to the Five Classics of Confucianism in China and the Hindu Vedas in India. Forms of writing using an alphabet developed in

ONS

the eastern Mediterranean region and were spread by the Phoenicians—a race of traders and sailors.

The Greek city-states became a test bed for new forms of political organization, including democracy, and the source of new ideas in the arts and philosophy. The influence of Greek culture spread as far as northern India, while India itself was the birthplace of Buddhism—the first "world religion," winning converts beyond its society of origin.

Growing populations

The ancient world reached the peak of its classical period around 2,000 years ago. The world's population had grown from around 20 million at the time of the first civilizations to an estimated 200 million. About 50 million of these lived in a united Han China, while about the same number were under the governance of the Roman Empire, which had extended its rule to the shores of the Atlantic and the borders of Persia. In large part, the empires were successful because of efficient communications by land and water, and the ruthless deployment of military power. Long-distance trade routes linked Europe to India and China, and cities had expanded to a great degree—Rome's population was estimated at over 1 million.

Civilizations in decline

The causes of the decline of these powerful classical empires from the 3rd century CE have long been disputed among historians. Bred in overcrowded cities and transmitted along trade routes, epidemic diseases certainly played a part. Internal power struggles were also a major factor, leading to political fragmentation and a decline in the quality of government. But perhaps most crucial was the geographical limitation of the civilized areas of Eurasia. Both the Roman and Han empires built walls to mark and defend the borders of their empires, beyond which lived mostly nomadic or semi-nomadic "barbarian" tribes. The civilized societies had little or no military advantage over these peoples, who increasingly raided or settled within their territories. The eastern part of the Christianized Roman Empire survived until 1453, and Chinese civilization revived to full vigor under the Tang dynasty from 618, but Western Europe would take centuries to recover the levels of population and organization that it had known under the rule of Rome. ∎

ALL THE LANDS HAVE FALLEN PROSTRATE BENEATH HIS SANDALS FOR ETERNITY

THE TEMPLES OF ABU SIMBEL (c. 1264 BCE)

IN CONTEXT

FOCUS
Pharaonic Egypt

BEFORE

c. 3050 BCE Narmer unifies the kingdoms of Upper and Lower Egypt.

c. 2680 BCE Khufu begins construction of the Great Pyramid in Giza—it is the largest pyramid in history.

c. 1480 BCE Thutmose III conquers Syria, extending his empire as far as the Euphrates.

AFTER

c. 1160 BCE Ramses III fights off invasions of Egypt by Libyans and raiding tribes known as the Sea People.

c. 1085 BCE Collapse of the New Kingdom; Egypt is divided with Libyan rulers in the north and Theban priest-kings ruling in the south.

7th century BCE Egypt is invaded by Assyrians and then Persians.

The magnificent temple complex at Abu Simbel was, remarkably, moved 656 ft (200 m) inland and 213 ft (65 m) higher up in 1964–1968 to rescue it from the rising waters of the Nile during the construction of the High Aswan Dam.

A round 1264 BCE, the Egyptian pharaoh Ramses II (c. 1278–1237 BCE) had two mighty temples hewn out of the cliffs on the west bank of the Nile in southern Egypt. The entrance was guarded by four vast statues of the pharaoh, seated in glory and wearing the symbols of divine kingship, including the double crown that signified his authority over Upper and Lower Egypt. The temples were designed to signify and embody the unique status, ambition, and power of the ancient Egyptian pharaohs.

The pharaonic tradition
Ramses II inherited a tradition that was already very ancient: about 1,800 years earlier, King Narmer (called Menes by the ancient Greek historian Herodotus) first unified the kingdoms of the Upper (southern) and Lower (northern) Nile. Narmer's deeds were recorded on a stone palette, which was recovered from a temple at Hierakonpolis in the 19th century and provides one of the earliest known depictions of an Egyptian king.

The palette is inscribed with many of the symbols and traditions that would come to typify the pharaohs for the next three millennia. For instance, Narmer is shown holding an enemy by the hair, about to smite him, and Ramses II was often depicted in the same way—military might and supernatural strength were hallmarks of Egyptian kingship. The pharaoh, like the gods, was frequently shown much larger than ordinary mortals.

The geographical situation of Egypt—with its stark contrasts between the fertile Nile Valley and its delta, which empties in the north into the Mediterranean Sea, and the surrounding expanses of uninhabitable desert—gave rise to the kingdom's unique culture and civilization. The pharaoh was viewed as a living god who could control the order of the cosmos, including the annual flooding of the Nile, which brought fertilizing silt to replenish the soil. Pharaohs were also often depicted as farmers in agricultural scenes, representing their role as guardians of the land.

The Old Kingdom

The Old Kingdom that followed Narmer was ruled by a succession of dynasties that were led by powerful pharaohs, who channeled the bureaucratic and economic might of the unified kingdom into monumental building projects, such as the construction of the pyramids. These, in turn, stimulated scientific, technological, and economic development, increasing trade with other kingdoms in the Near East and the Mediterranean. In the Old Kingdom the predominant gods were Ra, the sun god; Osiris, the god of the dead; and Ptah, the creator. In the Middle and New Kingdoms that followed, which were ruled by families from Thebes, Amun became the main deity. As supreme ruler, the pharaoh was closely associated with the gods, and was believed to be the living incarnation of certain deities.

The New Kingdom

In the 22nd century BCE, the Old Kingdom collapsed. After what is known as the Intermediate Period, the Middle Kingdom dynasties restored unified control of Egypt from 2134 BCE until around 1750 BCE, when they were invaded by the Hyksos (probably Semites from Syria). The Hyksos, in turn, were expelled from Egypt in about 1550 BCE, with the XVIII dynasty—arguably the greatest and most important—coming to power and establishing the New Kingdom. By this time, immortality was believed to be available not just to the pharaoh, but to priests, scribes, and others who could afford offerings, spells, and mummification, and many tombs were dug into the Valley of the Kings to be filled with extraordinarily rich grave goods.

Under expansionist pharaohs, such as Thutmose III and Ramses II, Egyptian control was extended into Asia as far as the Euphrates River, and up the Nile into Nubia. It was no coincidence that Ramses built Abu Simbel in Nubia: as well as representing the divine glory of Egypt's pharaohs generally, the temple was a symbol of Ramses' control over the recently conquered territory. ■

The **Nile Valley** is bordered by **inhospitable desert**, but is **highly fertile** because the longest river in the world flows through it and **irrigates it**.

↓

| A **sophisticated, coherent, and unified** civilization develops over a **vast stretch** of terrain. | → ← | **Trade and conquest** boost the economy and **population levels**. A large, prosperous kingdom emerges. |

↓ ↓

Vast monuments, such as the Abu Simbel temple complex, are constructed, reflecting Egypt's power, wealth, and belief systems.

ATTACHMENT IS THE ROOT OF SUFFERING
SIDDHARTHA GAUTAMA
PREACHES BUDDHISM (c. 500 BCE)

IN CONTEXT

FOCUS
The spread of Buddhism

BEFORE
1200 BCE Vedic (aka Aryan) culture extends across northern and central India.

1200–800 BCE Oral Vedic traditions are written down in Sanskrit as the Vedas.

c. 600 BCE The Mahajanapadas, the 16 competing kingdoms of Vedic India, emerge.

AFTER
322 BCE Chandragupta Maurya founds the Mauryan Empire.

3rd century BCE Sri Lanka converts to Buddhism.

185 BCE The Mauryan Empire collapses.

1st century CE Buddhism arrives in China and Japan.

7th century Buddhist missionaries are invited to establish a monastery in Tibet.

Siddhartha rejects material life and preaches Buddhist philosophy.

Ashoka the Great conquers India and **unifies the empire.**

Ashoka **makes Buddhism the state religion** and spreads it across South and East Asia.

After the collapse of the Mauryan Empire, **Buddhism declines in India.**

Buddhism flourishes in Sri Lanka, Southeast Asia, China, Japan, Tibet, and Central Asia.

Siddhartha Gautama, better known as the Buddha, was born at the end of the Vedic Age (1800–600 BCE) into a South Asia in transition. In the country's caste system, the priestly Brahmins and the warrior-elite Kshatriyas ranked highest, and it was into this latter group that Siddhartha Gautama was born.

India was then a ferment of sects and new ideologies, some of which espoused a philosophy renouncing the material world. Siddhartha developed a similar philosophy based on mystical Hinduism, but he also rejected the increasingly rigid strictures of Vedic ritual and the inherited piety of the Brahmins. Renouncing material possessions, he sought and eventually found enlightenment, and became the

Buddha. He preached in northeast India and founded the Sangha—the monastic order of Buddhism—to continue his ministry.

For the next two to three centuries, Buddhism remained one among several minor sects but, under the Mauryan emperor Ashoka the Great (304–232 BCE), it became India's state religion. Ashoka's reign had proceeded initially through bloody conquest, but in around 261 BCE he had a change of heart. From then he embraced a new model of kingship and religious philosophy based on a creed of tolerance and nonviolence. He extended Mauryan control and, his Buddhism proving a powerful unifying force, succeeded in joining all of India, except the southern tip, into an empire of 30 million people.

A world religion

Having established Buddhism as the state religion, Ashoka founded monasteries, and sponsored scholarship. He sent Buddhist missionaries to every corner of the subcontinent and abroad as far as Greece, Syria, and Egypt. His missions established Buddhism initially as an elite pursuit, but the religion went on to take root at all levels of society in Sri Lanka, Southeast Asia, along the Silk Road in the

Stone reliefs depicting the life of Buddha decorate gateways of The Great Stupa at Sanchi, commissioned by the emperor Ashoka in the 3rd century BCE.

Indo–Greek kingdoms (in modern-day Pakistan and Afghanistan), and later in China, Japan, and Tibet. In India—its birthplace—Buddhism started to decline after Ashoka's death in 232 BCE, affected by a resurgence of Hinduism and then the arrival of Islam. Outside India, however, its tradition and scholarship flourished, evolving into multiple strands including Zen Buddhism, Theravada or Hinayana Buddhism, Mahayana Buddhism, and Vajrayana Buddhism.

The first religion to have spread widely beyond the society in which it originated—so the first "world religion"—Buddhism is also one of the oldest, having been practiced since the 6th century BCE. ∎

The Buddha

The life history of Siddhartha Gautama is obscured by the myth and legend that has grown up around him. Different

traditions give different chronologies for his birth and death, but many agree on 563–483 BCE. Said to have been born miraculously through the side of his mother, Siddhartha was raised in luxury in the palace of his father, King Suddhodana Tharu, leader of the Shakya clan.

A the age of 29, Siddhartha rejected this luxurious life and left his wife and child, renouncing material things to seek enlightenment through asceticism. Having spent six years wandering and meditating, he achieved

enlightenment and became the Buddha, but instead of ascending to nirvana, the transcendent state that is the goal of Buddhism, he chose to remain and preach his new message, the *dharma*.

Gathering followers who formed the Sangha, a monastic order, the Buddha pursued his ministry until he died, at age 80. He urged his disciples to follow the *dharma*, instructing them: "All individual things pass away. Strive on, untiringly."

ADMINISTRATION IS IN THE HANDS OF THE MANY AND NOT OF THE FEW
ATHENIAN DEMOCRACY (c. 507 BCE)

IN CONTEXT

FOCUS
Greek politics and philosophy

BEFORE
14th–13th centuries BCE Mycenaean settlement at Athens, with fortification of the Acropolis.

c. 900 BCE Political union of small towns in Attica into a city-state centered on Athens.

c. 590 BCE Reforms of Solon open the political machinery of Athens to all citizens, regardless of class.

AFTER
86 BCE Athens sacked by Romans under General Sulla.

c. 50 BCE Beginning of the Roman philhellene movement; Athens becomes the focus of imperial benefactors.

529 CE Christian Emperor Justinian I closes Plato's school and drives out pagan scholars.

The term "democracy" comes from the Greek words *demos* (people) and *kratos* (rule). The democracy that developed in ancient Athens around 507 BCE and flourished in its purest form from 462 to 322 BCE, albeit with some interruptions, provided the model for what has become the dominant form of government in the world: by 2015, 125 of the world's 195 countries were electoral democracies. The democracy of ancient Athens, however, differed from its modern form, reflecting the history of Athens and the warring Greek states of the age.

Oligarchs and hoplites
After the chaos of the ancient Greek Dark Ages—a period that followed the breakdown of Mycenaean civilization around 1100 BCE and lasted until about the 9th century BCE—most of the emergent city-states evolved into oligarchies, with powerful nobles monopolizing government and serving their own interests. In Athens, the Areopagus—a council and law court consisting of men of aristocratic birth—controlled the machinery of state, appointing officials and serving as a civil court, while the lower classes (*thetes*) were excluded from office.

However, the development of the "hoplite" model of citizen-soldiery in the 8th to 7th centuries BCE proved disruptive to those who were in power, as it led to a certain level of egalitarianism. Hoplites were men in the heavy infantry, mainly free citizens, whose primary tactic was the phalanx—a military formation in which soldiers stood in tightly packed ranks, with each man's shield protecting the hoplite to his left. Any man who could afford the arms and armor would be putting his life on the line to defend the state. As a result, a kind of middle class emerged, which declared that service should bring full citizenship and political representation. At the same time, the lower classes were also making demands, and tensions between them and the higher orders over key issues, such

Pericles

Pericles (c. 495–429 BCE) became Athens' most famous democrat and the leading man of the city-state for about 30 years. He came to prominence around 462 BCE, when he helped the politician Ephialtes dismantle the Areopagus—the last bastion of oligarchic control. After Ephialtes' death, Pericles undertook further reforms, including the introduction of pay for those serving in the courts, making it possible for even the poorest citizen to have his say. He is also believed to have helped drive Athens' assertive foreign policy as the city sought to exploit its dominance of the Delian League. During the 440s and 430s BCE, Pericles was involved in an ambitious public building program that provoked controversy at home, where he fought off revolt, and abroad, where he was condemned for requisitioning money from the Delian League to pay for the Parthenon. Nonetheless, he was popular and was elected as general every year from 443 BCE.

as land reform and debt slavery, threatened to lead to civil breakdown.

Solon and Cleisthenes

In Athens, some of these tensions were eased around 594 BCE by the reforms of the statesman Solon. He established a law that declared all citizens could vote in matters of state, and that a law court should admit all citizens. At the same time, however, he mollified the upper classes by introducing a graded oligarchy in which power corresponded to wealth—the aristocracy was to control the highest offices, the middle class the lesser offices, and the poor could be selected by lot to serve on juries.

In the late 6th century BCE, Athens fell under the sway of the tyrant Pisistratus and his sons. In response, a faction of aristocrats led by Cleisthenes allied with lower-ranking members of society to take power. The institution of true democracy in Athens is traditionally dated to this point—around 507 BCE. Cleisthenes introduced true popular government, or direct democracy, enabling all citizens of Athens to vote directly on Athenian policy (unlike in a contemporary representative democracy, in which the people elect representatives to act as the legislature). He also reorganized the citizenry into units by geography rather than kinship, breaking the traditional ties that underpinned Athenian aristocratic society, and established sortition—the random selection of citizens for government »

Aristocratic oligarchy monopolizes **power**.

↓   ↓

| Poor farmers are forced into **debt slavery**, causing major **resentment**. | Middle-class hoplites achieve **military success**, leading to desire for **representation**. |

↓   ↓

Pressure for change is strong. The limited political reforms of Solon **fail to meet the demands** of the lower and middle classes.

↓

Pisistratus achieves **economic reforms**, but he **does not satisfy** continuing demands for political reform.

↓

Cleisthenes implements democracy and other reforms creating a more egalitarian government.

The Parthenon, built in 447–438 BCE as a temple dedicated to the goddess Athena, is often seen as a symbol of democracy and Western civilization.

The Athenian constitution relied on a careful separation of powers. This was essential to make the practical operation of direct democracy possible. It also ensured that all citizens (men aged 20 and above) could serve and that power could not be abused.

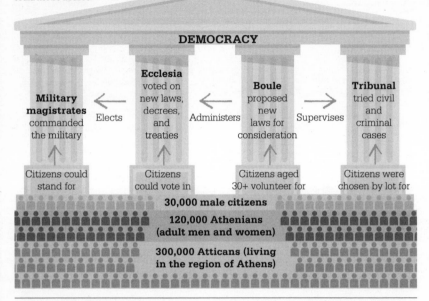

DEMOCRACY

Military magistrates commanded the military

← Elects

Ecclesia voted on new laws, decrees, and treaties

← Administers

Boule proposed new laws for consideration

→ Supervises

Tribunal tried civil and criminal cases

Citizens could stand for

Citizens could vote in

Citizens aged 30+ volunteer for

Citizens were chosen by lot for

30,000 male citizens

120,000 Athenians (adult men and women)

300,000 Atticans (living in the region of Athens)

positions rather than basing the choice on heredity. In addition, he restructured the Boule—a council of 500, which drew up legislation and proposed laws to the assembly of voters (*Ecclesia*). In 501 BCE, command of the military was transferred to popularly elected generals (*strategoi*).

In 462 BCE, Ephialtes became leader of the democratic movement in Athens and, together with his deputy Pericles, he dismantled the Areopagus council, transferring the majority of its powers to the Boule, the Ecclesia, and the citizen courts. Ephialtes was assassinated in 461 BCE and Pericles took over the political leadership, becoming one of the most influential rulers in the history of ancient Greece.

A perfect democracy?

Athens now had a genuine direct democracy, but many people were not allowed to participate in the system as they were not considered true citizens. Political rights were restricted to adult male Athenians; women,

foreigners, and enslaved people were excluded. In the 4th century BCE, out of the 300,000-strong population of Attica—the region of Greece controlled by Athens— just 30,000 men comprised the voting population. In theory, men became voting citizens at age 18, but as they were generally liable for two years of military service they were not enrolled on the rosters of the council until they turned 20, and did not come into their full political rights until the age of 30.

During the "Pentekontaetia"—the decades between Greek victory in the Persian War (479 BCE) and the start of the Peloponnesian War (431 BCE)—Athens reached the height of its glory. In 447 BCE, Pericles appropriated the treasury of the Delian League (the anti-Persian confederation that had become a vessel for Athenian hegemony) to build a magnificent temple (the Parthenon) on the rocky hill known as the Acropolis. Citizenship of Athens was highly coveted, and in 451 BCE Pericles passed a law restricting it to men whose parents were both Athenians.

A center of philosophy

As well as being the most powerful city-state in ancient Greece, Athens was also the crucible of a revolutionary new direction in philosophy, in large part due to Socrates (c. 469–399 BCE). Earlier Greek philosophers, collectively known as the pre-Socratics, had introduced a revolution of their own in human thought in the 5th and 6th centuries BCE. They rejected supernatural explanations for the world, the explanatory power of mythology, and the authority of tradition, and set out to discover the origins and workings of the natural world through reason and observation. The pre-Socratic natural philosophers developed theories about the elements, classifications of nature, and mathematical and geometric proofs.

Socrates turned his inquiries inward to more human matters—as Cicero said of him, "he brought philosophy down from heaven." Socrates' method was simply to ask questions—What is friendship? What is justice? What is knowledge? The Socratic method tended to lay bare the limits of existing thinking, often making people look foolish or pompous. Accordingly, Socrates was unpopular and eventually he was accused of two crimes by his enemies—corrupting youth by encouraging them to go against the government, and impiety, or lack of respect for the gods. Consequently, he was sentenced to death.

Socrates' successors

The fate of Socrates was taken as an indictment of democracy by his successors, particularly Plato (c. 428–348 BCE), who saw him as a martyr for truth. Plato ran a school (the Academy) and developed ideas about universal truths and metaphysics that have shaped all subsequent religion and philosophy in the Western world. His student Aristotle (384–322 BCE) became equally influential, setting up the Lyceum school and writing on such diverse topics as politics, ethics, law, and natural sciences.

Plato opposed democracy, because he believed that the people were not sufficiently equipped with philosophical grace to legislate, and if governance were left in the hands of the ordinary citizen

An Audience in Athens (1884), by Sir William Blake, captures the atmosphere at the Greek tragedy *Agamemnon* by Aeschylus c. 450 BCE. This period is regarded as the Golden Age of drama in ancient Greece.

tyranny would emerge. In his ideal republic, enlightened philosophers would rule as kings. He also challenged the basic principle of democracy—that of liberty (*eleutheria*)—which he believed could divert people from the proper pursuit of ethics and cause social disunity.

The fall of democracy

During the Peloponnesian War (431–404 BCE), in which Athens was ultimately defeated by the Spartans, Athenian democracy was twice suspended, in 411 and 404 BCE. Athenian oligarchs claimed that Athens' weak position was due to democracy and led a counterrevolution to replace democratic rule with an extreme oligarchy. In both cases, democratic rule was restored within one year.

Democracy flourished for the next eight decades. However, after the Macedonian conquest of Athens under Philip II and his son Alexander (later Alexander the Great) in 322 BCE, Athenian democracy was abolished. It was intermittently restored in the Hellenistic age in the 1st and 2nd centuries BCE, but the Roman conquest of Greece in 146 BCE effectively killed it off.

Although democratic rule had been quashed, Athenian science and philosophy lived on. The renown and influence of Plato and Aristotle endured through the ages that followed, and much of their work continues to influence Western thought to this day. ∎

THERE IS NOTHING IMPOSSIBLE TO HE WHO WILL TRY
THE CONQUESTS OF ALEXANDER THE GREAT (4TH CENTURY BCE)

IN CONTEXT

FOCUS
Hellenistic world

BEFORE
359 BCE Philip II of Macedonia begins his rise to power and develops innovative military technology and tactics.

338 BCE Philip II defeats the Greek states and becomes undisputed leader of Greece.

336 BCE On Philip's death, his son Alexander is proclaimed king of Macedonia.

AFTER
321 BCE After Alexander's death, squabbling between his generals breaks out into widespread civil war.

278 BCE Alexander's generals establish three Hellenistic kingdoms in Greece, the Middle East, and Europe.

30 BCE The Roman emperor Octavian annexes Egypt, the last Hellenistic kingdom.

East–West **cultural exchange** begins from an era of **Persian Wars**, with western provinces of Persian Empire becoming **Hellenized** and Macedonians adopting aspects of **Persian culture**.

Alexander's conquests force the rapid synthesis of Greek and Asian cultures, laying seeds of the Hellenistic age.

Hellenized societies in Egypt and West Asia **assimilated** into Roman Empire.

Hellenistic learning survives the fall of Rome in the **Byzantine Empire** and in the **Translation Movement** of the **Islamic Caliphate**.

I n one of the fastest and most daring military expansions in history, Alexander the Great, the young king of Macedonia in the Balkans, blazed a trail of conquest across most of the known world of his day, and set in motion a process of Hellenization—the spread of Greek culture and its fusion with non-Greek, Eastern traditions—which endured for centuries.

Alexander's father, Philip II, had transformed this peripheral state into a formidable military power, and had waged campaigns against his neighbors that culminated in Macedonia's domination over all of Greece. When he was assassinated in 336 BCE, Philip had been planning an expedition to West Asia, to free the former Greek city-states that had been reconquered by the Persian Empire. After securing the Macedonian throne by destroying his rivals, Alexander set about pursuing his father's quest, while satisfying his own thirst for glory.

King of the world

After forcing the other Greek city-states to accept his authority, in 334 BCE Alexander marched into Asia Minor (modern-day Turkey) at the head of an army of 43,000 foot soldiers and 5,500 cavalry. At its heart lay the Macedonian phalanx, a well-drilled, tight-knit corps of 15,000 men armed with the *sarissa*, a pike that was up to 23 ft (7 m) long. When combined with the shocking cavalry charge provided by the king's personal bodyguard, the Companions, the formation proved irresistible.

After an initial victory over the Persians at the Granicus River in the northwest, Alexander pressed on across Asia Minor. He stopped at Gordium in the central kingdom of Phrygia, where tradition held that he who could untie a complex knot made by the city's founder, would conquer the entire continent. Alexander, in a typically forthright move, cut the knot with his sword. He went on to twice defeat the far superior forces gathered by Darius III, the Persian emperor—at Issus (on the southern coast of Asia Minor) in 333 BCE and Gaugamela (in modern Iraq) in 331 BCE, subduing Egypt in the interval.

Having forced the Persians into submission, Alexander drove his troops eastward, across mountains, deserts, and rivers into Afghanistan and Central Asia, and on to the Indian Punjab, ruthlessly crushing all resistance. He would have pushed further into India, but in 325 BCE his exhausted men refused to go on.

The Hellenistic legacy

Alexander was now the king of a vast and ethnically diverse empire that included 70 newly founded cities, united by a common Greek culture, customs, and language, and linked by trade routes; although the process of Hellenization was already underway in the western half of Persia before his expedition, Alexander had accelerated its spread throughout the Middle East.

In 323 BCE, Alexander died—most likely from disease but perhaps by poisoning—without naming a successor. His empire was carved up by his leading generals, but some of the Hellenistic dynasties they founded, notably Seleucid Syria and Babylon and Ptolemaic Egypt, survived until Roman times. ∎

Alexander the Great

Throughout antiquity, Alexander was widely regarded as the most remarkable man who ever lived, and in terms of the breadth and duration of his renown, which saw him become a key figure in national literature from Central Asia to Western Europe, he is one of the most famous men in history.

Born in 356 BCE, to parents who claimed descent from demigods and heroes, Alexander's education under the philosopher Aristotle ensured he was steeped in Greek legend, and he came to believe he was invincible, even divine. As a general he was decisive, bold to the point of recklessness—with his own life and those of his men—and a brilliant tactician. He maintained the loyalty of his forces throughout his long and arduous campaign, but his quick and violent temper, fueled by his heavy drinking, occasionally spurred him to eliminate those closest to him, including his friends. Alexander died at age 32, at the height of his power. His funeral cortège was hijacked by Ptolemy, one of his generals, and diverted to Alexandria in Egypt, where his tomb was later visited by Julius Caesar, but is now lost.

IF THE QIN SHOULD EVER GET HIS WAY WITH THE WORLD, THEN THE WHOLE WORLD WILL END UP HIS PRISONER

THE FIRST EMPEROR UNIFIES CHINA (221 BCE)

IN CONTEXT

FOCUS
Han China

BEFORE
1600–1046 BCE Shang dynasty rules.

c. 1046–771 BCE Western Zhou dynasty.

771–476 BCE Spring and Autumn Period (the first half of the Eastern Zhou dynasty).

551–479 BCE Life of Kong Fuzi (known as Confucius).

476–221 BCE Warring States Period (the second half of the Eastern Zhou dynasty).

AFTER
140–87 BCE Reign of Han Emperor Wudi (Liu Che)—a time of imperial expansion.

220–581 CE Three Kingdoms and Six Dynasties Period.

581–618 Sui dynasty.

618–907 Tang dynasty.

China is probably the most enduring coherent state in world history, and to an extraordinary extent this is due to the will of one man: Qin Shi Huang, the self-styled First Emperor. Before he unified ancient China in 221 BCE, it was a region of diverse states, differing in culture, ethnicity, and language. During the era known to Chinese historians as the Spring and Autumn Period (771–476 BCE), the region was nominally under the control of Zhou dynasty kings, but in reality their feudal system of government meant that only a token authority rested with the royal throne, while feudal lords held genuine power over what were effectively autonomous states. Up to 140 small states competed for power and territory.

The Spring and Autumn Period gave way to the Warring States Period (476–221 BCE), in which power was consolidated into the hands of seven kingdoms: Qi, Chu, Yan, Han, Zhao, Wei, and Qin. At this point in China's history it was by no means certain that an over-arching Chinese identity or state would emerge. If anything, it was more likely that the considerable geographical, climatic, cultural, and ethnic differences between the various kingdoms would see the region develop in a similar fashion to Europe many centuries later, with multiple distinct and divergent national entities.

The rise of Qin
In 247 BCE, a 13-year-old prince named Ying Zheng succeeded to the throne of Qin. He inherited a militarized state, in which effective bureaucracy, powerful armies, and competent generals combined to produce a formidable and ruthless war machine. Zheng had rivals executed or exiled, appointed very effective generals and counselors, and conquered the six

other states in the region, so that by 221 BCE all seven states were unified under his rule. Disdaining the old title of king (*Wang*), he styled himself as emperor (*Huangdi*). Since he was the first (*Shi*) emperor of the Qin dynasty, he was known as Qin Shi Huang.

The governing philosophy of the Qin state had been legalism: strict centralization of power and severity in enforcing adherence to the law. The emperor now set about applying this philosophy throughout the whole of China, ruthlessly imposing cultural, linguistic, economic, and technological unity. All scripts except Xiaozhuan (small seal script) were banned. In addition, according to legend, the emperor gave orders for 400 Confucian scholars to be buried alive and all existing books to be burned; his reign was to mark a new "Year One" in the history and culture of China. He also introduced a host of economic reforms—there was to be a single, unified system of weights and measures, a uniform coinage, and even the gauge of cart tracks was standardized so that axle-widths could be the same across the empire.

The new order

The new social and political order of the empire reflected changes that had been underway since the Spring and Autumn Period. The feudal system was abolished, so the mass of peasantry now owed their allegiance to the state rather than feudal or clan lords. Over 100,000 noble families were relocated to the emperor's capital city Xianyang (near Xi'an, in the Shaanxi province), and their arms were confiscated, melted down, and then cast into giant statues. During the Warring States Period, the pressure of incessant military competition had generally favored the emergence of more meritocratic avenues for advancement, thereby facilitating social mobility while undermining the importance of noble lineage. In the Qin dynasty, aristocratic rule was replaced with a centralized bureaucratic administration and the country was divided into 36 commanderies, which were administrative divisions controlled by appointed (not hereditary) governors. Censors, or inspectors, traveled the country to enforce adherence to Qin law.

The Qin dynasty also saw the emergence of a new scheme of social stratification, with society divided into four classes: gentlemen (*Shi*), peasants (*Nong*), and two new classes that had emerged during the Zhou dynasty—artisans (*Gong*) and merchants (*Shang*). The educated gentry would replace the nobility as the main source of state officials. The merchant class was officially the »

Qin Shi Huang

As First Emperor of China, Ying Zheng (later known as Qin Shi Huang, 260–210 BCE) was a truly pivotal figure in Chinese history, uniting the country and ushering in a period of imperial rule that lasted nearly 2,000 years. He was a brutal despot but was also innovative, dynamic, and energetic—reports claim that he needed just one hour's sleep per night and he set himself a daily work quota, measured by the weight of papers that he needed to go through. He regularly walked the city streets in disguise to keep tabs on the populace, and he made five great tours of inspection of the empire. Highly paranoid and fearful of possible attempts on his life (he survived at least one assassination attempt), the emperor became obsessed with the quest for immortality, sponsoring expeditions to look for magic ingredients and mystics who could brew an elixir of life, to enable him to live forever. Ironically, his death at the age of 50 might well have been linked to his consumption of toxic mercury-based potions that he had taken to extend his life.

lowest and most despised of the orders, and was subject to legal discrimination; however, wealthy merchants were able to use their financial muscle to become important political players.

Great works

Among Qin Shi Huang's greatest achievements were his ambitious civil engineering projects, although there was a great human cost as many lost their lives in the process. He is traditionally credited with building the first part of the Great Wall of China, to keep out nomadic tribes in the north, by connecting parts of old walls erected by the Warring States and then adding thousands of miles of new wall. Other projects included constructing the Lingqu canal, which linked the Xiang and Li rivers so military supplies could be transported from northern to southern China, and building military roads including "the Straight Road," which was 497 miles (800km) long and ran from Xianyang to the Great Wall.

Most famous of all the emperor's ventures was the construction of his own elaborate mausoleum complex, which took 38 years and over 700,000 workers to construct. It consisted of a giant pyramid covered in earth to create an immense mound, 328ft (100m) high and 1,640ft (500m) across. Within the pyramid was a tomb in which his beloved empire was recreated in miniature, complete with liquid mercury rivers and seas. Buried around the tomb were large pits filled with thousands of life-size terra-cotta warriors, bureaucrats, and entertainers, all intended to serve the emperor in the afterlife. Workers on the tomb were killed after completing their tasks so the secrets of the mausoleum's location and contents died with them, and the tomb remained undiscovered for over 2,000 years.

Despite the megalomaniacal exertions of the First Emperor, the Qin dynasty was to prove short-lived. Peasant unrest caused by deep-seated resentment over the brutal extortions of money and the many years of forced labor, plus bankruptcy as a result of over-ambitious civil works, combined to undermine the carefully ordered administration of the emperor and his leading counselors, chief among them the chancellor Li Si.

When the First Emperor died in 210 BCE his youngest son, Hu Hai, under the influence of advisor and former tutor Zhao Gao, seized the throne and exiled—and later executed—Li Si. Hu Hai was subsequently murdered after just three years of being in

Guarding the tomb of Emperor Qin Shi Huang, these life-size terra-cotta soldiers were discovered in 1974 by workers digging a well. The figures were originally brightly painted and each has a unique facial expression.

Large region comprises many small, **culturally diverse** states.

Qin state conquers the other six states.

Chinese unity is strengthened further.

Seven major states emerge and engage in frequent **warfare** to gain **power** and **territory**.

Qin Shi Huang imposes unification, standardization, and homogeneity.

power and his successor, Zi Ying, found his authority so reduced that he adopted the title of king, rather than emperor.

The Han Dynasty

China collapsed into rebellion and civil unrest, and a few days after Zi Ying's accession, the Han general Liu Bang marched into Xianyang. The following year, in 206 BCE, he declared himself emperor of the Han dynasty, which would go on to rule China for 400 years, shaping its subsequent history to such an extent that the main ethnic group in China is now known as the Han.

The Han expanded Chinese territory in all directions—west to Xinjiang and Central Asia, northeast to Manchuria and Korea, and south to Yunnan, Hainan, and Vietnam. Most importantly, they consumed the powerful Xiongnu Empire in the north. They also reintroduced Confucianism as the official state philosophy: Confucian education and ethics soon became the cornerstones of the scholar-bureaucracy, eventually forming the basis for the all-important civil service examination system, which would give a meritocratic basis to imperial institutions and combat the power of the aristocracy for millennia to come.

Han success in building and maintaining a unified, centralized China was based on the foundations that had been laid down by the First Emperor. The Han dynasty finally collapsed in 220 CE, amid a foment of civil unrest and natural disasters that convinced the Chinese that

their dynasty had lost "the mandate of heaven," giving way to the violent and chaotic era known as the Three Kingdoms and Six Dynasties Period. Despite the devastating cost of this breakdown, which saw the Chinese population plummet from 54 million in 156 CE to 16 million in 280 CE, the concept of a unified China survived 360 years of division, enabling the Sui dynasty to reunify China in 581.

The influence of the First Emperor is still felt in modern China, and Chairman Mao Zedong (1893–1976) explicitly drew on the emperor for inspiration. "You accuse us of acting like Qin Shi Huang," Mao thundered in a 1958 tirade against intellectual critics. "You are wrong. We surpass him a hundred times. When you berate us for imitating his despotism, we are happy to agree! Your mistake was that you did not say so enough." ■

Confucius is generally considered to be the most influential philosopher in Chinese history. His teachings emphasized the importance of morality, integrity, humility, and self-discipline.

THUS PERISH ALL TYRANTS

THE ASSASSINATION OF JULIUS CAESAR (44 BCE)

IN CONTEXT

FOCUS
Fall of the Roman Republic

BEFORE
509 BCE Rome becomes a republic in which a small number of wealthy families share power.

202 BCE Rome defeats Carthage in North Africa and the empire expands rapidly.

88–82 BCE Civil war between rival generals Sulla and Marius tips the republic into crisis.

AFTER
31 BCE Octavian's victory at the Battle of Actium leads to his accession as Rome's first emperor and the end of the republic.

79 CE Vesuvius erupts, destroying Pompeii.

2nd century CE The Roman Empire reaches its greatest extent, with a population of around 60 million people.

The **oligarchic** political system in the **Roman Republic** is corrupt and decaying.

Rome's **nobility** dominate the **Senate**, protecting their privileges at the expense of political change, leading to a **crisis of the republic**.

After successful military campaigns, **Julius Caesar becomes dictator** and forces **political and social reforms** on the nobility.

Fearing Caesar's popularity and power, a group of senators assassinate him.

Octavian wins the **civil war** to determine Caesar's heir. Calling himself **Augustus**, he becomes the **first emperor of Rome**.

Augustus ensures that **the office of emperor** survives by making **Tiberius** his heir, transforming Rome into a **hereditary monarchy**.

O n March 15, 44 BCE, the life of Julius Caesar, dictator of Rome, came to a bloody end at the hands of a faction of aristocratic senators who were determined to rescue the Roman Republic from what they saw as Caesar's tyranny. In reality, the dictator's death did not save the republic: it merely unleashed the latest in a series of civil wars, which exhausted the Roman state. It was left powerless to resist the rise to absolute power of Caesar's great-nephew Octavian. Taking the title Augustus, Octavian created a new political arrangement that enabled him to rule as emperor, bringing the 500-year-old Roman Republic to an end in all but name.

Republican origins

From its ancient beginnings as a cluster of small villages on seven hills by the Tiber River, Rome grew into a city-state that was just one of many on the Italian peninsula. According to legend, Rome was first ruled by kings, but in 509 BCE, the monarchy was overthrown and it became a republic. A new constitution allowed the election of two top officials, known as consuls, to run the state, but in order to prevent abuse of power, their term was limited to one year. The office of king was also prohibited, and special provision was made for the appointment of a dictator to replace the consuls in times of crisis—his term being limited to six months.

The fledgling Roman Republic proved remarkably successful: between 500 and 300 BCE, it increased its extent and power through a combination of conquest and diplomacy until it incorporated the whole of Italy. Between 202 and 120 BCE, Rome came to dominate parts of North Africa, the Iberian Peninsula, Greece, and what is now southern France. Its conquered territories were organized into provinces, ruled by short-term governors who maintained order and oversaw the collection of taxes.

By the 1st century BCE, Rome was a Mediterranean superpower, yet its long tradition of collective government, in which no individual could gain too much control, was being challenged by the personal ambitions of a few immensely powerful military men. A series of bloody civil wars, internal political struggles, and civil unrest culminated with the dictatorship of Julius Caesar, a brilliant general and statesman, whose murder at the hands of his political enemies led to the demise of the republic and the birth of the Roman Empire.

The republic crumbles

In the period in which Julius Caesar came to prominence on the Roman political scene (around 70 BCE), Rome was in turmoil: beset with ever worsening social and economic problems and torn by political conflict. Early in Rome's history, the non-enslaved population had been officially split into two classes: the patricians (members of the ancient hereditary nobility and wealthy landowners) and the plebeians, or plebs for short (the common people). On the formation of the republic, only patricians had been entitled to hold office in the Senate—Rome's governing and advisory council—but in 368–367 BCE, a constitutional amendment allowed the election of wealthier plebs, too, and the result was a power-sharing arrangement.

However, in reality, a small group of patrician families known as the Optimates (the "Best Men") had long dominated the Senate and jealously guarded their privileges. In the late Roman Republic, those who championed the rights of the plebs—the Populares (the "People's Men")—sought popular support against the Optimates, either in the interests of the people themselves, or more often, in pursuit of their own careers. The self-interested Optimates resisted making the social and economic reforms that were urgently required to meet the changing needs of the Roman people. In Italy and the provinces an unequal system of taxation and corrupt governance were causing social unrest, while in the city of Rome itself, the infrastructure was barely able to cope with a growing population. The empire's rapid expansion had brought a flood of enslaved labor from the provinces, driving many Roman farm workers and smallholders off the land and into the city in search of work.

The rise of Julius Caesar

Meanwhile, a handful of military leaders in Rome's provinces had begun to use their armies to jockey for political prominence. Among them was Julius Caesar, a highly intelligent and ambitious general from a patrician family who had aligned himself with the Populares and risen swiftly through the political ranks. Caesar was » intent on making the reforms necessary to meet the challenges of the republic, and so he maneuvered himself into a position that would allow him to achieve his goal.

In 60 BCE, Caesar became consul, and two years later he was appointed governor of the province of Gaul, a role which enabled him to remain abreast of developments in the Senate while also offering a springboard to military glory. In a series of masterful campaigns over the next eight years, he conquered Gaul, bringing the whole of what is now France, along with parts of Germany and Belgium, under his rule. He also led two expeditions to Britain, in 55 and 54 BCE. Caesar's heroic military exploits left him immensely rich and increased his personal prestige; he enjoyed the loyalty of his armies and the love of the Roman mob, upon whom he could now afford to lavish feasts, games, and money.

Buoyed by his achievements, Caesar attempted to dictate the terms on which he would return to Roman politics, demanding to be allowed to stand for a second consulship while remaining in command at Gaul. This put him on a collision course with the Optimates in the Senate, since Roman law required military leaders to relinquish control of their armies before entering Rome, a prerequisite for running for office. Caesar knew that if he agreed to enter the city as a private citizen, without

his armies, his political opponents would most likely attempt to try him for abuse of power during his first consulship.

Back in Rome, the Optimates, alarmed by the implications of Caesar's meteoric rise, allied themselves to one of his main political rivals, the renowned general Pompey. The Senate passed laws intending to strip Caesar of his command when he returned from Gaul, and in 49 BCE they declared him *hostis*, or public enemy. In response to this direct threat, Caesar did the unthinkable: he marched his army on Rome. En route, he paused at the border between the Gallic provinces and Italy proper: a small river called the Rubicon. Caesar was acutely aware that crossing the river would constitute a declaration of war against the Senate but, quoting the Athenian poet Menander, he announced *alea iacta est* ("let the dice roll") and led his men onward.

Caesar's new order

In the ensuing civil war, Caesar finally triumphed over Pompey's forces at the Battle of Pharsalus in northern Greece in 48 BCE. The defeated Pompey fled to Egypt for sanctuary, where he was assassinated. After crushing the remaining pockets of resistance, Caesar finally returned to Rome in 45 BCE, to consolidate his political position. In 46 BCE he accepted the dictatorship for 10 years; two years later, he was granted the

---

Julius Caesar

Gaius Julius Caesar was born in Rome in 100 BCE, to a patrician family of distinguished ancestry. From an early age, he grasped that money

was the key to power in a political system that had become hopelessly corrupt. He also quickly learned that forging a network of alliance and patronage would be crucial to his success.

After serving in the war to crush the slave revolt led by Spartacus in 72 BCE, Caesar was briefly taken hostage by pirates. Once he returned to Rome in 60 BCE, Caesar spent vast sums on buying influence and positions, eventually teaming up with the two other leading men in Rome,

Crassus and Pompey, to form the so-called First Triumvirate. Between 58 and 50 BCE, he formed a provincial power base in Gaul where, without the sanction of the Senate, he launched a series of campaigns that made him master of Western Europe, with fabulous wealth and powerful armies. However, these campaigns also earned him many opponents among the governing classes, who would eventually cut short both his career and his life.

The Cursus Honorum was the sequence of offices through which Roman patricians aspiring to power had to progress as they aged in order to reach the highest rank: consul.

Consuls
were chief judges, who chaired the Senate and commanded the army.

A separate series of ranks
governed offices for plebeians (those not of noble birth). The rank of aedile was the highest plebeians could hope to achieve.

Praetors
acted as judges and commanded armies in Rome in the consuls' absence.

Aediles had responsibility for maintaining the public buildings and temples, and for ensuring the city's grain supply.

Plebeian aediles
had a lower status than patrician aediles.

Quaestor was the first elected office. They supervised the use of state finances.

Tribunes
protected plebs from abuses of power by vetoing legislation or judgments.

Senators directed other magistrates and controlled the granting of public money.

office for life. Now in a position to begin the monumental task of reconstructing the Roman state and restoring stability to the empire, Caesar initiated far-reaching social and political reforms. He extended Roman citizenship; he enlarged the Senate, bringing in allies from among the provincial aristocracy; he established colonies outside Italy, to help spread Roman culture and knit the empire together; he spent lavishly on grandiose public works and buildings; he cut taxes; and he even reformed the Roman calendar, introducing the system of leap years that is still in use today. »

A murder plot

Caesar's pragmatic solutions for reestablishing unity in the empire after years of chaos found favor with many parts of society, yet at the same time, his increasingly autocratic attitude to power was alienating fellow members of the ruling class. They felt that Caesar was trying to destroy the cherished traditions of the Roman state, and to undermine the prestige of the nobility, and spread the rumor that he was planning to make himself king. Unfortunately, Caesar failed to quell the suspicions. He accepted unprecedented honors, such as assuming the title "Imperator" ("Victorious General") as a family name; he also allowed temples and statues to be erected in his honor, and had coins minted bearing his image. And when he adopted his grand-nephew, Octavian, there were fears that he was trying to establish a dynastic succession. Some members of the Senate concluded that the only solution to the problem was to assassinate Caesar, and so they hatched a conspiracy to carry it out.

Representing those opposed to the dictator's reforms—and the leading agent in the plot to murder him—Gaius Cassius Longinus was a general who had risen to political prominence during a largely disastrous campaign in Persia. Ancient Roman historians argued that Cassius's involvement was prompted by a combination of jealousy and greed. He is also said to have recruited the most important conspirator, Marcus Junius Brutus, a trusted colleague and confidante of Caesar, opposed to the dictator's presumed monarchic ambitions.

Death of a dictator

The assassination plot grew rapidly, eventually including 60 senators, among them many of Caesar's close colleagues. The plotters decided to strike at a meeting of the Senate that had been called for March 15, (the Ides of March). On the day, they gathered at Cassius's home, each senator concealing a dagger beneath his robes, before moving on to Pompey's Theater—part of a great civic complex that Caesar's old rival had constructed—where the Senate was meeting. A group of gladiators had been stationed in the theater itself, to help control any crowd problems. However, many of the conspirators were nervous and ready to flee, convinced that the plot had been uncovered.

Caesar had indeed been warned: a list of the plotters had been thrust into his hands, but he ignored it. His wife pleaded with him not to attend the Senate meeting, but one of the conspirators, stationed at Caesar's house, helped calm her fears. When Caesar arrived at the meeting, a conspirator distracted his deputy, Mark Antony, delaying him outside the theater. As Caesar took his seat, the conspirators drew their daggers and struck, stabbing him 23 times. In an ironic twist, Caesar breathed his last slumped against the base of a statue of his old rival Pompey.

The Second Triumvirate

Seized with manic fervor, the conspirators dipped their hands in Caesar's blood and rushed out into the Forum to proclaim their tyrannicide. In the power vacuum that followed, Mark Antony, and Caesar's heir, Octavian, promptly assumed control of the state, forming in 43 BCE a triumvirate (a group of three men holding power) with Lepidus, one of Caesar's former allies.

Needing to gather enough funds to stabilize their authority, and to remove political opposition, the triumvirate drew up a list of those who had supported Caesar's murderers, and declared them outlaws. Around 200 senators and more than 2,000 equites ("knights" or minor nobility) were either killed or had their estates confiscated. The treasury's coffers now filled, the triumvirate hunted down and destroyed Brutus and Cassius.

In 40 BCE, the triumvirs met again, this time to carve up the Roman world. Africa was given to Lepidus, the East to Mark Antony, and the West to Octavian. However, it was not long before Octavian went to war against Antony in north Africa, and, after defeating his forces at Actium in western Greece in 31 BCE, Octavian became the master of the Roman world.

Rome's first emperor

Octavian returned to Rome in 28 BCE and, instead of following Caesar's example, he renounced the dictatorial powers granted to him in order to wage his war against Antony. In 27 BCE, in gratitude for his service to Rome, the Senate bestowed on him the name Augustus ("revered personage") and granted him wide-ranging legal powers. Eventually, through political sleight of hand, he became Rome's sole ruler, controlling all aspects of the Roman state and command of the army.

An emperor in all but name (he was careful to spurn such titles, styling himself instead as princeps, or "first citizen"), over the next four decades, Augustus set about transforming the ruins of the republican system into an imperial autocracy, all the while maintaining the illusion that his authority was dependent on the will of the people. He loosely established the boundaries of the empire, pushed through reforms to clean up both private and public life, and crushed dissent. After the long periods of exhausting civil war, many in the empire were grateful for peace.

The Pax Romana

Indeed the might of the Roman military and the consequent improvements in security and stability across a vast stretch of territory, in what became known as the Pax Romana ("Roman Peace"), led to a growth in trade, economic activity, population, and general prosperity. The arts and culture flourished, public and private building works proliferated, and the provinces outside Italy underwent a process of Romanization, in which the Roman language, culture, laws, and institutions were embedded into diverse societies and across ethnic boundaries. Provincials were even granted full Roman citizenship after a period of military service.

However, for the regions beyond the bounds of empire, Augustus's Pax Romana often meant just the opposite. Even after reducing the army from 80 legions to a

The Ara Pacis Augustae altar in Rome is dedicated to Pax, the Roman goddess of peace. The processional frieze shows members of the Roman Senate with a priest.

permanent force of just 28, Augustus had to find employment for 150,000 soldiers. He launched a series of campaigns to extend borders, suppress and harry rebels and "barbarians," and enslave people from conquered areas.

An imperial legacy

By the end of his life in 14 CE, Augustus had established a new imperial system that would endure for centuries. For some years before his death, Augustus had prepared the way for an heir to succeed him, and retain control of the state. His step-son Tiberius was gradually granted powers until he could effectively be considered to be a co-emperor. This smoothed the transition of authority on Augustus' death, preventing a vacuum of power and ensuring continuity.

Augustus thus established the principle of direct succession and ensured the survival of the office of emperor. The system continued through multiple dynasties, with the empire reaching its height under the Nerva-Antonine dynasty when the emperor Hadrian ordered the building of a wall in northern Britain to mark the empire's outer limit.

The transition from republic to monarchy, while drastic, gave Rome a new stability. Masquerading as a democrat, Augustus created a new autocratic system of government, which, despite restricting political participation, was much better able to resist the compulsive upheavals that had plagued the Roman Republic a generation before. ■

BY THIS SIGN CONQUER
THE BATTLE OF MILVIAN BRIDGE (312 CE)

IN CONTEXT

FOCUS
The spread of Christianity

BEFORE
33 CE Crucifixion of Jesus.

46–57 Missionary journeys of St. Paul the Apostle.

64–68 CE When a fire breaks out in Rome, Emperor Nero kills hundreds of Christians as scapegoats; martyrdom of saints Peter and Paul.

284–305 Diocletian and Galerius suppress Christianity throughout the empire.

AFTER
325 The first Council of Nicaea defines the nature of orthodox Christian belief.

c. 340 Ulfilas, the "Moses of the Goths," begins to spread Arian Christianity to the Germanic tribes.

380 Christianity becomes the Roman Empire's official faith.

391 Pagan worship is banned in the Roman Empire.

Constantine I's adoption of Christianity after his victory at the Milvian Bridge gave the faith a huge boost: it rapidly gained more followers and began edging out the pagan cults.

I n October, 312 CE, Emperor Constantine I was stationed at the Milvian Bridge near Rome, waiting to join battle with Maxentius, his rival for control of the Western Roman Empire (in 285, the empire had been split into two halves, eastern and western, each ruled by an emperor and a deputy). Tradition says that in the days before the encounter, Constantine had a vision of a flaming cross in the heavens bearing the inscription *in hoc signo vinces* ("by this sign conquer"). This convinced him that he had the support of the god of the Christians, and this belief was upheld when his army went on to defeat Maxentius's men. In fact, the Christian god was not the first deity Constantine had auditioned; an earlier version of his vision had involved the Greek and Roman god Apollo. He appears to have been looking for theological "backup" to legitimize his ambition to become sole emperor, and a monotheistic supreme being may have seemed to him a good fit: a heavenly mirror image of his own position on Earth. Despite the legend of his divine vision, Constantine's conversion to Christianity seems to have been gradual rather than immediate—he was not baptized until many years later, on his deathbed. However, soon after his victory at the Milvian Bridge, he began the process of rehabilitating, and then exalting, Christianity; in 313 CE, he issued the Edict of Milan, a proclamation that established religious toleration for Christianity within the empire.

A multi-faith empire

For almost 300 years after the life of Jesus Christ, the religion based on his teachings remained a minor sect within the Roman Empire, practiced alongside many other faiths, both mono- and polytheistic. Some aspects of Christianity, such as its egalitarian nature, made it suspicious to the imperial authorities, however, and Christians were periodically persecuted.

All across the ancient world at this time, changing social, political, and economic conditions were reflected in cultural and religious changes; Christianity was just one of a number of monotheisms gaining popularity in the Roman Empire, including the Persian cult of Mithraism, with which it had much in common.

The rise of Christianity

In 324, after disposing of the emperor in the East, Constantine became sole ruler of the Roman Empire, and then sought to use Christianity as a unifying force across his diverse and fractious realm. To make the increasingly dominant eastern half easier to govern, he founded a new city called Constantinople (now Istanbul), consecrating it with both Christian and pagan rites, but allowing only Christian churches to be built. Although it would take time for all Roman citizens to convert to Christianity, in Constantine's reign, the higher ranks of society, seeking political advancement and personal favor with the emperor, flocked to the Church, and the emperor built basilicas across the empire.

Christianity, however, was not a single, uniform religion at this time, and splits, or schisms, formed. In 325, Constantine convened the Council of Nicaea—the first universal council of the Christian Church— mainly to settle the Arian schism, a theological dispute over whether Jesus was of the same substance as God.

Roman emperors derive authority and legitimacy from **pagan religions**.

Christianity's egalitarianism threatens to **disrupt the strict social order** of the Roman Empire.

Constantine sees Christianity, with its one supreme deity, as a **tool for unity**, and a **validation of imperial authority**.

After the Battle of Milvian Bridge, Constantine adopts Christianity. It later becomes the official religion of the Roman Empire.

The Church is refashioned in the image of the **Roman state**, with a **strict hierarchy** and **centralization of dogma**.

Rome is Christianized

In the mid-300s, Emperor Julian, an adherent of the old religion, tried to revive paganism, but it was too late: Christians had become a majority, at least in the East. The faith was increasingly bound up with empire, as the Roman state adopted and molded the Church into an instrument of social and political control, unity, and stability.

Under Emperor Theodosius I (reigned 379–395), pagan temples and cults were suppressed, heresy was outlawed, and Christianity became the official religion of the Roman Empire. Eventually, it also became the faith of the barbarian successor states in the Roman Western Empire, as well as of the Byzantine Empire in the East. Over the course of many centuries, the western (Catholic) and eastern (Orthodox) churches grew apart in doctrine and organization, but Christianity endured. ■

THE MEDIE
WORLD
500–1492

Historians call the period from 500 to 1500 "the Middle Ages," seeing it as a separate era sandwiched between the ancient world and modern times. In reality, there was never a clear break with the ancient world. In the eastern Mediterranean, the Roman Empire continued for almost 1,000 years after the fall of Rome, although it was rebranded by historians as the Byzantine Empire. The ancient tradition of a united China ruled by an emperor was revived in the 6th century and continued to the Ming dynasty, albeit with interruptions. Even in Western Europe, where the breakdown after the Roman Empire's collapse was most evident, Christian religion survived in Rome as the key marker for the distinction between what were considered "civilized" and "barbarian" societies.

The rise of Islam
The dominance of two mutually hostile monotheistic religions—Christianity and Islam—was the most distinctive characteristic of this period across much of Eurasia. The founding of Islam in the 7th century was a transformative event, and Arab armies inspired by the faith

altered the political landscape: Muslim rule spread from Spain in the west to central Asia in the east.

Although a united Islamic caliphate could not be sustained, the religion ensured a continuity of civilization even when power shifted from the Arabs to other peoples such as the Turks. The great cities of the Muslim world surpassed any in Christendom in size and sophistication, and Muslim scholars preserved the science of the ancient Greeks and built upon it. Islamic civilization remained dynamic and expansive throughout the entire medieval period.

Western European fortunes
In Western Europe, civilization fell drastically from the level achieved under the Roman Empire. Warrior kings ruled over a thinly spread population sustained by subsistence agriculture, and the area remained prey to non-Christian raiders and invaders, such as the Vikings and the Magyars, into the 10th century.

A nostalgia for ancient Rome led to King Charlemagne being crowned emperor in 800, but the Holy Roman Empire, based on the tradition Charlemagne founded, failed to unify Western Europe politically. In the absence of strong centralized state systems, feudal relationships held societies together.

From the 11th century, a revival of Western European culture, trade, and urban life gathered pace. The "Medieval Warm Period" (950–1250), when Europe experienced above-average temperatures, improved yields from agriculture; it was also a time when great cathedrals and castles were constructed. But even when the Christian crusaders fought their way to Jerusalem at the heart of the Muslim world, the flow of civilization was the other way, with Islamic scholars far advanced in medicine, philosophy, astronomy, and geography.

Expansion and contraction

By the 13th century, the world's population is believed to have risen to around 400 million—double its total at the high point of the ancient empires. A wide-ranging network linked Europe to China and the thriving trading kingdoms of Asia, by land along the Silk Road and by sea across the Indian Ocean. Cairo and Venice both became wealthy cities as focal points at the western end of this trade.

However, civilized life remained precarious. The Mongols—nomadic warriors from the Asian steppes—seized major cities from the Middle East to southern China, carrying out large-scale massacres. Lethal diseases were also highly prevalent. Carried along the trade routes in the mid-14th century, the Black Death epidemic may have killed a quarter of the world's population.

Inventions and progress

Technological progress was slow but cumulatively substantial. As the world's most advanced country, China was the ultimate source of most inventions, from paper and printing to the magnetic compass and gunpowder. Even relatively backward Europe benefited from improvements in shipbuilding and metalworking, and the invention and spread of the plow and the windmill transformed agriculture.

By the end of the Middle Ages, Western European kingdoms had developed from "feudal" states, based on oaths of loyalty, to more stable and centralized states, able to channel their key resources into the large projects of colonization and exploration. In the Americas, meanwhile, civilizations such as the Aztecs and Incas continued to evolve independently, untouched by developments in Eurasia and Africa, until the Spanish conquistadors arrived in the 16th century. ■

TRUTH HAS COME AND FALSEHOOD HAS VANISHED

MUHAMMAD RECEIVES THE DIVINE REVELATION (c. 610)

IN CONTEXT

FOCUS
The rise of Islam

BEFORE
c. 550 CE Fall of the Himyarite Kingdom in southern Arabia.

570 Birth of Muhammad.

611 Persian Khusrau Shah conquers the Byzantines in Egypt, Palestine, and Syria.

AFTER
622 Muhammad and his followers flee Mecca and take up residence in Medina.

637 Muslim army captures Jerusalem after a siege.

640 Muslim general Amr ibn al-As conquers Egypt.

661 Umayyad caliphate established by Muawiya at Damascus, Syria.

711 Muslim armies cross into Spain and conquer the Christian Visigothic kingdom.

A round 610 CE, in a cave in the hills above the town of Mecca, central Arabia, Muhammad—a 40-year-old man from a merchant family—declared that he had received a divine message from the angel Gabriel. This was followed by similar revelations over the coming months and years and led to the founding of a new

In this 16th-century miniature The Kaaba, considered the house of God and the holiest shrine in Islam, is decorated by angels on the occasion of the Prophet Muhammad's birth.

monotheistic religion: Islam. Within 20 years, this creed had come to dominate the Arabian peninsula, and a century later its followers had shattered the ancient Byzantine and Persian Empires, creating a state that stretched from Spain in the far west to Central Asia in the east.

Arabia before Islam

From the first millennium BCE there were sophisticated kingdoms in southern Arabia, which derived their wealth from the spice trade. In the early days, the trade routes ran along the northwest coast, but by the 7th century these had diminished as merchants increasingly used a maritime route up the Red Sea, leaving many places that had been relatively prosperous in decline. There were a few scattered towns, such as Medina (then known as Yathrib) and Mecca, which were dependent on more local trade in wool and leather, along with a few key imports such as grain and olive oil. The central desert regions of the Arabian peninsula were very poor: Bedouin tribes followed a nomadic lifestyle, and competition for scarce resources shaped a society in which primary loyalty was to a kinship group, or tribe.

At the time of Muhammad, Arabia was in a state of religious and political ferment. Strong Jewish communities had become established in Yemen in the south and in northwestern oasis towns, such as Medina, while Christianity had gained footholds in Yemen and eastern Arabia. Although monotheistic faiths were making inroads against the traditional polytheistic paganism of the Bedouin Arabs, paganism still remained strong. Conflict between tribes was also common, and in Mecca, in the sacred enclosure known as the *haram*, a truce was enforced so men of different tribes could trade freely without violence.

Muhammad in Mecca

The Meccan *haram* was controlled by the powerful Quraysh clan, of which Muhammad was a member. Muhammad's rejection of paganism, and his bold proclamation that there was but a single God, and that believers needed to follow a prescribed set of religious observances—including praying five times a day and fasting during Ramadan—set his followers apart. His preaching of a single religious community that cut across social boundaries was perceived as threatening by the traditional leaders, who felt it undermined the source of their authority.

The flight to Medina

By 622, the atmosphere in Mecca had become so tense that Muhammad and his handful of followers fled north to Medina— an event called the *hegira* (meaning immigration), which marked the real foundation of the Islamic community. The Medinans, who resented the power of the Mecca-based Qurayshi, were sympathetic to Muhammad's cause and allowed him to preach freely, giving him the opportunity to attract further converts.

The Qurayshi were not content to see Muhammad's power base grow in Mecca and within two years violence had broken out between the established powers there and Muhammad's supporters. Muhammad outmaneuvered the Qurayshi, first by raiding their caravans, then defeating them in a pitched battle in 627, and finally negotiating the right to return to Mecca on a pilgrimage in 629. By the time he died in 632, Muhammad was reestablished in Mecca, and his diplomatic and military successes in attracting other tribes to his cause had made his position unassailable. As his authority spread, so, too, did the reach of his religious message and the numbers of new Muslim converts.

After Muhammad's death, Islam entered a crisis and the fledgling religion might easily have been crushed. Tribes in the east broke away from the Muslim religious community (the *umma*) and declared allegiance to one of their commanders, while the Medinans were unhappy about the dominance of Meccans in the movement. The choice of Abu Bakr, »

Muhammad

The Prophet Muhammad was born in Mecca around 570 CE to a branch of the influential Quraysh tribe. Tradition relates that he was an orphan, whose first marriage to a wealthy widow named Khadijah secured his economic future. The religious revelations that were imparted to Muhammad over a period of more than 20 years from about 610—and which were later written down as the Quran—caused a rupture with the traditional Meccan elites when he began to preach against pagan polytheism and practices such as female infanticide. Muhammad's flight to Medina in 622 marked a key moment in the spread of Islam, as its acceptance outside Mecca showed that its appeal might transcend traditional kinship structures. Muhammad proved an inspirational leader, and his adept handling of the challenges facing the new religion meant that by the time of his death in 632, two years after imposing his rule on Mecca, its adherents had spread throughout Arabia.

Muhammad's father-in-law, as caliph (successor) overcame the division within the Islamic community and this decision, together with a series of successful military campaigns against the malcontents, enabled the *umma* to survive.

Conquests beyond Arabia

Having secured their position, Muhammad's successors, in particular Umar (634–644), initiated campaigns of conquest further afield. They were fortunate in that profound changes had occurred on the northern fringes of Arabia. Between 602 and 628, the two long-established empires in the area—the Byzantines to the northwest and the Persian Sassanids to the northeast—had been engaged in a long, vicious war that ended in catastrophe for both parties. Their coffers had been drained by the costs of the conflict and some regions within their territories had been utterly devastated. Both sides had also become reliant on Arabs to defend their borders and small, semi-independent Arab states had emerged on the peripheries of the two empires.

The Battle of Uhud (in 625) was one of several bloody conflicts fought between the Muslims of Medina, led by Muhammad, and the larger Qurayshi army from Mecca.

Rapid defeat

The Arab armies that swept northward in the 630s faced far less resistance than they would have half a century earlier. Provinces fell easily as weakened garrisons and the doubtful loyalty of citizens undermined resistance. Although relatively small in number and lightly armed, the Arab armies were very mobile and did not need to defend fixed positions, giving them a huge advantage over their opponents. When they defeated the Byzantines at Yarmuk in 636, the whole edifice of imperial control in Palestine and Syria came crashing down. In the case of Persia, it took Arab generals just nine years to dismember the Sassanid Empire.

Islamic society

The newly conquered lands became part of an Islamic caliphate. Many of its inhabitants converted, while those who did not were tolerated if they were Christians, Jews, or Zoroastrians, provided they paid a special tax. Islam transformed the lands it absorbed in many ways. As well as sweeping away the old imperial structures, it imparted a new sense of religious community, often uniting the conquerors and the conquered. Islamic scholars resurrected the works of Greek philosophers and scientists that had languished forgotten for centuries, translating them into Arabic, and beautiful mosques began to adorn the towns. Areas that had been marginalized under the Byzantine or Sassanid Empires now found themselves at the heart of a new, vibrant civilization.

Success, however, brought its own problems for Islam. Acquiring lands far more urbanized than Arabia meant that the caliphs had to adapt from being warrior chiefs commanding a tight-knit group of followers, to monarchs ruling over a huge area with complex economies and societies. In addition to this, Muslims were initially in the minority, and not wholly united.

Growing divisions

Tensions over the succession to the caliphate resulted in a major schism in Islam. A struggle between Ali, Muhammad's son-in-law, and Muawiya, the Governor of Syria, led to a civil war that ended in Ali's murder and Muawiya taking

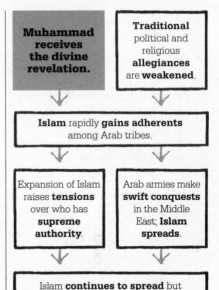

Muhammad receives the divine revelation.

Traditional political and religious **allegiances** are **weakened**.

Islam rapidly **gains adherents** among Arab tribes.

Expansion of Islam raises **tensions** over who has **supreme authority**.

Arab armies make **swift conquests** in the Middle East; **Islam spreads**.

Islam **continues to spread** but **divides** into **Sunni and Shia** factions and **competing caliphates**.

control of the caliphate in 661. While Muawiya's descendants (the Umayyads) ruled from the Syrian city of Damascus, Ali's followers opposed their authority, claiming the caliph should be chosen from among Ali's offspring. After the murder of Ali's son Husayn at Karbala in 680, the split between the Shia (those who supported the right of Ali's descendents to rule the caliphate) and the more mainstream Sunni (who rejected this) became definitive—a division that continues to this day.

Islamic unity was fractured in other ways, too; ruling over such a vast empire was almost impossible when messages from the eastern and western extremities might take months to reach the caliph's court. Independent Muslim dynasties emerged in peripheral areas and rival caliphs appeared in the 10th century in Spain and Egypt. Yet even though its political unity had been shattered, and its religious unity compromised, Muhammad's creed was so popular and successful that by the 21st century there were about 1.5 billion Muslims worldwide. ■

A SURGE IN SPIRIT AND AN AWAKENING IN INTELLIGENCE
THE FOUNDING OF BAGHDAD (762)

IN CONTEXT

FOCUS
Islamic society and science

BEFORE
711 A Muslim Arab and Berber army conquers the Visigothic Kingdom of Spain.

756 Umayyad prince Abd al-Rahman I establishes a court at Cordoba in Spain.

AFTER
800 The first Islamic hospital is established in Baghdad.

825 Al-Khwarizmi introduces decimal notation (derived from India) to the Islamic world.

1138–1154 Al-Idrisi compiles a world map for Roger II of Sicily.

1258 The sack of Baghdad marks the end of the Abbasid caliphate.

1259 An astronomical observatory is founded at Maragha.

Islamic conquests result in many collections of **Greek manuscripts** being held in **Arab-controlled areas**.

Al-Mansur founds Baghdad and the city becomes a center of Muslim science and learning.

Translation of Greek scientific texts in the **House of Wisdom** in Baghdad leads to **Arab scientific advances**.

↓

Arabic translations of Greek authors appear in Europe where they are **translated into Latin**, so diffusing knowledge of lost classical texts.

I n 762, the second ruler of the newly ascendant Abbasid dynasty moved the capital of the powerful Islamic Caliphate from Damascus to the newly-founded city of Baghdad. The move is often seen as marking the beginning of an Islamic golden age in which science, art, and culture flourished. The extent of Muslim technological development was demonstrated in 802 when the Abbasid caliph Harun al-Rashid dispatched an embassy to the Frankish ruler, Charlemagne, which included the gift of a water clock that chimed the hours by dropping brass balls onto cymbals at the mechanism's base. This sophisticated timepiece was just one of the advances the Arabs had made—advances that left their European counterparts far behind.

The rise of the Abbasids

After the death of the Prophet Muhammad in 632, his successors ruled over a growing Islamic empire (or caliphate). Following the murder in 744 of the caliph al-Walid, a member of the Umayyad family that had ruled from Damascus since 661, civil war broke out, ending only when the Abbasid dynasty came to power in 750. The Abbasids spent their first decade pacifying the empire, with the help of troops from Khurasan in northeastern Iran. These troops, a mixture of Arab-speakers, Persians, and central Asians, had been among the Abbasids' principal backers and had provided them with a power base independent of the Arab tribes based in northern Arabia, Syria, and Iraq who had supported the Umayyads.

It was in part to provide land for his Khurasani soldiers that al-Mansur, the second Abbasid caliph, established the city of Baghdad in 762. He chose the site for its mild climate and its location on the trade routes between Persia, Arabia, and the Mediterranean. It was also just 20 miles to the southeast of the Persian royal seat at Ctesiphon, which it soon eclipsed, enabling the new dynasty to portray themselves as masters of a culture that stretched back to Cyrus the Great in the 6th century BCE. The heart of the new capital was a mile-wide, circular enclosure in which sat the caliphal palace and main government offices.

Search for knowledge

The Abbasids laid claim not only to their predecessors' political heritage, but also to their cultural and scientific achievements. Although the Umayyad Empire had included ancient seats of Greek learning such as Alexandria in Egypt, under their rule there had been little sponsorship of scientific endeavor. This changed under the Abbasids, who spent their time consolidating Islamic rule rather than on campaigns of conquest. They sponsored scholars to explore knowledge gained from foreign works, rather than relying solely on the guidance found in the Quran and the *hadiths* (the sayings of the Prophet Muhammad).

The earliest advances were made in medicine. During the mid- to late 6th century, a philosophical school at Gundeshapur in south-western Iran became a center of medical scholarship. It was staffed mainly by Christians from the Nestorian sect, which had been persecuted in the Byzantine Empire. In 765, al-Mansur is said to have summoned staff member Jurjis ibn Jibril ibn Bukhtishu to Baghdad to diagnose a stomach complaint. So pleased was the caliph with his treatment that he prevailed upon Jurjis to stay on as his personal physician, and for eight generations until the mid-11th century, members of the Bukhtishu family occupied the position at the Baghdad court, bringing with them knowledge of Greek and Hellenistic texts and medical practices. In 800, Caliph Harun al-Rashid asked Jibril »

Harun al-Rashid

Harun (763–809) succeeded as caliph in 783 after the mysterious death of his older brother al-Hadi, who had reigned for just one year. For the first 20 years of his reign,

the Barmecide family, who helped strengthen a powerful central administration, dominated court. Under Harun's rule, Baghdad became the most powerful city in the Islamic world, and flourished as a center of knowledge, culture, invention, and trade. Even so, for almost two decades Harun based himself at Raqqa, closer to the frontiers of the Byzantine Empire, against which he launched a raid in 806, personally commanding an army of many thousands. Harun's

gift of an elephant to Charlemagne in 802 was part of a series of diplomatic exchanges with the Frankish court that were intended to put further pressure on the Byzantines.

Harun's House of Wisdom, a translation bureau, library, and academy for scholars and intellectuals from across the empire, contributed to his nickname al-Rashid ("the Just"). He died in 809 while on an expedition to Khurasan in the northeast of Iran.

ibn Bukhtishu, Jurjis's grandson, to head the new hospital in Baghdad, the first in the Islamic world.

Al-Mansur established a library in Baghdad to house his collection of manuscripts. This venture was made easier by the Arab adoption of paper as a medium for books, and the establishment in Baghdad in 795 of a paper mill. However, since Arabic speakers had no access to this learning, the library did little to advance an indigenous Arab scientific tradition.

House of Wisdom

To remedy this, Harun al-Rashid (caliph from 786 to 809) and al-Mamun (reigned 813–833) established the *Bayt al Hikma* (House of Wisdom), which not only housed the growing library, but also acted as an academy for scholars and a center for the translation of key scientific works into Arabic. Among its leading scholars were Hunayn ibn Ishaq (808–873), a Nestorian Christian from al-Hira in Iraq, who translated more than 100 mostly medical and philosophical works; and Thabit ibn Qurra, a member of a pagan sect known as the Sabaeans, who translated *Elements*, Euclid's great work on geometry, and the *Almagest*, Ptolemy's key work on astronomy.

Translation became a highly prestigious endeavor. One Arab patron paid an extravagant 2,000 dinars a month to ensure his association with a translation of a work by the Greek physician Galen (a dinar, made of pure gold, weighed the same as 72 grains of barley). Within around 150 years, almost all of the key Greek texts that had been discovered had been rendered into Arabic. Many of them were not available in Western Europe at all, and even if they had been, knowledge of Greek had all but disappeared there. The Muslim world was therefore well set by around 850 to build on the scientific traditions of Classical and Hellenistic Greeks transmitted and developed under the Roman Empire—and to acquire a centuries-long lead over Christian Western Europeans.

Complex calculations

An understanding of mathematics and astronomy is essential to the calculation of the times at which Muslims must observe their five daily prayers (times that varied widely across the vast Islamic Empire), therefore both disciplines were studied assiduously. Another, separate, intellectual tradition contributed to the development of these calculation techniques, arriving in 771 with a delegation of Hindu scholars. The scholars were visiting al-Mansur's court (which in itself illustrates the comparative openness and tolerance of the early Abbasids), and brought with them India's relatively advanced mathematics, including the use of trigonometry to help solve

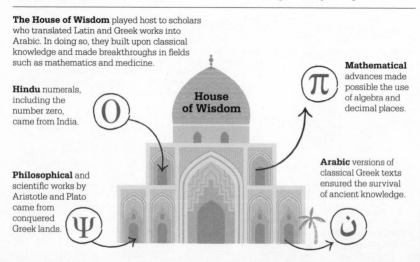

The House of Wisdom played host to scholars who translated Latin and Greek works into Arabic. In doing so, they built upon classical knowledge and made breakthroughs in fields such as mathematics and medicine.

Hindu numerals, including the number zero, came from India.

House of Wisdom

Mathematical advances made possible the use of algebra and decimal places.

Philosophical and scientific works by Aristotle and Plato came from conquered Greek lands.

Arabic versions of classical Greek texts ensured the survival of ancient knowledge.

algebraic equations. Crucially, the Hindu mathematicians also employed a decimal notation, which one of the members of the House of Wisdom, Al-Khwarizmi (c. 780–830), adopted and described in *The Book of Addition and Subtraction According to Hindu Calculation*.

Furthermore, Al-Khwarizmi also explained a method of calculating the square roots of numbers, and pioneered work on algebraic equations. He and his fellow scholars made rapid strides in geometry, taking as their starting point Euclid's and Archimedes's work on spheres and cylinders.

Astronomy and medicine

Al-Khwarizmi compiled the first known tables of daily prayer times at Baghdad, his calculations assisted by direct astronomical observation. The early Islamic astronomers drew from Ptolemy's *Almagest*, adopting his view that the Earth was at the center of the solar system, and that the planets rotated around it along the lines of eight spheres. They also learned from Hindu astronomers, translating and perfecting Indian *zij*, or tables of planetary positions, and continued to refine Ptolemy's system, only occasionally (as in the work of the 10th-century astronomer al-Biruni) toying with a heliocentric system that had the sun at its center. Their calculations were made simpler when in the mid-eighth century they adopted the astrolabe, an instrument in which the celestial sphere was projected onto a flat plane marked with latitude and longitude lines.

The Canon of Medicine by ibn Sina or Avicenna (980–1037) set the standard for medicine in the Islamic world and medieval Europe, and remained an authority for centuries.

By the 13th century, Islamic astronomy was at its zenith, and in 1259 a great observatory was constructed at Maragha in eastern Iran. Here Nasir al-Din al-Tusi and his successors made fine adjustments to account for slight discrepancies in the orbit of the planets, assisted by mechanical clocks that enabled them to record their observations in fine detail. Muslim scholars made advances in many other areas, too, first building on the base of Greek manuscripts translated into Arabic, and then making their own discoveries. They did not accept the theories of the ancients uncritically: al-Haytham (died 1039) produced a key work, the *Book of Optics*, in which he speculated that sight was the result of light traveling from an object to the eye, rather than the other way around as Ptolemy had theorized. Arab physicians continued to make progress, combining their practical observations with theoretical analysis. Al-Razi (died 925) produced the first description of smallpox and measles, as well as compiling a medical compendium that began a tradition of such encyclopedias, culminating in the *Canon of Medicine* by ibn Sina (who was known as Avicenna in the West). Composed around 1015, it included separate sections for diseases that are specific to one body part, and those that afflict the body as a whole.

Islamic science spreads

The Islamic expansion that began in the mid-7th century not only absorbed ancient centers of learning such as Alexandria, but also brought the Muslim world to the fringes of Western Europe through the conquest of Spain (from 711) and Sicily (from 827). A tradition of Islamic learning embedded itself in both areas, and particularly in the Iberian Peninsula, known to the Arabs as al-Andalus. The court established there in 756 by Abd al-Rahman I, a refugee Umayyad prince who had escaped the Abbasid revolution, became a magnet for scholars from the East, and its libraries became a repository of precious ancient texts that had been translated into Arabic. »

In 967, the French cleric and scholar Gerbert of Aurillac (who in 999 would become Pope Sylvester II) arrived in Spain for a three-year period of study at a monastery in Catalonia. There he had access to manuscripts that had filtered over the border from Muslim-held al-Andalus. He took back to France knowledge of Arabic technology such as the water clock and the astrolabe, and of a type of abacus that used a decimal system. This was the first example of the system's use in medieval Europe. It was a small beginning, and one paralleled in southern Italy where a medical school was established at Salerno in the 9th century. A few Islamic manuscripts reached the school in the early years, but many more arrived in the late 11th century when Muslim doctor Constantine the African returned from Qairawan in Tunisia. He had gone there to study medicine, and brought back with him works such as the *Complete Art of Medicine* by Ali ibn al-Abbas al-Majusi (known in the West as Haly Abbas), parts of which he then translated into Latin. This translation gave Western doctors and scholars access to comparatively advanced Muslim medical knowledge.

Classical Greek texts arrived directly from the Byzantine Empire to the West (in particular Pisa, which had a trading quarter

The ancient Greek thinker Aristotle teaches Muslim students how to measure the positions of the sun, moon, and stars in this imagined scene from an Arabic manuscript.

in Constantinople), including works by the philosopher Aristotle. The main channel for the transmission of Islamic learning into Europe, however, continued to be Spain. As Islamic Spain shrank, pressurized by the Reconquista, the flow of materials accelerated. The Christian reconquest spread increasingly into Muslim emirates until, in 1085, Alfonso VI of Castile captured Toledo. The city became a center for the translation of Arabic works by an international group including the Englishman Robert of Ketton, Slav Hermann of Carinthia, the Frenchman Raymond of Marseilles, Jewish scholar Abraham ibn Ezra, and Italian Gerhard of Cremona. In the mid-12th century, the group translated many Arabic texts into Latin, including works on mathematics, medicine, and philosophy. Western Europe now had access to Ptolemy's *Almagest*, and to the medical works of Galen, as well as access to new works by Arabic writers who had built on or summarized the work of their ancient predecessors, such as ibn Sina's *Canon of Medicine*. This five-book encyclopedia became one of the most widely used treatises in European medical schools until the 16th century.

Royal patronage

This transmission of knowledge to the West mirrored the process by which the Islamic world had absorbed Greek learning during the great period of translation into Arabic in the 9th and 10th centuries. Noble and royal patrons played similar roles in both phases of the transmission. King Roger II of Sicily (which by 1091 had been reconquered from the Muslims) invited Arab scholar al-Idrisi to his court in 1138 with a commission to construct a map of the world based on Islamic geographical and cartographic works. The result, which took more than 15 years to complete, was by far the most accurate world map yet available to Europeans, and showed areas as far east as Korea. The map was accompanied by the *Book of Pleasant Journeys into Faraway Lands*, in which al-Idrisi's royal patron could have read of wondrous things such as cannibals in Borneo, and the gold trade in Ghana.

A tradition of learning

Roger's grandson Frederick II, Holy Roman Emperor from 1220 until 1250, continued his grandfather's tradition of sponsoring translations of Arabic texts. A remarkable polymath who knew at least four languages, Frederick so impressed his contemporaries with his learning that he became known as Stupor Mundi ("the Marvel of the World"). Among his protégés were the Scottish scholar Michael Scot, who translated key works of Aristotle on zoology, and the Pisan Leonardo Fibonacci, who had been sent by his merchant family to study mathematics at Bougie in Muslim North Africa. There Fibonacci learned of the decimal system, and in 1202 he published the *Book of Calculations*, the most detailed account yet seen in Europe of the Arabic system of numbering.

By the early 13th century, the Abbasid Empire had all but collapsed. The difficulties of ruling such a far-flung empire and the effects of a series of civil wars had led to key provinces such as Spain, Tunisia, and Egypt breaking away to make themselves independent. Even in Baghdad, where the

Roger II invited scholar al-Idrisi to create an accurate map of the known world in 1138. Al-Idrisi presented the planisphere, and an accompanying book, to his patron in 1154.

Abbasid caliphs clung on, they were only notionally sovereign. Real power was held by other dynasties such as the Shia Buyids and, from 1055, the Seljuks, a Turkish group originating in central Asia. The final blow was dealt by the Mongols, who surged westward into the Islamic world in the early 13th century. In 1258, the Mongol Great Khan Möngke unleashed an army against Iraq, which laid siege to and then sacked Baghdad, inflicting an appalling massacre on its inhabitants. The last ruling Abbasid caliph al-Musta'sim was executed, and political and cultural leadership of the Islamic world passed first to the Mamluks in Cairo and then, after their conquest of Egypt in 1517, to the Ottoman Turks.

By this time Europeans had rediscovered Greek and Roman learning in almost every field of scholarship through the medium of Arabic texts. It had taken centuries for the new material to be absorbed, and a further wave of interest in classical manuscripts in the 15th century to spark the Renaissance in Europe. The House of Wisdom founded by the Abbasid caliphs had played a key role in ensuring the survival of Greek and Roman science in the Islamic world, allowing its transmission centuries later to Christian Europe. ∎

NEVER BEFORE HAS SUCH A TERROR APPEARED IN BRITAIN
THE VIKING RAID ON LINDISFARNE (793)

IN CONTEXT

FOCUS
Viking raiders

BEFORE
550–750 In Sweden, the Vendel period is a time of increased prosperity.

737 Construction of Danevirke fortifications in Denmark shows growing royal authority.

AFTER
841 Vikings establish a permanent settlement in Ireland, which will grow into the city of Dublin.

845 Viking raiders advance along the Seine and sack Paris.

867 Danish Vikings take control of Northumbria in northeast England.

911 Vikings found Duchy of Normandy in northern France.

10th century Swedish "Rus" Vikings are dominant in Kiev and Novgorod in Russia.

Population **pressure** and **political instability** in Scandinavia.

↓

News of **rich targets** across the North Sea attracts **rootless young men** to war leaders.

↓

Attack on Lindisfarne Monastery.

↓

Success of Lindisfarne **attack attracts more** warriors to join new raids.

↓

Raids lead to **permanent** Viking settlements.

O n a calm June day in 793, a group of men landed on the shore of the holy island of Lindisfarne in northern England, and mounted a ferocious attack on its monastery. The invaders murdered some of the monks, dragged others away into slavery, and plundered the church's treasures before slipping away.

This unexpected assault was the first recorded raid by Vikings—pagan seafaring warriors from Denmark, Norway, and Sweden—and news of it sent waves of horror and fear across Christian Europe. Over the next 200 years, Vikings would ravage and loot settlements across large parts of the continent. But they were also colonists and traders with a sophisticated artistic culture who left a lasting imprint on the places they invaded and settled.

An unstoppable force

Within six years of the Lindisfarne raid, bands of Vikings—or "Danes" as they were known in Anglo-Saxon England—were targeting the wealth of other Christian sites in England, Scotland, Ireland, and France. Key to the success of these missions was the Viking longship, a slender vessel with a shallow bottom that enabled its crew to sail far up waterways and alight stealthily on shores. Each ship could carry up to 80 warriors, recruited by a warlord whose authority depended on his military prowess and his success in capturing booty for his followers.

No single motive drove the Vikings to venture across the sea. In parts of Scandinavia, population growth may have forced young men into a piratical lifestyle; in others, perhaps the increasing strength of local clan leaders sparked power struggles that pushed the losers into exile. And the newly rich trading towns in northern Europe were irresistible targets for a warrior society in which a reputation for valiant deeds was a great asset.

Conquest and settlement

As the Vikings' raiding parties grew in size, many of the men started to settle in the territories they invaded, including those in Britain and France. In the late 9th century, England was divided into a number of kingdoms that offered no coherent resistance to the Viking challenge, while France was consumed by civil war.

This disunited opposition helped the Vikings to conquer northern and central England—where they established a kingdom that lasted almost 100 years—and to occupy land in northern France, where their descendants became French-speaking Normans. In the east, Vikings traded and raided along Russia's rivers, which brought them silver from the Islamic world and contact with the Byzantine Empire.

By the 11th century, most of the Scandinavian kingdoms had adopted Christianity, and turned from raiding and pillaging to more organized settlement and conquest. Cnut of Denmark created a Viking North Sea empire that included Denmark, Norway, and England. Yet it did not survive his death, and in 1066, an unsuccessful attempt to claim the English throne by the Norwegian King Harald Hardrada, was the final flourish of the Viking age that began with the sack of Lindisfarne. ∎

Viking expansion in the North Atlantic

The Vikings used their knowledge of winds and currents to navigate the seas and discover new lands. Around 800, they colonized the Faroe Islands, and used them as a stepping stone to explore the North Atlantic. By the 870s, their ships had reached Iceland, where settlers founded a colony that grew politically independent.

In 982, Erik the Red, exiled from Iceland for murder, stumbled upon Greenland and established a new colony there. A Norse saga tells how, 18 years later, Erik's son, Leif Erikson, was driven off course at sea and landed in a region teeming with hardwood forests and wild grapes that he called Vinland (Land of Wine).

Subsequent expeditions to this area, which is located in what is now Newfoundland in eastern Canada, led to a tiny Viking colony, but this was abandoned after attacks by hostile indigenous people. Nevertheless, Leif and his crew had been the first Europeans to set foot on North American soil.

The Vikings were among the most skilled shipbuilders, sailors, and navigators in the Western world of the early Middle Ages.

A MAN DESTINED TO BECOME MASTER OF THE STATE
MINAMOTO YORITOMO BECOMES SHOGUN (1192)

IN CONTEXT

FOCUS
Shogunate Japan

BEFORE
1087 The *Insei* system begins: emperors withdraw from court but retain authority, in order to counter the power of regents and the rising warrior class.

1156 The Minamoto challenge the Taira for the first time, and are crushed.

1180 The Genpei War between the Minamoto and the Taira breaks out.

1190s Minamoto Yoritomo builds power in the provinces.

AFTER
1221 Emperor Go-Toba fails to reestablish imperial power in the Jokyu Disturbance.

1333 The Ashikaga family overthrows the Kamakura shogunate.

1467 The Onin Wars, the first of a series that plague Japan for over a century, break out.

The **imperial court** at Kyoto becomes inward-looking and **loses touch with the provinces**.

↓

Lawlessness in the provinces **leads to the rise of the samurai** military class.

↓

After victory over the Taira, Minamoto Yoritomo is appointed shogun.

↓

Samurai clans become semi-independent as **shogunate authority weakens**.

↓

The shogunate collapses and **power devolves to the *daimyo***.

W hen in 1192 the Japanese clan leader Minamoto Yoritomo became the military commander-in-chief, or shogun, it marked the ascent to power of a Japanese military class, the samurai, and established a line of military rulers who would govern Japan for the next 750 years.

The Japanese imperial court had been dominated since the mid-7th century by regents from the Fujiwara family, who had reduced the emperors to mere figureheads. The situation became entrenched after the capital moved (following the emperor) to Kyoto in 794. Non-Fujiwara nobles were denied preferment at court, so sought positions in the provinces. The gulf widened between the Kyoto-based bureaucrats and the regional nobility, the samurai, who assumed a dominant role in local government. The Kyoto court appointed the most talented samurai as governors (*zuryō*), both to bind them to the imperial government and to prevent them from building their own power bases. However, the samurai developed loyalty to their extended family, or clan, and its leader rather than to the emperor, and fought one another from their power bases in the provinces. The Minamoto and Taira clans engaged in a series of these struggles which culminated in the Genpei War, during which the Taira were utterly crushed.

The shogunate

Following his victory, clan leader Minamoto Yoritomo established a parallel government based at Kamakura, about 250 miles east of Kyoto. Other clan chieftains became his vassals or *gokenin*, and he dispatched military estate governors to cement his control over the provinces. In 1192, Yoritomo accepted from the emperor the title of shogun, becoming the de facto military ruler of Japan.

Over the following centuries, the emperors made periodic vain attempts to reassert authority over the shogunate, but the shoguns in turn could not maintain control of the samurai and their warlords, who controlled their areas and fought among themselves. Japan dissolved into a patchwork of military warlords or *daimyo*, each with its own power base and retinue of samurai warriors.

Establishment of the office of shogun, which had seemed to offer Japan stability in 1192, ultimately led to the Sengoku, a civil war lasting almost 150 years. This war ended with the reunification of Japan under the new shogunate of Tokugawa in 1603. ∎

At the time of the Genpei Wars the Samurai fought as mounted bowmen, but by the 15th century the sword, in particular the long-bladed *katana*, had become their principal weapon.

Minamoto Yoritomo

A descendant of the royal emperor Seiwa, Yoritomo was the heir of the Minamoto clan, which had been crushed by the Taira clan after a civil war in 1159. After the war, the now orphaned Yoritomo was exiled to Hirugashima, an island in Izu province. Here he remained for 20 years before issuing a call to arms and rising up against the Taira. He established a headquarters in Kamakura, from which he began to organize the warlords and samurai into an independent government.

A decisive victory over the Tiara in 1185 sealed Yoritomo's military success, and he emerged the undisputed leader of Japan.

Yoritomo developed policies to relieve the strain between the military lords and the court aristocrats, and set up an administrative network that soon took over as the central government, but much of the remainder of his life was spent in suppressing those clans who had not accepted Minamoto dominance.

THAT MEN IN OUR KINGDOM SHALL HAVE AND KEEP ALL THESE LIBERTIES, RIGHTS, AND CONCESSIONS
THE SIGNING OF THE MAGNA CARTA (1215)

IN CONTEXT

FOCUS
The development of subjects' rights

BEFORE
1100 Henry I's Coronation Charter promises to abolish unjust oppression.

1166 The Assize of Clarendon extends the power of royal justice at the expense of baronial courts.

1214 Normandy is lost at the Battle of Bouvines; barons bridle at the campaign's cost.

AFTER
1216 The Magna Carta is reissued on the accession of Henry III, and again in 1225 in exchange for a tax grant.

1297 The Magna Carta is again confirmed and written into statute law by Edward I.

1970 A bill repealing ancient statute laws leaves untouched four chapters of the Magna Carta, including Chapter 39.

O n June 15, 1215, King John of England signed a charter at Runnymede, a meadow beside the Thames. Designed to make peace between the king and a group of rebel barons, the Magna Carta, as a form of the document became known, at first seemed ineffectual. However, its assertion of the rights of subjects against arbitrary actions of the Crown—the essential principle of the rule of law—provided a blueprint which, more than eight centuries later, is still viewed as a fundamental guarantee of rights in the US and elsewhere.

Feudal society

When King John acceded in 1199, England was a feudal society, a land-based hierarchy headed by the king, who owned all the land. The tenants-in-chief (or barons) received land from the king in exchange for loyalty and military service. They in turn leased the land to their own armed retainers, who leased to peasants, or villeins. Yet monarchs, especially in England, were levying an ever-increasing series of taxes and additional financial burdens on their barons. English kings from Henry I (1100–1135) onward also sought to centralize administration, partly by establishing a series of royal courts. These royal courts raised revenue for the Crown through fines and charges—but at the expense of the barons, who had previously raised those funds from their own local tribunals.

The exactions of King John

The barons' discontent at these growing demands intensified under King John. Ruinously expensive campaigns against the French in 1200–1204 had already resulted in the loss of Normandy. Scutage, a further cash levy that left many barons in debt to money-lenders, was bitterly resented. Not only was the king proving lamentably unsuccessful in war, but he had

Centralization of royal administration **reduces barons' power and income**.

Financial demands to fund wars in France **increase**.

Barons revolt and force King John to sign a charter of rights.

Rights of individuals against arbitrary punishment by the Crown are **established**.

The principle that **new taxes** can be raised **only after consultation** with a royal council evolves.

also broken the unspoken contract between himself and the barons, that allowed them to run their lands as they chose.

Hoping for support from the pope, who had excommunicated John in 1209, the rebellious barons confronted the king. Attempts at diplomacy failed, and by May 1215, the barons had occupied London, forcing John to enter into a treaty with them to avoid a civil war. After careful direction of negotiations by Archbishop Stephen Langton of Canterbury, the agreement— more a truce than a peace—was signed.

Provisions of the charter

The charter was known as the Magna Carta, or Great Charter, to distinguish it from a more restricted Forest Charter issued in 1217. Much of the Magna Carta dealt with redressing baronial grievances, but the section that has exerted the most influence down the ages was Chapter 39.

This open-ended clause protected all "free men" from arbitrary actions by the Crown such as arrest or confiscation of land. The charter survived the civil war that broke out soon after the Magna Carta was agreed, and the papal repudiation of the charter's terms in August 1215, which led to the barons' excommunication. Chapter 39 was extended under a 1354 law of Edward III to protect not only "free men" (a small minority in England where most people were technically serfs), but also any man "of whatever estate or condition he may be." It survived longer than most of the other provisions, including the security clause that allowed barons to seize all the king's land if he failed to fulfill his obligations under the agreement.

What had seemed a small concession that day in Runnymede provided a long-lasting rallying cry for opponents of royal tyranny. ∎

Influence of the Magna Carta

The Magna Carta has acquired an almost mythical status as the constitutional bedrock of subjects' rights. It contributed to the development of parliament from the 13th century, and was used by 17th-century rebels to argue against the divine right of kings propounded by the Stuart monarchs Charles I and James II. Several American colonies' charters contained clauses modeled on it, while the design of the Massachusetts seal chosen at the start of the Revolutionary War depicts a militiaman with sword in one hand and the Magna Carta in the other. Revolutionary feeling was fueled by Americans' belief that the Crown had breached the fundamental law enjoyed by all English subjects, and both the United States Constitution, enacted in 1789, and the Bill of Rights adopted two years later, were influenced by the Magna Carta's limitations on the arbitrary powers of a government against its subjects.

I DID NOT TELL HALF OF WHAT I SAW, FOR I KNEW I WOULD NOT BE BELIEVED

MARCO POLO REACHES SHANGDU (c. 1275)

IN CONTEXT

FOCUS
Rise of international trade

BEFORE
106 BCE The first caravan to travel the full length of the Silk Road carries Chinese ambassadors to Parthia.

751 CE Defeat of the Chinese army at the Talas River prevents Chinese expansion west along the Silk Road.

1206 Genghis Khan unites the Mongol tribes, beginning Mongol conquest of Central Asia and China.

AFTER
1340s The Black Death spreads along the Silk Road, reaching Europe in 1347.

1370–1405 Tamerlane makes extensive conquests, briefly reviving the Mongol empire and the Silk Road.

1453 The Ottoman conquest of Constantinople blocks Europeans' land route to Asia.

Long-distance trade from China to the Middle East is **damaged** by the collapse of traditional powers.

↓

Mongols conquer lands through which the Silk Road runs, **improving** the route's **security**.

↓

Trade along the route increases, attracting European merchants including Marco Polo.

↓

The **collapse of Mongol rule** and rise of the Ottoman Empire render the route's territory **less secure**.

↓

European powers seek **alternative maritime trade routes** to the east.

Venetian merchant Marco Polo's arrival at Shangdu, the capital of the Great Khan Kublai, in 1275 marked the end of a four-year journey. He had traveled from Italy to the Mongol capital Shangdu along the length of the Silk Road, an ancient network of routes that had been carrying precious goods between China and Europe for centuries. The Silk Road had first become a conduit for trade when the Chinese Han Dynasty pushed into Central Asia in the late 2nd century BCE. From then on, goods such as jade and silk were carried west, passed from caravan to caravan by a series of merchants, to be met by caravans of furs, gold, and horses traveling in the opposite direction. Chinese inventions ranging from gunpowder and paper to the magnetic compass were also brought to the west along the route, arriving at Constantinople and the Black Sea ports, the western end of the route where Genoa and Venice chiefly traded.

Mongol revival of the route

By the 13th century, empires that had controlled sections of the Silk Road had fragmented. This left the route less secure for travelers, and so deterred merchants from using it. However, following Mongol conquest of the area between 1205 and 1269, the area was controlled—if loosely—by a single authority, the Great Khan, so a merchant could travel from Khanbaliq (Beijing) to Baghdad without leaving Mongol territory. This renewed stability encouraged a revival of trade.

At around this time, European merchants' horizons were also expanding. In the early Middle Ages, traders could work only locally, and transport their goods to points where they might connect to longer distance trade routes. From the 12th century, Italian city-states such as Pisa, Genoa, and Venice, pioneered maritime trade across the eastern Mediterranean, which enabled merchants to connect directly with sea routes that linked West Asia and Egypt to China via the Indian Ocean.

The profits for merchants taking advantage of the "Pax Mongolica," or Mongol peace, could be huge. In the late 13th century, the costs of setting up a caravan might amount to 3,500 florins, but the cargo, once sold in China, could yield seven times that sum, and by 1326 Genoese traders were a common sight in the principal Chinese port of Zaiton.

Decline of land trade

The Silk Road flourished for a further century, but the collapse of the Mongol Ilkhanate of Persia in 1335, and the overthrow in 1368 of the Yuan, the Mongol ruling dynasty in China, once again left the route divided between politically weak powers. It was also blocked to European traders at the western end by the growth of the Muslim Ottoman Empire.

A taste of the profits of long-distance trade in luxury goods encouraged European powers to seek alternatives to the now defunct Silk Road, this time by sea. In 1514, Portuguese merchants arrived off the coast of China, near Guangzhou, eager to take up the direct trading links with China that had been pioneered two and a half centuries earlier by their illustrious predecessor, Marco Polo. ∎

Marco Polo

At just 17 years old, Marco Polo (1254–1324) set off from Venice to the court of the Mongol ruler, Kublai Khan. He traveled with his father and uncle, who had previously visited China and been entrusted by Kublai with a message for the pope. Polo was received with great favor at the Mongol court and stayed in China for 17 years. He traveled extensively throughout the country in the Khan's service, leaving for home at last in around 1291.

During a naval battle in 1298, Polo was captured and imprisoned by the Genoese. The stories he told of his sojourn in the lands of the Great Khan attracted the attention of his cell mate, Rustichello, who wrote them down, embellishing them as he went along. The resulting book was translated into many languages and includes much invaluable information about late-13th-century China. After his release, Polo returned to Venice, where he lived for the rest of his life.

THOSE WHO UNTIL NOW HAVE BEEN MERCENARIES FOR A FEW COINS ACHIEVE ETERNAL REWARDS
THE FALL OF JERUSALEM (1099)

IN CONTEXT

FOCUS
The Crusades

BEFORE
639 A Muslim army captures Jerusalem.

1009 Caliph al-Hakim orders Jerusalem's Church of the Holy Sepulchre to be destroyed.

1071 Seljuk Turks defeat and capture Byzantine emperor, Romanus Diogenes.

1095 Byzantine emperor Alexios sends to pope for help.

AFTER
1120 The Order of the Knights Templar is founded.

1145 The Second Crusade is launched.

1187 Muslim leader Saladin captures Jerusalem, and the Third Crusade is launched.

1198 Baltic Crusade begins.

1291 Muslim forces complete the reconquest of Palestine and Syria.

Victorious crusaders flooded into Jerusalem, and in a ruthless assault seized the city from the Fatimid caliphate, laying the foundations for a new kingdom.

O n July 15, 1099, some 15,000 Christian knights surged into Jerusalem after a month-long siege. The victorious crusaders slaughtered Muslim defenders and Jews alike in a bloody act that marked the beginning of 200 years of Muslim–Christian warfare in the Holy Land.

Defending Christianity
Jerusalem had fallen into Muslim hands in 639. Neither the Byzantine emperors in Constantinople nor the Christian kings in Western Europe had the political willpower or the strength to reverse the conquest, although the city was sacred to both.

In the 11th century, however, the advances of a new group, the Seljuk Turks, disrupted the pilgrimage routes to Jerusalem, and the Turks' defeat of the Byzantines at Manzikert threatened to push the frontiers of Christianity back to the gates of Constantinople. In 1095, Emperor Alexios I Komnenos sent emissaries to Pope Urban II asking for help to bolster the Byzantine retaliation.

Emperor Alexios **appeals for help** to defend the **Byzantine Empire**.

Pope Urban II calls upon **Christian knights** to launch a **military expedition** to Jerusalem.

Crusading armies capture Jerusalem and establish states in Palestine and Syria.

Further crusades are launched to **defend the crusader states** against Muslim counterattacks.

The **crusading movement spreads** to eastern Europe and southern France.

The Just War

Pope Urban readily seized a cause that would enhance papal prestige. In a sermon of 1095, he described atrocities against Christians in the Holy Land, calling for an expedition to free them. Christian warriors rallied to the cause, eager to gain both salvation and plunder by joining a so-called Just War in God's name.

Some 100,000 crusading knights, mostly French and Norman, set out in 1096. Progress to Jerusalem was slow: the crusaders suffered several setbacks at the hands of the Seljuk Turks, and the long siege of Antioch severely tested their morale, yet they pressed on and, led by the French knight Godfrey of Bouillon, at last captured the Holy City.

In the conquered area, the crusaders established four states, at Edessa, Antioch, Tripoli, and the Kingdom of Jerusalem, known collectively as Outremer. To withstand the Muslim counterattacks, the crusaders built a dense network of fortresses such as Beaufort, Margat, and Krak des Chevaliers, which dominated strategic routes into the Holy Land.

As the initial crusading impulse waned, Outremer began to suffer from a shortage of manpower. This was partly resolved by the founding of crusading orders such as the Templars and Hospitaller knights, organizations who swore monastic vows to defend the Holy Land.

Further Crusades

However, even this was not enough, and when Muslim armies captured Edessa in 1144, a Second Crusade was called. This,

and the Third Crusade mustered in response to the catastrophic loss of Jerusalem in 1187, attracted participation at an even higher level, as monarchs such as Louis VIII of France, Richard I of England, and the Holy Roman Emperor Frederick Barbarossa assumed their leadership.

By 1270 there had been eight further crusades, and the movement had extended to include attacks on Muslims in North Africa; joining the Reconquista (the Christian reconquest of Islamic emirates in Spain); launching expeditions against pagan groups in eastern Europe, and even Christian heretics, such as the Cathars in southern France. In the Middle East, however, the emergence of stronger Muslim states, such as the Mamluks in Egypt, able to mount a strong resistance to crusader pressure, rendered the later expeditions largely ineffectual.

Jerusalem fell to the Muslims for a final time in 1244. The last crusader stronghold in the Holy Land, the city of Acre, was taken by the Mamluks in 1291. ∎

 A race absolutely alien to God has invaded the land of Christians, has reduced the people with sword, rapine, and flame.
Pope Urban II, 1095

GIVE THE SUN THE BLOOD OF ENEMIES TO DRINK
THE FOUNDATION OF TENOCHTITLAN (1325)

IN CONTEXT

FOCUS
The Aztec and Inca empires

BEFORE
c. 1200 Emergence of the Incas in the Cuzco valley, Peru.

c. 1250 Aztecs arrive in the Valley of Mexico.

1300 Aztecs establish settlements on land owned by the lord of Culhuacán.

1325 Aztecs flee south from Culhuacán and enter the land around Lake Texcoco.

AFTER
1376 Acamapichtli becomes the first Aztec ruler.

1428 Inca expansion begins. Establishment of the Aztec Triple Alliance.

c. 1470 Incas capture Chimor, center of the Chimú culture.

1519 Spanish arrive in Mexico.

1532 Spanish arrive in Peru.

Small, competing states in central Mexico and Peru **attract Aztec and Inca migrants** who fill the power vacuum.

↓

The Aztecs and Incas found capital cities at Tenochtitlan and Cuzco respectively.

↓

The Aztec Empire expands using military **aggression** and **fear of reprisals** to **retain power**.

The Inca empire expands by **coopting conquered peoples** and seeking to **integrate** them.

↓

Neither model of empire can survive the **Spanish invasion**.

I n 1325, a band of Central American refugee warriors, known as the Aztecs, saw a sign their patron god Huitzilopochtli had long ago prophesied— an eagle perched on a cactus, marking the spot they had been told to settle. Before long, they had built a temple that became the nucleus of their capital, Tenochtitlan.

Within two centuries, the city was the center of the most predominant empire in the history of Mesoamerica—a large region that shared a pre-Columbian culture and extended from modern-day central Mexico southward to Belize, Guatemala, El Salvador, Honduras, Nicaragua, and northern Costa Rica. This progress was paralleled by the growth at much the same time of Cuzco, the capital of the Incas— an Andean people of humble beginnings, who in just a few decades created the largest state South America had yet seen.

Aztec foundations

The Aztecs may have begun their wanderings in northern Mexico around 1200. For the next 100 years they eked out a miserable existence as mercenaries or barely tolerated squatters, their plight not aided by their reputation as cruel warriors. Frequently, they had to flee after committing violent acts, at times involving human sacrifice; indeed, their flight to Tenochtitlan was prompted by one such incident. The Aztecs had asked their host, the lord of Culhuacán, whether he would give his daughter as a bride for their chief. He agreed, believing she would be greatly honored as queen; however, to his horror they killed and flayed her as a sacrifice to their deity Xipe Totec. Driven out by the lord and his soldiers, the Aztecs fled southward toward the future site of Tenochtitlan.

Although the soil around Lake Texcoco, on which the island of Tenochtitlan was situated, was marshy and there was very little timber available, the capital was easily defensible and the Aztecs used it to consolidate their position. Initially shielded by a treaty with the Tepanec ruler Tezozomoc, who dominated the Valley of Mexico from 1371 to 1426, the Aztecs went on to form a Triple Alliance with the cities of Texcoco and Tlacopan in 1428—a union that kick-started a period of imperial expansion.

Aztec expansion

In the early days, Aztec society had little formal hierarchy. It was based around communities (*calpulli*), that owned land in common and whose chiefs, together with priests, ruled on important decisions. In 1376, the Aztecs chose for the first time an overall leader (*tlatoani*), who came to serve as war leader, judge, and administrator for the burgeoning empire. Under Itzcoatl (1427–1440), Montezuma I (1440–1469), Axayacatl (1469–1481), and Ahuitzotl (1486–1503) Aztec armies subdued their neighbors in the Valley of Mexico and then spread outward, reaching Oaxaca, Veracruz, and to the edges of land controlled by the Mayan people in the east of modern-day Mexico and Guatemala.

As the Aztec Empire expanded, society was transformed. A warrior elite emerged, while at the bottom of society bondsmen (*mayeques*), who owned no land, were bound by labor service to their lords. The militaristic nature of Aztec society was accentuated by an education system in which all males received military training (in separate schools for nobles and commoners). This reinforced the warrior ethos and gave the Aztecs an incalculable advantage over neighboring tribes in Mexico.

The imperial system

Tenochtitlan was adorned by many temples to the gods of the Aztec pantheon. Each god had their own temple, with the Templo Mayor having twin shrines dedicated to Huitzilopochtli and Tlaloc, the rain god. At these temples a stream of human victims was sacrificed—up to 80,000 at the rededication of the Templo Mayor in 1487—by burning alive, decapitation, or cutting open the chest and removing the heart.

Many of the Aztec battles were "flower wars": ritual affairs in which opponents were captured (rather than killed) and sacrificed to placate the Aztec gods, who were believed to need blood to sustain them and keep the sun moving across the sky.

Tenochtitlan also exacted tribute from its subjects. Although there was very little in the way of an organized government bureaucracy, there were tax collectors, who crisscrossed the 38 provinces of the Aztec Empire and levied tribute, which included 7,000 tons of maize, 4,000 tons of beans, and hundreds of thousands of cotton

blankets each year. The empire depended on this tribute to reward the nobility and »

The founding of Tenochtitlan is illustrated in the *Codex Mendoza*: a record of Aztec history and culture created c. 1540 by an Aztec artist for presentation to Charles V of Spain.

the warriors, who ensured that the towns subjugated by the Aztecs remained submissive—little mercy being shown to those who revolted.

While the Aztecs provided some security to their subjects, they gave little else. At Tenochtitlan, artificial islands (*chinampas*) were created at great expense to expand the land available to produce food, but no such works were carried out for the subject cities. Defeated states did not provide troops for the Aztec army, and so did not share in the spoils of future victory, and little effort was made to propagate the Aztec language. It was an empire built on fear and in the end it proved brittle: when it was invaded by a small party of Spaniards led by Cortés in 1519, the subject peoples rallied to the newcomers rather than defending the Aztecs, and the empire collapsed within two years.

Inca beginnings

The Incas, whose heartland lay high in the central Andes around Cuzco, in modern-day Peru, had similarly humble origins to the Aztecs, but their rise to imperial status was, if anything, even more meteoric. They began as a small, somewhat disregarded tribe and developed their own strategies to coopt neighboring groups into a successful empire.

The Incas' origin myth told of their emergence from a cave in the high mountains, from where their first leader—Manco Capac—led his people to Cuzco. It is generally believed that the Incas arrived in the region around 1200, and for two centuries

they remained a relatively insignificant farming group, with their society divided up into clans (*ayllus*) of roughly equal status.

Inca expansion

The Incas began to make their mark as a major power around 1438, when the neighboring Chanka people attempted to push the Incas out of the Cuzco valley. By this time, the Incas had a supreme leader (the Sapa Inca), and although the incumbent Viracocha was unequal to the task, his son Pachacuti defeated the invaders, and then led Inca armies to conquer the rest of the Cuzco valley and the southern highlands around Lake Titicaca. Under Pachacuti's son Topa Inca Yupanqui and grandson Huayna Capac, the Incas overcame Chimor (the largest coastal state) in about 1470. They then absorbed the rest of the northern highlands and extended to parts of modern-day Ecuador and Colombia and south to the deserts north of Chile.

Unlike the Aztecs, the Incas recruited troops from among the conquered peoples (placed under the command of Inca officers), thus providing them with the lure of plunder in return for their loyalty.

Inca communication

The empire of the Incas was highly centralized; censuses recorded the number of peasants, who all owed labor service (*mitad*) to the Sapa Inca. This level of organization enabled the construction of public works on a vast scale. Particularly vital was the extensive road network,

Tlacaelel

As the Aztec Empire expanded and conquered new territories, it became increasingly necessary to create a more complex system of administration. After Itzcoatl became ruler (*tlatoani*) in 1427, he introduced the new post of chief adviser (*cihuacoatl*). The office's first incumbent was Itzcoatl's nephew,

Tlacaelel (1397–1487), who held the office until his death. Tlacaelel served through several reigns and he provided invaluable continuity. In addition, he created impetus for his reforms (mostly benefiting the royal family and nobles) by ordering the destruction of earlier chronicles and the rewriting of Aztec history to establish the basis of Aztec imperial ideology.

He also presided over the formation of the Triple Alliance, solidifying the Aztec position and ensuring a steady stream of sacrificial victims. Given that Tlacaelel was never the Aztec's ruler, his immense influence in Tenochtitlan shows that the Aztec system of authority was not as monolithic as it might at first appear.

Society in the expansionist Aztec Empire was deeply
militaristic. A boy had to prove himself a warrior before
he could be considered a man. Noble Aztec youths joined
warrior societies and progressed through the ranks by
taking more captives for sacrifice.

The Shorn Ones Deadly
warriors who swore not
to step back in battle.

Otomies Named after
skilled allies of the
Aztecs, Otomies may
have been the first
warriors to enter battle.

Jaguar Warriors Men had to take
four human captives before they
could be admitted to the ranks of
the Eagle and Jaguar Warriors.

Eagle Warriors Alongside Jaguar
Warriors, these may have been the
lowest rank of the elite Aztec warrior
societies. Their resplendent uniforms
resembled their namesakes.

which extended nearly 25,000 miles (40,000
kilometers) long and was dotted at regular
intervals with rest houses that facilitated
rapid transit for the army and provided a
very efficient system of communication
across the far-flung Inca domains. At
the same time, the Inca domestication of the
llama as a beast of burden made it easier to
transport heavy loads across the empire.

Unlike the Aztecs, the Incas actively
sought to spread their own language
(Quechua) and system of religious beliefs,
which was initially based around the
worship of Inti (the sun god), but which
came to feature prominently Viracocha—
a supreme creation god and therefore
considered a more suitable deity for a
conquering power. They also dispatched
colonists (*miqmaq*), shifting troublesome
groups into more pacified areas to dilute
their resistance and creating networks of
loyal settlers on the fringes of the empire.
Although definitive population statistics
are not known, by the early 16th century
the Inca Empire—which the Incas called
Tawantinsuyu ("The Realm of Four
Quarters")—consisted of about 4–6 million
people in total, operating to the advantage
of the Inca minority and their subjects.

Despite its many strengths, the highly
centralized nature of the Inca Empire
proved fatal in the early 1530s, when

Spanish invaders led by Pizarro captured
the Sapa Inca Atahualpa; without their
leader, the Incas rapidly collapsed.

The new colonizers
The Aztecs and the Incas built the first true
empires in their regions of the Americas.
They were able to do so by creating food
surpluses through irrigation projects, thus
releasing a large proportion of their population
to fight in the armies that conducted
their campaigns of expansion. They also
reorganized the traditional tribal structure to
favor a warrior and noble elite. In both cases,
the momentum of conquest demanded
further wars to reward the warrior caste or
to provide an incentive for newly conquered
peoples to remain loyal and thus to gain the
rewards of participation in new campaigns.

Neither the Aztecs nor the Incas
survived long enough to govern after their
expansion slowed down. Had they done so,
they might have developed strategies to
bring long-term stability to their empires,
or might have declined to the status of
competing city-states fighting to control
limited resources. Instead, the Spanish
conquest of the Aztecs in 1521 and their
defeat of the last Incas by 1572 put an end
to the ambitions of both empires and left
the Spanish firmly established as colonial
rulers in the region for the next 300 years. ■

SCARCE THE TENTH PERSON OF ANY SORT WAS LEFT ALIVE

THE OUTBREAK OF THE BLACK DEATH IN EUROPE (1347)

In late November 1347, a galley entered the Italian port of Genoa, having fled a Tatar siege of Kaffa in the Crimea. It bore a deadly cargo: the bubonic plague. Within a mere two years this lethal pestilence had killed more than a third of the population of Europe and the Middle East, and altered the regions' economic, social, and religious makeup forever.

Spread of the Black Death

Having probably originated in Central Asia or western China in the 1330s, the plague's initial progress westward was slow, but after it reached Crimea and Constantinople in 1347 it spread rapidly along maritime trade routes. Having hit Genoa, it appeared quickly in Sicily and Marseilles; by 1348 it had struck Spain, Portugal, and England, and it reached Germany and Scandinavia by 1349.

The epidemic's main vector was infected fleas and the rats that harbored them, both of which flourished in the unsanitary conditions of the time. The main symptoms of the disease were swellings, known as buboes, that appeared in the groin, neck, or armpits. These were followed by black blotches on the skin (hence "Black Death") and then, in around three-quarters of cases, by death.

Contemporaries ascribed the causes of the pestilence variously to divine punishment for immorality, adverse conjunctions of the planets, earthquakes, or bad vapors. There was no cure, but preventive advice included abstinence from hard-to-digest food, the use of aromatic herbs to purify the air, and—the only effective measure—avoiding the company of others.

Disease spreads west from Central Asia **along trade routes**.	Plague **rats and fleas flourish** in unsanitary living conditions.

⬇   ⬇

Black Death kills over a third of Europe's population.

⬇   ⬇

Fall in population leads to demands for **better living conditions** and wages.	Church authority **diminished** by mortality among priests and monks.

More than a hundred million people may have died of the plague; estimates put the world population at 450 million before it arrived, and 350 million afterward. Its effects were more deadly in some areas than in others—in Egypt, about 40 percent of the population are thought to have died. Populations did not reach pre-plague levels again for nearly three centuries.

Reactions to the plague

Survivors reacted in varying ways. Jewish communities in Germany were accused of causing the plague by poisoning wells, and many were attacked. In Strasbourg alone, 2,000 Jews were killed.

With the population diminished, landholdings fell vacant, labor became scarce, and peasants' bargaining power increased. By 1350, English laborers could demand five times the wages they had asked in 1347, and tenants were paying rent in cash rather than with compulsory labor. Governments tried to clamp down on wages—the 1351 Statute of Labourers aimed to freeze rates at 1346 levels—but peasants responded with outbursts such as the Jacquerie in France in 1358, and the Peasants' Revolt in England in 1381.

By the time it ended, the Black Death had killed proportionately as many clergy as laity, and some clergy deserted their posts. As a result the church's authority, like that of the nobility, was greatly weakened. The plague had loosened the ties that had previously bound medieval society together, leaving a freer and more volatile population to face the challenges posed by the Renaissance, Reformation, and the economic expansion of the 16th and 17th centuries. ∎

Shattered society

The plague's catastrophic toll cast a long shadow over contemporary social attitudes. A landscape of mass graves, abandoned villages, and an all-pervading fear of death deepened the sense that God had abandoned his people, and diluted the claims of traditional morality. Crime rose: the incidence of murder in England doubled in two decades from 1349. Flagellants roamed the countryside, scourging themselves with knotted ropes, until a Papal bull banned the practice in 1349. Bequests to charitable foundations—hospitals in particular—rose as the rich gave thanks for their survival. Artistic production tended to the morbid: depictions of the Dance of Death appeared, showing Death cavorting among the living; and writers such as Boccaccio, who chronicled the plague in his *Decameron*, stressed the briefness and fragility of life.

Death selects his victims indiscriminately from among the social orders in the allegorical *Danse Macabre* or Dance of Death.

I HAVE WORKED TO DISCHARGE HEAVEN'S WILL

HONGWU FOUNDS THE MING DYNASTY (1368)

IN CONTEXT

FOCUS
Ming China

BEFORE
1279 Kublai Khan overthrows the Song and establishes the Mongol Yuan dynasty.

1344 In central China, the Yellow River begins to shift course, leading to droughts and a subsequent upsurge in peasant rebellions.

1351 Outbreak of Red Turban revolt against the Yuan.

AFTER
1380 Hongwu takes on the role of chief minister, laying the basis of an authoritarian political culture.

1415 Yongle revives and extends the Grand Canal, enabling it to carry goods from southern China to Beijing.

1520 The first Portuguese trading missions to China.

c. 1592 Publication of *Journey to the West*, one of the masterworks of Chinese classical writing.

1644 Chongzhen dies by suicide, ending the Ming era.

Military and economic decline under the late Yuan dynasty leads to **widespread peasant revolts**.

↓

Hongwu founds the Ming dynasty and institutes reforms that restore stability, and also give the emperor absolute authority.

↓

Autocratic, highly centralized system provides centuries of stable rule and economic prosperity.

↓

A series of **weak rulers** means centralized system ceases to operate efficiently.

↓

Ming dynasty collapses in the face of Manchu invasion and peasant uprisings.

Surrounded by officials at the imperial palace in Nanjing, Zhu Yuanzhang, the son of poor peasant farmers, offered sacrifices to Heaven and Earth as he was proclaimed first emperor of China's Ming ("brilliant") dynasty.

It was the culmination of a remarkable rise to power by the monk turned rebel general, who had ousted the despised Yuan dynasty—founded by Kublai Khan, the Mongol conqueror of China—the country's rulers since 1279. Zhu reigned as emperor Hongwu ("Vastly Martial"—a reference to his military prowess) from 1368 until his death in 1398, by which time he had firmly established one of China's most influential, but also most authoritarian, dynasties. He and his successors brought three centuries of prosperity and stability to the country, establishing its government and bureaucracy in a form that would endure, with slight modifications, until the demise of the imperial system in 1911, and broadening the base of its economy.

Driving out the Mongols

Zhu's new dynasty arose from the chaos that accompanied the decline of the Yuan. In the 1340s and '50s, factionalism in the Mongol court, rampant government corruption, and a series of natural disasters, including plagues and epidemics, resulted in wholesale breakdown in law and order and administration as peasant groups rose up against their faltering foreign overlords. Zhu himself lost most of his family in an outbreak of plague in 1344, and after a few years spent as a mendicant monk, begging for food, he joined the Red Turbans, one of a constellation of native Han Chinese peasant secret societies in rebellion against the Yuan. Determined, ruthless, and an able general, the young rebel climbed the ranks to the leadership of the Red Turbans, and later overcame his rivals to become the national leader against the Yuan.

Zhu took control of much of southern and northern China and declared himself emperor before pushing the Mongols out of their capital at Dadu (Beijing) in 1368. The rest of the country was then subdued, although the Mongols resisted in the far north until the early 1370s, and the unification of China was not achieved until the defeat of the last Mongol forces in the south in 1382.

Reform and despotism

Zhu's first priority as emperor Hongwu was to establish order—decades of conflict had ravaged China and impoverished its rural population. His humble beginnings may

The tribulations of Hongwu's early life led him to improve the lot of China's rural poor, but they also created a cruel and irrational man who murdered all those he suspected of disloyalty.

have influenced some of his early policies: responsibility for tax assessment was entrusted to rural communities, sweeping away the problem of rapacious tax collectors who had preyed on poorer areas; slavery was abolished; many large estates were confiscated; and lands owned by the state in the under-populated north of the country were handed to landless peasants, to encourage them to settle there.

From 1380, Hongwu instituted government reforms that gave him personal control over all matters of state. After executing his prime minister, who had been implicated in a plot to overthrow him, he abolished the prime ministership and the central secretariat and had the heads of the next layer of government, the six ministries, report directly to him, ensuring he oversaw even minor decisions.

From then on, Hongwu acted as his own prime minister. His workload was almost unbearable—in a single week-long stint, he had to scrutinize and approve some 1,600 documents—and as a result, the state became incapable of responding swiftly to crises. Although in time a new grand secretariat emerged—an advisory board through which the emperor responded **»**

The **Forbidden City**—the imperial palace in Beijing—adhered to hierarchic Confucian ideology: the higher one's social status, the further one could enter into the city.

1 Meridian Gate The grand entrance had five gates. The central one was always reserved for the emperor.

2 The Golden Water Bridge Crossing points like the bridges were arranged in odd numbers. Only the emperor could use the central passage, with the next highest rank able to use the neighboring paths.

3 Outer Court This area was reserved for state affairs and ceremonial purposes.

4 Inner Court Only the emperor and his family could enter the Inner Court.

5 The Palace of Heavenly Purity To fool assassins, the palace had nine bedrooms: the emperor slept in a different one each night.

to the six ministries and other government agencies—the Ming retained a more autocratic and highly centralized structure than that of previous Chinese dynasties. This was reflected in the protocol of the Ming court, too: under the Song dynasty (960–1279), the emperor's advisers had stood before him to discuss matters of state, but under the Ming they were required to *kowtow*—kneel and knock their heads to the floor—before him, a reverential acknowledgment of his absolute power and superiority.

Curbing the military

In the later years of the Yuan dynasty, the state had been torn apart by competing power bases outside the central court, and in a bid to avoid this scenario, Hongwu diluted the strength of the army. Although he adopted the Yuan military system—establishing garrisons in key cities, particularly along the northern frontier, where the threat of nomad incursions was ever-present, and creating a hereditary caste of soldiers that supported itself on land granted by the government—he also ensured that military units were periodically rotated through the capital for training, and that a group of centrally selected officers shared authority in the army with the garrison commanders, thus preventing the rise of influential warlords with a strong local base.

Perfecting the civil service

Hongwu also had a deep mistrust of the elite scholar class that had been at the heart of government for centuries. However, he was aware that they played a vital role in the efficient running of the state, and so he promoted education and trained scholars specifically for the bureaucracy. In 1373, he suspended the traditional examinations used to recruit civil servants and ordered the establishment of local county and prefectural schools. From these, the best candidates would be called for further study at a national university in the capital, where eventually 10,000 students from the original intake were enrolled. The civil service examinations were restored in 1385, when the emperor considered the well-trained graduates of the university ready to take them, and were so competitive that soldiers were stationed outside the cubicles where the examinees sat to avoid any collaboration or illicit use of reference materials.

The pool of potential recruits into the administration was thus widened, but civil servants still received a very conservative education based on the Four Books and Five Classics of Confucianism and a selection of neo-Confucian works that expounded the virtues of loyalty to the emperor and adherence to Chinese tradition. Innovation was discouraged and bureaucrats became set in their ways. Those who were perceived as having stepped outside their brief were publicly flogged, sometimes to death.

This maltreatment of public servants was a sign of the cruel side of Hongwu's personality. He was also violently paranoid, and vicious in his suppression of dissent. In 1382, he established a secret police, the Embroidered Brocade Guard, whose 16,000 officers stamped out all signs of resistance. The Guard's reach and influence was wide, and as a result, until the very last years of its rule, the Ming dynasty experienced no significant rebellions by either the military or the aristocracy.

International diplomacy

The dynasty's self-confidence appeared to grow even further under Hongwu's successor, Yongle (reigned 1402–1424), who moved the capital from Nanjing to Beijing, and embarked on an ambitious program of reconstruction and public works, including measures to improve the navigability of the Grand Canal. He also built the extravagant Forbidden City, which housed an imperial palace complex containing more than 9,000 rooms.

Yongle's initially aggressive foreign policy led to four campaigns against Mongolia and an attack on Annam (Vietnam) in 1417 that resulted in its incorporation into the Ming Empire. He also sought recognition from the rulers of faraway states: between 1405 and 1433, he launched six large-scale maritime expeditions to Southeast Asia, East Africa, and Arabia. Led by the great fleet admiral Zheng He, their purpose was to confirm China's domination over the area by exacting tribute and other gestures of homage to the emperor.

The later Ming

However, the enormous cost of Zheng He's ambitious ventures put great strain on the treasury, and to ensure they would never be repeated, all records relating to them were destroyed. Official ideology »

The voyages of Zheng He

A Muslim of Mongol descent, Zheng He was captured by the Ming as a boy, castrated, and sent into the army, where he acquired military and diplomatic skills and distinguished himself as a junior officer. He went on to become an influential eunuch in the imperial court, and in 1405, Yongle chose him to lead a grandly conceived maritime expedition around the rim of the Indian Ocean, as both fleet admiral and diplomatic agent.

Over the next 28 years, Zheng He commanded one of the largest naval forces in history: the first mission had 63 vessels, including 440-ft- (130-m-) long "treasure ships" carrying more than 27,000 crew.

Although these voyages were dramatic in their conduct and scope—the last three sailed as far south as Mombasa on the east coast of Africa—they were not in any real sense commercial or exploratory ventures. Their intention was strictly diplomatic, designed to enhance China's prestige abroad and to extract declarations of loyalty and exotic tributary gifts for Yongle.

This silk scroll records one of the most celebrated tribute gifts from Zheng He's voyages: a giraffe brought back from Africa in 1414.

Hongwu's final resting place, the Xiaoling Mausoleum, lies at the foot of the Purple Mountain in Nanjing, and is guarded by an avenue of stone statues of pairs of animals, including camels.

regarded China as the center of the world, and the later Ming saw no reason to encourage further maritime contact. The Chinese did not regard relations with foreign powers as possible on an equal basis: where diplomatic relations were conducted, the foreigners were considered (by the Ming, at least) as tributaries. The confidence and stability of the Ming bureaucracy also created a sense of self-sufficiency, with little use for external influences.

Ocean-going vessels were made to report all the cargo they landed, and private maritime trade was periodically banned (until it was legalized again in 1567 for all except trade with Japan). In Beijing, a shopkeeper's unauthorized contact with foreigners could result in the confiscation of his stock.

Diplomatic isolation was reinforced by military uncertainty: Annam became independent once more in 1428, while huge resources were devoted to containing the threat posed by the Mongol tribes on China's northern borders. In 1449, Emperor Zhengtong personally led a disastrous expedition against the Mongol leader Esen Khan in which the majority of the 500,000 Chinese soldiers died of hunger, were picked off by the enemy, or perished in a final battle as they retreated.

Extending the Great Wall
In the 1470s, the building of the final stages of the Great Wall—begun by the Qin dynasty in the 3rd century BCE—was not only a bid to prevent a similar disaster, but also to compensate for the Ming's waning energy. Like their predecessors, they were

unable to absorb the lands of the nomadic groups to the north of the border, or to send out expeditions that had any lasting effect on discouraging their raids. Therefore, a fixed, strongly garrisoned border defense was the best compromise.

During the 16th century, a succession of short-lived emperors who were dominated by their consorts, mothers, or by eunuch (castrated) advisers, was capped by the long reign of Wanli (1573–1620), who simply withdrew from public life entirely: for the last decades of his reign, he refused even to meet with his ministers. The dynasty began to decline: the machinery of government faltered and the army had little strength to respond to the serious threat posed by the Jurchen in Manchuria (now in northeast China). In 1619, this tribal people, who later renamed themselves Manchu, began to encroach on China's northern borders.

Global trade
Economically, however, Ming China's great productivity was a magnet for European maritime states seeking new commercial connections in East Asia, and in the early 16th century, European traders finally reached the coast of China. In 1514, a Portuguese fleet appeared off Canton (now Guangzhou) in the south, and by 1557, Portugal had established a permanent base at Macao. Spanish and Portuguese merchants (the former operating from Nagasaki in Japan and Manila in the Philippines)—and from 1601, the Dutch—secured an important share in trade with China.

Even though Ming policy discouraged foreign maritime trade, individual Chinese merchants had participated actively in the revived economy. Before long there were flourishing Chinese colonies in Manila and on Java in Indonesia, near the Dutch-controlled trading city of Batavia, and Chinese merchants controlled a large share of local trade in Southeast Asia. The technical sophistication of the Chinese porcelain industry under the Ming led for the first time to the mass production of ceramics for export to European markets.

The effects, though, of this growth in trade were not wholly positive: while a huge influx of silver from the Americas and

Japan, used by the Europeans to pay for Chinese goods such as silk, lacquerware, and porcelain, stimulated economic growth, it also caused inflation.

Technological change

Ming China had inherited a legacy of scientific and technological innovation from the Song dynasty, which had left the country at the forefront of many scientific fields, including navigation and the military applications of gunpowder—a substance discovered during the Tang era whose use had spread to Europe from China in the 13th century. Under the Ming, though, the pace of progress slowed and by the later part of the dynasty, ideas had begun to flow in from Europe.

The Chinese military began to use artillery of European manufacture, and knowledge of European mathematics and astronomy was introduced to the country through Jesuit missionaries, including Matteo Ricci, who lived in Beijing from 1601 to 1610. He translated the ancient Greek mathematician Euclid's *Geometry* into Chinese, as well as a treatise on the astrolabe (an astronomical instrument used for taking the altitude of the sun or stars). In 1626, the German Jesuit Johann Adam Schall von Bell wrote the first treatise in Chinese on the telescope, bringing Heliocentrism (an astronomical model in which the sun lies at the center of the universe) to a Chinese audience.

On taking the throne, Hongwu issued his own traditional bronze coinage, although a shortage of metal led to the reinstatement of paper money, made of mulberry bark.

The Ming collapse

The late Ming began to suffer many of the same issues that had led to the fall of the Yuan. Crop failures reduced the productivity of China's vast agriculture, and famines and floods led to widespread unrest in rural areas. The army's pay began to fall into arrears, leading to discipline problems and desertions, while localized peasant uprisings coalesced into more general revolts. Meanwhile, on the northeastern frontier, the Manchus had built a state along Chinese lines at Mukden in Manchuria—calling their regime the Qing dynasty in 1636—and were now poised to take advantage of the Ming's imminent collapse. They were aided in this by a revolt led by Li Zicheng, a rebel leader whose forces entered Beijing in 1644 unopposed, prompting the emperor to commit suicide. In desperation, the Ming military called on the Manchus for help. The tribesmen swept into the capital and drove out the rebels, but then seized the throne, and proclaimed the Qing dynasty in China.

An enduring legacy

Although the Ming had fallen victim to an agrarian crisis that coincided with renewed nomadic activity on its frontiers, this was a combination that had also brought down dynasties before it. The bureaucracy that had given China centuries of constancy and reduced the possibility, or even the need, for internal dissent, was slow to adapt itself to times of fast-moving crisis.

Yet even so, the Ming era had brought great wealth and success to China. The population expanded from around 60 million at the start of its rule, to around three times that number by 1600. Much of this growth was centered in medium-sized market towns, rather than in large cities, and an increase in agricultural production led to the rise of an affluent merchant class in the provinces. Many of the elements of orderly government that Hongwu had inaugurated were carried over into the succeeding Qing dynasty, providing China with a degree of unity, stability, and prosperity that the European states of that period could only envy and admire. ∎

I HAVE NEWLY DEVISED 28 LETTERS

KING SEJONG INTRODUCES A NEW SCRIPT (1443)

IN CONTEXT

FOCUS
Chosŏn Korea

BEFORE
918 The Goryeo dynasty is founded.

1270 Goryeo comes under the structural, military, and administrative influence of the Mongol Yuan dynasty.

1392 Yi Sŏngyye founds the Chosŏn dynasty.

1420 King Sejong founds the Chiphyŏn-jŏn research institution.

AFTER
1445 A 365-volume medical encyclopedia is published.

1447 The first work printed in Han'gŭl is published.

1542 The first sŏwŏn private academy opens. The academies become centers of debate and house neo-Confucian texts.

1910 Japan annexes Korea and deposes the last Chosŏn ruler.

I n 1443, the Korean court of King Sejong announced the creation of Han'gŭl, a national alphabet for the Korean language, and launched a program of publications in the new script. The measure was one of a number of strategies encouraged by Korea's king that were designed to stabilize Korea and improve prosperity, and enabled his Chosŏn (or Yi) dynasty to survive for another 450 years.

Rise of the Yi dynasty

The Mongol Yuan dynasty had interfered in the Korean Peninsula from the late 12th century until 1368, when it was overthrown by the Ming dynasty. Korea was left in chaos as its Koryŏ kings tried to reverse the effects of a century's authoritarian domination. The redistribution of land and the sacking of pro-Mongol ministers led almost to civil war, but in 1392 Sejong's grandfather Yi Sŏngyye, a former general, stepped in, deposed the last Koryŏ king, and assumed the throne as King Taejo.

King Taejo's immediate priority was to secure stability, and the installation of a state ideology based on neo-Confucianism was key to achieving that. This ideology sought to reestablish proper relations between the ruler and his people, and conferred privileged status on a bureaucratic class that would act as guardian of the social hierarchy. Buddhism had been the dominant ideology under the Koryŏ dynasty, but Taejo undermined its hold in the region by breaking up large estates controlled by Buddhist temples and redistributing the land, some to Confucian shrines.

Neo-Confucianism emphasized the importance of education as a way of producing a class of literati capable of ensuring the harmonious running of the state. Taejo's grandson, King Sejong (reigned 1418–1450) raised this principle

Neo-Confucianism

The neo-Confucianism that became dominant in Korea under the Choson dynasty had evolved in China during the 11th and 12th centuries as a means to revive Confucianism, which had declined in favor of Taoism and Buddhism under the Tang and early Song. A more rationalist and secular form of Confucianism, the new philosophy rejected superstitious and mystical elements that had influenced Confucianism during and after the Han dynasty. Writers such as Confucian scholar Zhu Xi stressed the importance of morality, respect for social harmony, and education as means of understanding the Supreme Ultimate (*tai qi*), the underlying principle of the universe. In practice, however, neo-Confucian virtues such as loyalty, determination, and the belief that a supreme monarch should rule the state to parallel the Supreme Ultimate that governed the universe, tended to favor a hierarchical, bureaucratic state staffed by scholars who jealously maintained the status quo.

Hyanggyo were Confucian schools, built throughout provincial Korea and used for both ceremonial and educational purposes.

to new heights, founding in 1420 the Chiphyŏn-jŏn (Hall of Worthies), an elite group of 20 scholars tasked with research that would promote the better running of the kingdom.

Encouragement of wider literacy was an important neo-Confucian ideal, and Taejo had already ordered the foundation of government-sponsored schools. At the time, however, Korean was written in Chinese characters, which were not well adapted to express the sounds of the language. Sejong himself is said to have developed the simplified script, the Han'gŭl, whose principles were explained in *Proper Sounds for the Education of the People*, a book published in 1445. Having only 28 characters—later reduced to 24— the script was far easier than Chinese was to learn, but its introduction faced bitter resistance from traditionalist nobles. They feared it might open civil service examinations to people from other social classes, which would risk diluting their power. As a result Han'gŭl faded from use, relegated as the "vulgar letters" of the lower orders, until its rediscovery in the 19th century, since when it has thrived as a vehicle for Korean nationalism.

The reforms of Taejo and Sejong, however, broadly survived, creating a class of yangban—elite government officials dedicated to the perpetuation of the state. The yangban also acted as a break on any tendency to autocracy among the Yi monarchs, which helped the resulting dynasty endure for more than five centuries. ∎

Decline in Mongol power leads to the rise of the Chosŏn.

The Chosŏn promote **wider education**.

Sejong devises the Han'gŭl alphabet.

Yangban scholars **enhance the stability of the Chosŏn** regime.

The dynasty endures and the **Han'gŭl alphabet is revived** in the 19th century.

THE EARLY
MODERN E

1420–1795

The course of world events always looks different in retrospect from the way that it appears at the time, but the contrast in perspective is rarely as extreme as in the Early Modern Era, which spanned the 15th, 16th, 17th, and 18th centuries. This period is often viewed today as the age during which Europe climbed toward world domination, but to Europeans living at the time it often seemed to be full of unprecedented disasters. The unity of Christendom was split by the Reformation, and sectarian conflict between Catholics and Protestants, combined with power struggles between competing royal dynasties, made Europe a place of frequent warfare—a continent tearing itself apart. Meanwhile, the Muslim armies of the Ottoman Empire threatened the heartland of Europe, seizing the Byzantine city of Constantinople and twice penetrating as far as Vienna.

Yet historical retrospect certainly recognizes changes underway that were to make European nations the founders of the modern world. The flowering of arts and ideas in the Renaissance meant that Europe ceased to be a cultural backwater. Printing and paper, both originally invented in China, were used by Europeans to create mass-produced books that went on to revolutionize the dissemination of information. Gunpowder weapons, also invented by the Chinese, were deployed most effectively by European armies and navies. Above all, explorers and sailors from Europe's western seaboard established oceanic trade routes that laid the foundations for the first global economy.

The start of colonialism

The importance of Christopher Columbus's transatlantic voyage in 1492 cannot be exaggerated. It established a permanent link between two entire ecosystems that had evolved in isolation from each another for almost 10,000 years. The impact on the inhabitants of the Americas was catastrophic. Eurasian diseases and the infamous brutality of the Spanish conquistadors decimated the population. A remarkably small number of European invaders conquered the most sophisticated American states with startling ease, laying potentially the entire New World open to European exploitation and colonization.

However, the arrival of European sailors in Asia did not have the same dramatic impact. Powerful countries, including India, Imperial China, the Mughal Empire, and the Japanese shogunate at first merely tolerated the Europeans as traders, allowing them to control only a few islands or enclaves along the coast, as long as they did not interfere or become too troublesome.

Economic growth

From the second half of the 17th century, signs of economic growth accelerated in Europe. Productivity of labor in trades and agriculture increased notably in areas like the Dutch Netherlands. New financial institutions, such as central banks and joint stock companies, laid the foundations of modern capitalism. Complex patterns of maritime trade linked European colonies in the Americas to Europe, Africa, and Asia. Enslaved people, mostly bought by European traders in West Africa, were transported in vast numbers to work on colonial plantations, so that in some parts of the New World people of African descent greatly outnumbered both Europeans and the native population. At home, Europeans consumed luxury goods from China and India, and products such as sugar and coffee from plantations in the Caribbean and Brazil. North America, the West Indies, and India were all regions of colonial contention—the precipitous decline of the Mughal Empire having opened up parts of India to European territorial conquest.

Intellectual movements

Even at this stage, the degree of European ascendancy should not be exaggerated. China had gone through difficult times in the mid-17th century transition from the Ming to the Qing dynasty, but in the 18th century, imperial China was enjoying a golden age of power and prosperity. The population of Europe had begun a steep increase to unprecedented levels—a result of improved food production and declining epidemic diseases—but China also experienced rapid population growth.

What really marked out Europe as unique at this time was the development of knowledge and thought. The 17th-century scientific revolution began a transformation of our understanding of the universe. The rationalist movement known as the Enlightenment challenged all preconceptions, traditions, and conventions. The modern world was under construction in the European mind. ■

AS MY CITY FALLS, I SHALL FALL WITH IT

THE FALL OF CONSTANTINOPLE (1453)

I n 1453, the Ottoman Turks attacked and took the city of Constantinople, the capital of the Byzantine Empire. The loss of this millennium-old Christian empire, which had once stretched virtually all the way around the Mediterranean, was a profound shock to the Christian world. As if to symbolize the Muslim victory Hagia Sophia, one of the greatest cathedrals in Christendom, was converted into a mosque.

The Ottoman Turks had already conquered much of the surrounding territory before Sultan Mehmed II (1432–1481) laid siege to the city and bombarded it with heavy artillery. Having breached its walls, his army of more than 80,000 men then overwhelmed the small force inside. Constantine XI, the last Byzantine emperor, was killed, and with the fall of the city, his empire ended. Constantinople then became the capital of the Ottoman Empire, which lasted until 1922.

A weakening empire

The Byzantine Empire was already in terminal decline by the time Constantinople was taken. It had shrunk to include only the capital city, some land to its west, and the southern part of Greece. The decline began at the Battle of Manzikert (1071), during which the army of the Turkish Seljuk dynasty drove the Byzantines out of their crucial territory in Anatolia. From this point, rival claims for the Byzantine crown, disputes over tax, loss of trade revenue, and poor military leadership all contributed to the contraction of the empire.

In 1203, the Fourth Crusade—a western European expedition originally intended to conquer Jerusalem—became entangled in the empire's politics. Some of the crusade leaders pledged to help restore the deposed Byzantine Emperor Isaac II Angelos in return for support for their expedition. They were initially successful: Angelos' son was crowned as co-emperor but, in 1204, he in turn was deposed by a popular uprising.

The Byzantine senate elected a young noble, Nicolas Kanabos, as emperor, and he refused to back the crusaders. Denied their promised payments, the crusaders and their allies, the Venetians, responded with a ruthless attack on the city. They raped and killed civilians, looted churches, and demolished priceless works of art. Constantinople was all but destroyed.

Rise of the Ottomans

Before capturing Constantinople, the Ottoman Empire had already expanded from Anatolia into the Balkans. Afterward, in the 16th century, it expanded into the eastern Mediterranean, along the banks of the Red Sea, and into North Africa. The defeat of the Mamluks in Egypt in 1517, and wars against the Safavids, one of Persia's most significant ruling dynasties, gave the Ottomans control of a whole swathe of the Arab Middle East.

The Ottoman Empire was a Muslim State and the sultans saw it as their duty to promote the spread of Islam. Nevertheless it tolerated Christians and Jews in a subsidiary status and made extensive use of enslaved people. Many languages were

When lighted tapers were put to the "innumerable machines" ranged along a four-mile section of the city walls, the world's first concerted artillery barrage exploded into life.

spoken and faiths followed within its domains, but it dealt with the conflicting religious and political differences by setting up vassal (subordinate) states in some regions. Territories such as Transylvania and Crimea paid tribute (made regular payments) to the emperor, but they were not ruled by him directly, and acted as buffer zones between Muslim and Christian areas. Some vassal states, including Bulgaria, Serbia, and Bosnia, were eventually absorbed into the larger empire; others retained their vassal status.

Government and military

The Ottomans evolved a strong system of government that combined local administration with central control. The sultan—whose brothers were customarily murdered at his accession—was supreme ruler. He had a council of advisers, later a deputy, who ruled on his behalf. Local areas were ruled by military governors (beys) under the emperor's overall control, but local councils kept the beys' authority in check.

Non-Muslim communities within the empire were allowed a degree of self-rule through a system of separate courts called millets. The millets allowed Armenian, Jewish, and Orthodox Christian communities to rule according to their own laws in cases that did not involve Muslims. This balanced combination of central and »

Janissaries wore distinctive uniforms and, unlike other military units, were paid salaries and lived in barracks. They were the first corps to make extensive use of firearms.

local control enabled the Ottomans to hold together a large and diverse empire for much longer than would have been possible with a more wholly centralized system.

The Ottoman army was also crucial to the empire's success. It was technically advanced—employing cannon from the siege of Constantinople onward—and tactically sophisticated. Its high-speed cavalry units could turn what looked like a retreat into a devastatingly effective flanking attack, surrounding the enemy in a crescent-shaped formation that would take them by surprise.

At the heart of the army were the Janissaries, a unit of infantry that began as the imperial guard and expanded to become the most feared elite force of the period. Initially, the unit was made up of men who, as children, had been abducted from Christian families in the Balkans. Under the *devsirme* system, which was also known as the "blood tax" or "tribute in blood," boys aged from 8 to 18 were taken by Ottoman military, forcibly converted to Islam, and sent to live with Turkish families, where they learned the Turkish language and customs. They were then given rigorous military training, and any who showed particular talent were selected for specialized roles ranging from archers to engineers.

Janissaries were not permitted to marry until they retired from active duty, but they received special benefits and privileges designed to secure their sole allegiance to the ruler. Although they made up only a small proportion in the Ottoman army, they had a leading role and played a key part in many victories, including those over the Egyptians, Hungarians, and Constantinople.

Mehmed II

Mehmed (1432–1481), the son of the Ottoman emperor Murad II, was born in Edirne, Turkey. As was usual for an heir to the Ottoman throne,

Mehmed had an Islamic education, and at 11 years old was appointed governor of a province, Amasya, to gain experience of leadership. A year later, Murad abdicated in favor of his son, but shortly afterward was called back from his retirement in Anatolia to lend military support. "If you are the Sultan," Mehmed wrote, "come and lead your armies. If I am the Sultan, I order you to come and lead my armies."

Mehmed's second, main, rule was from 1451 to 1481. His victory at Constantinople was followed by a string of further conquests: the Morea (southern Greece), Serbia, the coast of the Black Sea, Wallachia, Bosnia, and part of Crimea. He rebuilt Constantinople as his capital and founded mosques there, while also allowing Christians and Jews to worship freely. Known for his ruthless military leadership, he also welcomed humanists to the capital, encouraged culture, and founded a university.

Naturalistic motifs in cobalt blues and chrome greens surround Islamic calligraphy in these Iznik wall tiles, commissioned for the Topkapi Palace during the classical age of Turkish art.

The Ottoman heyday

The empire reached its peak under Emperor Suleiman the Magnificent. He forged an alliance with the French against the Hapsburg rulers of the Holy Roman Empire, and signed a treaty with the Safavid rulers of Persia that divided Armenia and Georgia between the two powers and put most of Iraq into Ottoman hands. Suleiman conquered much of Hungary, and even laid siege to Vienna, although he did not succeed in taking it.

The Ottomans took their Islamic faith to their territories, building mosques everywhere—and with the mosques came scholarship and education. Ottoman cities were impressive. Constantinople itself was virtually rebuilt: the Ottomans reinforced its fortifications as well as adding many mosques, bazaars, and water fountains. The city's dazzling centerpiece was the royal palace of Topkapi, commissioned by Sultan Mehmed II in around the 1460s. Masons, stonecutters, and carpenters were summoned from far and wide to ensure the complex would be an enduring monument. It contained mosques, a hospital, bakeries, and a mint among much else, and attached to it were imperial societies of artists and craftsmen who produced some of the finest work in the empire.

Internal divisions **weaken the Byzantine Empire** from within.

↓

The Ottomans attack and capture Constantinople.

↓

Ottoman armies **conquer and pacify** large parts of eastern Europe and the Middle East.

↓

The Ottomans govern conquered lands by **respecting local customs** and **allowing limited self-rule**.

↓

The large, pluralist Ottoman Empire **spreads Islam** but fails to create a **single united culture**.

Gradual decline

This cultural flowering continued after Suleiman's death, but the empire faced serious challenges in other arenas. A rising population was putting pressure on available land; there were military threats and internal revolts; and defeat by a coalition of Catholic forces at the sea battle of Lepanto in 1571 prevented the empire's expansion further along the European side of the Mediterranean.

The Ottoman empire steadily lost prestige and influence until its decline earned it the title "the sick man of Europe." Incapable of responding to the convulsions of the 19th century, it lost territory and struggled against a rising tide of nationalism among its conquered peoples. Its long history finally ended with defeat in World War I and the foundation of the modern Turkish state by Kemal Atatürk. ∎

FOLLOWING THE LIGHT OF THE SUN WE LEFT THE OLD WORLD

CHRISTOPHER COLUMBUS REACHES AMERICA (1492)

IN CONTEXT

FOCUS
Voyages of discovery

BEFORE
1431 Portuguese navigator Gonçalo Velho sails on a voyage of exploration to the Azores.

1488 Bartolomeu Dias rounds the Cape of Good Hope, discovering the passage around southern Africa.

1492 King Ferdinand and Queen Isabella of Spain agree to sponsor Columbus's voyage.

AFTER
1498 Vasco da Gama's fleet arrives in Calicut, India.

c. 1499 Italian explorer Amerigo Vespucci discovers the mouth of the Amazon.

1522 Ferdinand Magellan's Spanish expedition to the East Indies, from 1519 to 1522 results in the first circumnavigation of the Earth.

hristopher Columbus (c. 1451–1506), an Italian-born navigator and trader from Genoa, made a journey in 1492 that initiated a lasting contact between America and Europe, and changed the world.

When he set out, Columbus was expecting to reach Asia, since no Europeans at the time knew that an entire continent blocked this route. When he reached an island in the Bahamas after sailing for over two months, he believed that he had arrived at the outer reaches of Indonesia. From there, Columbus continued to explore the Caribbean, visiting Cuba, Hispaniola, and several of the smaller islands. He met with a mostly peaceful response from the native people, whom he observed might make good servants or enslaved people. He also noticed their gold jewelry, and took a sample of local gold, as well as some native prisoners, back to Europe.

Columbus was to return to the Caribbean on three later voyages, bringing in his wake countless European visitors and settlers.

Motivation to explore
The rulers and merchants of Western Europe wanted to explore the Atlantic for primarily economic reasons. Spices that would not grow in Europe's climate, such as cinnamon, cloves, ginger, nutmeg, and pepper, were prized not only for their taste but also because they could help preserve foods. There was also an enthusiastic market for luxury goods such as silk and precious stones, commodities that came primarily from the islands of the Indonesian group, such as the Moluccas, which were known in Europe as the Spice Islands.

Bringing such commodities across Asia by land was difficult and dangerous because of local wars and instabilities along the route; it was also costly, since during their journey goods would pass through many different merchants' hands. There were certainly excellent economic

Europeans develop **a taste for Asian spices** and luxury goods.

Land routes to Asia are hazardous and **blocked by the Ottoman Empire**.

The **Portuguese** explore **Indian Ocean routes**.

After the fall of Granada, **Spanish religious zeal** turns outward.

The **Spanish Crown supports** the exploration of a potential route **to Asia across the Atlantic Ocean**.

Columbus sets sail westward across the Atlantic to Asia, but instead reaches America.

reasons to develop sea routes: anyone who could find a more direct way of importing these goods to Western Europe would become very rich.

Another reason why Europeans started to explore sea routes in the late Middle Ages was to investigate the possibility of establishing European colonies in Asia. These could act not only as trading posts, but also as bases for missionaries, who could convert the locals to Christianity. This they believed would help reduce the perceived threat of Islam.

By the 14th and 15th centuries, the Spanish, Portuguese, English, and Dutch had developed ocean-going ships, and trained sailors who could navigate over long distances. Explorers used various types of vessels, among the most successful of which was the caravel—a fast, lightweight, and extremely maneuverable ship that was usually equipped with a mix of square and lateen (triangular) sails. The lateen sails made it possible to sail to windward (into the wind), which allowed explorers to make progress even in variable wind conditions. Explorers also used the carrack, or nau, a larger vessel that was similarly rigged. On his first transatlantic voyage, Columbus took two caravels, each probably of 50–70 tons, and one carrack of about 100 tons, the extra capacity being useful for carrying stores.

Skills and technology quickly developed in both shipbuilding and navigation. Sailors used the cross-staff—a basic sighting device—or later a mariner's astrolabe, to calculate a vessel's latitude. They achieved this by measuring angles, such as the angle of the sun to the horizon. They used a magnetic compass to gauge direction, and their charts and knowledge of prevailing winds and currents improved with each voyage.

Portuguese navigators

European navigators had been striking out into the Atlantic for many decades. Sailors from Bristol, England, were sailing in the 1470s in search of a mythical island called "Brasil," thought to be west of Ireland. The Portuguese established trading colonies on Madeira, and Prince Henry the Navigator, son of Portugal's King John I, commissioned numerous journeys of exploration to the Azores in the 15th century. Henry had started the first school for oceanic navigation, with an astronomical observatory at Sagres, Portugal, in about 1418. Here he promoted the study of navigation, map-making, and science. Henry sent ships down the west coast of Africa, to which he was particularly attracted by the potential to trade in enslaved people and gold. His ships pushed southward, setting up trading posts along the way. Subsequent rulers continued to sponsor voyages and, in 1488, Portuguese » captain Bartolomeu Dias rounded the southern tip of Africa. Soon another Portuguese navigator, Vasco da Gama, led the push to round the Cape and pressed on across the Indian Ocean, linking Europe and Asia for the first time by ocean route.

Since Portugal dominated the sea route along the African coast, Portugal's European neighbor and rival Spain needed to find an alternative route, if it was to gain access to the riches of the East. Although educated people knew by this time that the Earth was round, they did not know about the existence of the Americas. An alternative way to the East seemed, therefore, to be to sail west across the Atlantic. This route seemed especially attractive to the many seamen—including Christopher Columbus—who believed the planet's diameter to be rather smaller than it actually is.

Seeking sponsorship

In 1485, Columbus presented to John II, king of Portugal, a plan to sail across the Atlantic to the Spice Islands. John refused to invest in the scheme, however. This was partly because Portugal was already exploring the West African coast with some success, and partly because the experts John consulted about the proposal were skeptical about the distances involved.

Columbus cast his net more widely, seeking backing from the powerful maritime cities of Genoa and Venice, and sending his brother to England to do the same—but still he received no encouragement. He therefore turned to Ferdinand of Aragon and Isabella of Castile, the "Catholic Monarchs" who jointly ruled Spain. At first they turned him down, their navigational consultants also skeptical about the length of his proposed route, but eventually, after protracted negotiations, they agreed to sponsor the voyage. Securing a new trade route would certainly bring material rewards, but Isabella also saw the voyage in terms of a religious mission that could bring the light of Christianity to the East.

Columbus sails west

Having been granted viceroyship and governorship of any lands he could claim for Spain, plus other benefits including

Columbus's voyage was a bold undertaking. Despite a general understanding that the world was spherical, many believed the westward journey was doomed to fail, fearing the crew would die of thirst before ever reaching land.

Start

The voyage to America and back lasted seven months, from August 3, 1492–March 15, 1493.

Provisions on board the ships included vinegar, olive oil, wine, salted flour, biscuits, dry legumes, and salted sardines.

On August 3rd, 1492, Columbus departed Spain with three ships: the Niña, Pinta, and Santa Maria.

The crew consisted of 87 men—20 on the Niña, 26 on the Pinta, and 41 on the Santa Maria.

Christopher Columbus

Born in Genoa, Christopher Columbus became a business agent for several prominent Genoese families and undertook trading voyages in Europe and along the African coast.

Columbus followed his voyage to America with a second in 1493, during which he explored the Lesser and Greater Antilles, and set up a colony at La Isabela in what is now the Dominican Republic. His third voyage (1498–1500) took him to the Caribbean island of Hispaniola and on to Trinidad, where he found the coast of South America and guessed, from the size of the Orinoco River, that he had found a huge land mass. During this time, settlers complained to the Crown about the way he ran his Caribbean colony, and he was dismissed as governor.

On his last voyage (1502–1504) he sailed along the Central American coast, hoping to find a strait to the Indian Ocean. He returned to Spain in poor health and an increasingly disturbed state of mind, feeling he had not received the recognition and benefits he had been promised. Columbus died in 1506.

10 percent of any revenues they yielded, Columbus set sail westward in 1492. He called at Gran Canaria before sailing west, sighting land five weeks later. In early 1493 he returned to Europe with two ships, the third having been wrecked off the coast of present-day Haiti, and was duly appointed Governor of the Indies.

On October 12, 1492, the ships finally reached the Bahamas.

Finish

olumbus calculated that sia was 2,400 miles away om Spain. In fact it is ound 12,200 miles away.

Columbus's second expedition was organized just a few months later. This involved 17 ships loaded with some 1,200 people who would found Spanish colonies in the Caribbean. As well as farmers and soldiers, the colonists included priests, who were specifically charged with converting local people to Christianity. Religious conversion became a key part of European colonization, illustrating the colonist's ambition to impose their own culture and exert control over newly colonized peoples.

Columbus's achievement in 1492 is often described as the European "discovery" of America. This is a problematic claim not only because Columbus thought he had reached Asia, but also because Vikings from Scandinavia had reached North America some 500 years earlier— archaeological remains at L'Anse aux Meadows in Newfoundland reveal that they even settled there. However, the Viking settlement was not long-lived, and was unknown to Columbus and his contemporaries.

Nevertheless, Columbus's 1492 journey did inaugurate a lasting contact between the Americas and Europe. The pitiless destruction he and his men wrought upon the indigenous peoples of the West Indies, whom he encountered when he first arrived in the Americas, also began a process of decimation of Native American populations that would continue for a century. ∎

THIS LINE SHALL BE CONSIDERED AS A PERPETUAL MARK AND BOUND
THE TREATY OF TORDESILLAS (1494)

IN CONTEXT

FOCUS
Spanish and Portuguese American conquests

BEFORE
1492 Columbus makes his first journey to the New World, signaling the beginning of Spanish interest in the area.

AFTER
1500 Pedro Álvares Cabral claims Brazil for Portugal.

1521 Hernán Cortés completes his conquest of the Aztec Empire.

1525 The first Spanish settlement in Colombia, Santa Marta, is established.

1532 Francisco Pizarro begins the Spanish campaign to conquer the Inca Empire.

1598 Juan de Oñate founds the first Spanish settlement in California.

Spain and Portugal signed a treaty on June 7, 1494, at Tordesillas in Spain, that resolved the countries' disputes about the possession of newly discovered territory. The rulers settled on a meridian 370 leagues west of the Cape Verde Islands as a line of demarcation. All the lands to the west of this line would belong to Spain; all those to the east would belong to Portugal. The line was chosen because of its location: it lies roughly halfway between the Cape Verde Islands, which already belonged to Portugal, and the Caribbean islands, which Christopher Columbus had claimed for Spain in 1492.

By the 1490s both countries were discovering substantial territories, including lands in the New World, although at this point the size and extent of the Americas was unclear to Europeans. In spite of the fact that the Spanish Crown had funded Columbus's voyages, Spain's claim to his discoveries was not clear-cut. The 1479 Alcaçovas treaty between the Catholic Monarchs of Spain and the rulers of Portugal gave all newly discovered lands south of the Canary Islands to Portugal. When Columbus landed at Lisbon after his first voyage, he told John II, king of Portugal, that he was claiming Hispaniola and Cuba for his Spanish backers. John wrote to Spain's rulers immediately to say that he was preparing to send his own ships to claim the Caribbean for Portugal.

Legalizing possession

To prevent such disputes erupting each time a navigator made a fresh discovery, the leaders of both countries decided to

> ❝ I and my companions suffer from a disease of the heart that can be cured only with gold.
> **Hernán Cortés, 1519** ❞

European traders see potential for **rich profit** in Asian spices and **luxury goods**.

Spanish and Portuguese **navigators compete** to gain **new territories**.

Exploration opens eastern and western **sea routes**.

The Treaty of Tordesillas resolves territorial conflicts between Spain and Portugal.

review the terms of the Alcaçovas treaty. The papacy had been involved in the 1479 treaty, and now Pope Alexander VI (a Spaniard) proposed a combined north–south and east–west dividing line, suggesting that any lands west and south of a line 100 leagues west and south of the Azores and Cape Verde Islands be allocated to Spain. John rejected the proposition, considering it to be biased in favor of his rivals, and eventually all parties agreed on the meridian between the Cape Verde Islands and the Caribbean. The resulting treaty set the agenda for future colonization, and influenced the fate of vast swathes of the world.

Portuguese colonies

By the time the Tordesillas treaty was signed, Portugal had already made headway in exploring Africa and southern Asia. Working south from a North African base at Ceuta, explorers established a series of trading posts on the West African coast, gradually pushing south until, in 1498, Vasco da Gama rounded the Cape of Good Hope and sailed into the Indian Ocean. In the 16th century, Portugal had settlements in India, the Moluccas, Sumatra, Burma, and Thailand, and by 1557 they had established their long-standing enclave in Macau, which became a hub for their trade with many Asian communities.

The treaty line passed through South America, allocating a north-western portion to the Portuguese. In 1500, explorer Pedro Álvares Cabral landed on the coast of Brazil and claimed it for Portugal. The conquistadors exploited their new colony, forcing indigenous peoples to cultivate sugar cane, grow coffee, and mine gold. The laborers died in huge numbers, both from diseases introduced by the colonists, and as a result of their ruthless treatment, and enslaved people were brought in from Africa to replace them. Brazil, ruled from the mid-16th century by Portuguese governors-general, remained a colony until the early 19th century.

The Spanish in America

Following Columbus's transatlantic voyages and the settlement of the treaty, Spain turned increasingly to the Americas, sponsoring expeditions that combined exploration with conquest and colonization. The first of these, led by Hernán Cortés, was to Mexico, which was then home to the small but rich Aztec Empire. The empire's large, central capital was at Tenochtitlan (modern Mexico City). With just a small force of about 600 men, Cortés overthrew the million-strong empire, eventually killing its ruler, Montezuma. Another Spanish leader, Francisco Pizarro, conquered the Inca Empire, which centered on Peru but also included Chile, Ecuador, and large parts of Bolivia and northwestern Argentina. Again with just a small force (180 men), Pizarro laid the foundations of another Spanish stronghold and source of great wealth in precious metals. Peruvian silver became the main source of Spain's income from its colonies. »

> 66 Those regions which we found and explored with the fleet … we may rightly call a New World.
> **Amerigo Vespucci, 1503** 99

Several factors contributed to Cortés' and Pizarro's astounding conquests. The Aztecs were overwhelmed by a kind of battle unknown to them, involving firearms and the single-minded slaughter of opponents—Aztec practice was to capture prisoners, whom they would later kill in ritual sacrifice. The Spanish were also helped by alliances they made with local peoples who were hostile to the Aztecs. The result for Spain was a flow of wealth across the Atlantic and a secure base for building on their involvement in the Americas.

Further Spanish colonization followed, including that of Colombia, known to the Spanish as New Granada. By the end of the 17th century, much of western and central South America was in Spanish hands. Conquered areas, and the people who lived in them, were parceled out to the Spanish conquistadors, who undertook to convert the locals to Christianity. They did convert them, but they also made them perform forced labor, especially in the silver mines. Laborers fell victim to disease and exploitation—like their counterparts in Brazil, but on a lesser scale—and enslaved people from Africa were brought in to supplement their numbers.

The Spanish Crown tried to control this large empire, appointing viceroys to rule over the settlers and the native American

The siege of Tenochtitlan, the Aztec capital, was decisive in the Spanish conquest of Mexico, and brought the Spaniards a step closer to their goal of colonizing the Americas.

CONQVISTA DE MEXICO POR CORTES 7

peoples, and taking a fifth of the profits from silver mining. Settlers increasingly resisted this external interference, however, and by the 19th century the empire was diminishing as areas from Colombia to Chile won their independence.

Circumnavigation

The Treaty of Tordesillas set the seal of approval on Spain's activity in America, but this deterred neither Spain nor Portugal from looking for a westward route to eastern Asia, a potential source of spices, luxury goods, and great wealth for traders from Europe. Amerigo Vespucci, an Italian navigator working for the Portuguese Crown, was one of the first to take this exploration further. He explored the coast of South America, and is remembered because the Americas are named after him. The Portuguese navigator Ferdinand Magellan was next to explore this route, this time on behalf of Spain. He believed that the Spice Islands could be less than halfway around the world when sailing west from the treaty line, which would give Spain a claim to them. In 1519 he set out with five ships in an ambitious attempt to make the first circumnavigation of the globe. Although Magellan himself died en route, some of the expedition survivors completed the voyage, giving Spain a basis for its claim to land in Southeast Asia.

In 1529 the rival Crowns signed another treaty at Zaragoza. This agreement assigned the Philippines to Spain and the Moluccas to Portugal.

The treaty's heritage

European countries not party to the Tordesillas agreement simply ignored it, and soon began to move in to develop their own empires. Britain colonized North America, for example; the Dutch moved into the Spice Islands; and several European countries set up colonies in the Caribbean. The treaty did, however, influence a significant proportion of the world. It underlined a development that was already beginning in Europe in which wealth and influence were passing from the old central European powers (based in the Holy Roman Empire) to the coastal, maritime powers that looked to build empires in new territories. These empires brought both Spain and Portugal enormous riches, and their overseas empires left a significant cultural legacy: much of South and Central America is Spanish-speaking, and there is a major Portuguese heritage in parts of Africa and Asia, the greatest of all being in Brazil. ∎

Ferdinand Magellan

Born into a noble Portuguese family, Magellan (1480–1521) was orphaned as a boy, and sent to the Portuguese royal court to act as page.

As a young man, he became a naval officer. He served in Portugal's colonies in India and took part in the conquest of the Moluccas, but after a disagreement with the Portuguese king, he went to Spain to look for support for his venture westward. By 1518 he had the backing of the Spanish king Charles I, and set off the following year with five ships.

After losing one ship to the weather and another to a desertion, Magellan navigated the narrow sea route (named the Strait of Magellan in his honor) between what is now mainland South America and Tierra del Fuego. He emerged in an ocean he named Pacific, because of its calmness. He crossed this expanse of water, stopping at Guam, and then in the Philippines, where he was killed. Only one ship, under Juan Sebastian del Cano, made it back to Europe in 1522, having achieved the first circumnavigation of the globe.

THE ANCIENTS NEVER RAISED THEIR BUILDINGS SO HIGH

BRUNELLESCHI DESIGNS THE DOME OF FLORENCE CATHEDRAL (1420)

IN CONTEXT

FOCUS
The Renaissance

BEFORE
1296 Building work begins on the Santa Maria del Fiore cathedral (Il Duomo), Florence.

1305 Giotto completes his frescoes at the Arena (Scrovegni) Chapel in Padua.

1397 The Medici bank is founded in Florence; becomes the largest bank in Europe.

AFTER
1434 Cosimo de' Medici becomes de facto ruler of Florence and supports the arts.

1447 Francesco Sforza comes to power in Milan. His court becomes a center of culture.

1503 Leonardo da Vinci starts work on the *Mona Lisa*.

1508 Michelangelo begins to paint the Sistine Chapel ceiling in the Vatican.

In 1418, the wealthy Guild of Wool Merchants of Florence launched a competition to find a design for a dome to complete their unfinished cathedral— the Cattedrale di Santa Maria del Fiore, commonly known as Il Duomo. The city of Florence was one of the richest in Italy, a center of banking and trade and it was on the basis of this wealth that the city could afford to commission a cathedral dome of unprecedented size.

This lavish spending on art and architecture would soon be echoed across Italy, as the region's growing prosperity meant that rulers and rich citizens could spend money to beautify their towns and enhance their prestige. The strong economy and deep civic pride in Italy laid the foundations for one of the most significant intellectual movements in history: the Renaissance.

Il Duomo

At the time of the competition, Florence's cathedral featured a vast octagonal space toward its eastern end, but since work on

Dominating the skyline of Florence, Brunelleschi's groundbreaking dome remains the tallest building in the city, rising majestically from the surrounding red-tiled roofs at 374 ft (114 m) high.

the building began in 1296 no one had figured out how to make a dome to cover it. The dome would have to be the largest cupola constructed since the late Roman period and the guild specified that it should be built without external buttresses, favored by their political rivals in France, Germany, and Milan and also considered old-fashioned. This seemed an impossible task. The young goldsmith and clockmaker-turned-architect Filippo Brunelleschi won the competition with his daring plan for a huge eight-sided brick dome, but many doubted that he would be able to construct it.

The main problem was being able to support the structure in such a way that it did not spread and collapse under its own weight. Brunelleschi's ingenious solution was to construct two concentric domes—an inner supporting dome and a larger outer one. The domes were then joined together with huge brick arches and a complex interlocking system of "chains" made from rings of stone and wooden beams that were attached by iron clamps to prevent the dome from expanding outward.

The result—which was finally completed in 1436—remains the largest masonry dome in the world. Combining the style of antiquity with new engineering techniques, it exhibited the blend of ancient wisdom and modern knowledge that typified the Renaissance.

Michelangelo's painted ceiling at the Sistine Chapel in the Vatican combines the Renaissance interest in physical beauty and realism with religious subject matter.

The Renaissance in Italy

Meaning "rebirth," the Renaissance was a movement that started in Italy and began to spread across Europe from the mid-15th century. Its roots lay in the rediscovery of the culture of ancient Greece and Rome and it influenced all the arts, as well as science and scholarship. Painters, sculptors, and architects broke free from the traditions of medieval art. They visited the monuments of ancient Rome, looking at classical statues and the carvings on Roman buildings, and created works of art in the classical style. This new movement inspired architects, such as Leon Battista Alberti and Brunelleschi, and a wave of great artists, including Michelangelo and Leonardo da Vinci. Most of these figures were active in many fields—Brunelleschi was a sculptor and engineer as well as an architect; Michelangelo painted, sculpted, and wrote poetry; while da Vinci's achievements spanned both the arts and the sciences.

Renaissance painters and sculptors sought to represent the physical world in a more realistic way than their Medieval predecessors: they valued anatomical accuracy and developed scientific methods of illustrating perspective. As in classical art, there was more focus on human beauty and the nude. »

There was also a revival of interest in classical learning, which was influenced by Greek scholars from the Byzantine Empire, who settled in Italy when Constantinople (the empire's capital) fell in 1453. The émigrés brought with them ancient Greek literary, historical, and philosophical texts, which had been lost to the West, and taught the Italians Greek so they could read and translate the works. This led to the emergence of Renaissance Humanism in Italy, which involved studying the humanities—grammar, rhetoric, history, philosophy, and poetry—and, more broadly, a high regard for the dignity and potential of the human race.

At the time of the Renaissance, life, business, and politics in Italy were dominated by a number of powerful city-states—mainly Florence, Milan, Ferrara, and Venice—together with Rome, from where the pope could exercise great secular ("temporal") power as well as being the spiritual head of the Catholic Church. The city-states generated a lot of wealth from trade and—as in the case of Florence—banking. Their ruling families, such as the Gonzaga in Mantua, the d'Este in Ferrara, the Sforza in Milan, and the Medici in Florence, spent lavishly on palaces, churches, and works of art, and became patrons of many great Renaissance artists. These wealthy families also encouraged the revival of classical learning by employing scholars as tutors for their children. In addition, several members of the Medici family became popes.

The idea of the Renaissance Man, whose expertise and curiosity extends to a range of diverse subjects, reflects the great thinkers of the era: polymaths such as Leonardo da Vinci, who mastered disciplines from art to science.

Humanism placed mankind at the center of the universe. It gave the credit for human accomplishments to people instead of God.

The rediscovery of classical texts inspired thinkers to emulate and even surpass the work of philosophers such as Aristotle.

Science and a growing knowledge of how the world works contributed to fields as diverse as architecture and medicine.

Renaissance artists made several great achievements, which were inspired by the discovery of lifelike Greek and Roman sculpture, and aided by a new understanding of perspective.

Spread of the Renaissance

From the end of the 15th century, the Renaissance spread from Italy to other parts of Europe and a Northern Renaissance emerged. Northern countries, particularly the Netherlands and Germany, produced their own great artists, such as Albrecht Dürer (1471–1528) and Hans Holbein the Younger (1497–1543)—both gifted realists. Renaissance Humanism also spread northward, but northern writers and philosophers, most notably Erasmus of Rotterdam (1466–1536), tended to place more emphasis on Christianity, education, and reform than their Italian counterparts.

The invention of printing using movable type by Johannes Gutenberg in Germany in the 1430s enabled Renaissance ideas to spread even more quickly. Before Gutenberg, the only way printed text was possible was for each page to be carved by hand into a block of wood, but as this was so laborious books were invariably written out by hand. Gutenberg's method involved arranging individual metal letters and punctuation symbols in lines and pages; when many copies of a page had been printed, the type could be taken apart and reused. He combined this new idea with the existing technology of paper-making and the kind of press used in wine production, and the result was the printing of multiple copies of books for the first time.

Gutenberg's invention had a major impact. It meant that books, which had previously been costly and took months to produce, were now easily available and much more affordable, so ideas and information could circulate quickly and reach more people. While the church had used mostly Latin as its universal language, writers now wrote in their local tongues, and as a result literature in French, English, German, and other languages flourished. In addition, copies of the ancient classics were reproduced in quantity, thus helping spread ideas that were central to both the Renaissance and Humanism.

The Renaissance's impact

By the mid-16th century, the influence of the Renaissance was waning in southern Europe, but it lasted slightly longer in the north. However, many great Renaissance works endured and they continued to inspire future generations of painters and architects. Indeed, the long-standing popularity of oil paintings and classical style of architecture, and the rise of Humanism, would all have been impossible without the movement that began with Brunelleschi in Florence in the 15th century. ∎

Filippo Brunelleschi

Born in Florence, Filippo Brunelleschi (1377–1446) was the son of a civil servant, who educated Filippo in the hope that he would follow in his footsteps. However, Filippo was artistically talented and instead trained as a goldsmith and a clockmaker before becoming an architect. When he was around 25, he traveled to Rome with his friend, the sculptor Donatello, where he studied the remains of ancient Roman buildings and read the treatise *On Architecture* by the Roman writer Vitruvius. In 1419, he won his first major commission—the design of an orphanage, the Ospedale degli Innocenti in Florence, which, with its arched loggia, is one of the first great Renaissance buildings. A number of other fine works, including chapels in Florentine churches and fortifications for the city, cemented his reputation, but the stunning dome of Il Duomo is his masterpiece. In addition to his buildings, Brunelleschi did important work on the theory of linear perspective, and designed machinery to produce special effects in theatrical productions.

MY CONSCIENCE IS CAPTIVE TO THE WORD OF GOD

MARTIN LUTHER'S 95 THESES (1517)

IN CONTEXT

FOCUS
Reformation and Counter-Reformation

BEFORE
1379 English reformer John Wycliffe criticizes church practices in *De Ecclesia*.

1415 Czech reformer Jan Hus is burned at the stake.

1512 During a stay in Rome, Martin Luther's eyes are opened to church corruption.

AFTER
1520 Lutheran services are held regularly in Copenhagen.

1534 Henry VIII of England breaks from Rome and becomes head of the church in England.

1536 John Calvin begins his church reforms in Switzerland.

1545–1563 The Council of Trent reaffirms Catholic doctrines, beginning the Counter-Reformation movement.

 Injury is done to the Word of God when, in the same sermon, an equal or larger amount of time is devoted to indulgences than to the Word.
Martin Luther, 1517

I n the fall of 1517, Martin Luther, a monk and teacher of theology at the University of Wittenberg in Germany, set off a chain reaction that would transform Europe. Deeply concerned by what he saw as corrupt practices in the Catholic Church, he wrote a series of 95 theses—arguments—against them, which he then circulated within the university. According to some reports, he also nailed them to the door of the Castle Church in Wittenberg. The theses were soon published more widely, prompting Pope Leo X to charge Luther with heresy. Luther responded by breaking with the Catholic faith, so initiating the Reformation—the rise of churches based on reformed practices, and a focus on scripture rather than on priestly authority. Because of the churches' origin in protests against Catholic practices and beliefs, they became known as Protestant churches.

Spread of the Reformation

Luther was not alone in seeking religious reform. Swiss preacher Ulrich Zwingli (1484–1531) led a Protestant church based in Zurich, and Frenchman John Calvin broke from the Catholic church in around 1530. Forced to flee France, he went to

Geneva, Switzerland, where he supported the reform movement, eventually helping shape Protestant doctrine.

Reformers' beliefs did not necessarily concur. Calvinists were markedly different from Lutherans, and Anabaptists were persecuted by Protestants as well as Catholics for their radical views. Luther himself supported the brutal suppression of the Anabaptist-led Peasants' Revolt in the 1520s. What the Protestants had in common was that their views brought them into fundamental theological conflict with the Catholic church.

Reformers' ideas spread via the relatively new technology of the printed word. Before movable type and presses made printed books possible in the 1450s, books were all written by hand in Latin, the international language of the church. Print allowed information to be reproduced cheaply and quickly, and demand rapidly grew for books written in the vernacular. Luther wrote his theses in Latin, but before long they had been translated and printed in German, French, English, and other languages. Books and pamphlets describing church abuses and outlining Protestant theology soon followed, and were printed in large numbers.

Importance of The Word

A central idea in Protestant theology was that authority came not from the priesthood, but from scripture itself. For this reason, access to the Bible was essential both for the reformers and their followers. Bibles printed in native European languages were appearing by the 16th century; Luther's German translation of the New Testament was published in 1522, and a translated version of the whole Bible including the Apocrypha followed in 1534. A year later, Miles Coverdale (1488–1569), sometime friar, preacher, and Bishop of Exeter, produced the first complete Bible in English. A French translation by theologian Jacques Lefèvre d'Étaples (c. 1450–1536) appeared between 1528 and 1532. »

At the Diet of Worms in 1521, Luther refused to recant: "Unless I am convicted of error by the testimony of Scripture ... I cannot and will not retract .... Here I stand. God help me!"

By the mid-16th century, Reformation ideas had been widely disseminated. Lutheranism spread across Germany and Scandinavia; Calvinism took hold in much of Switzerland, and made significant inroads in Scotland. There were also Calvinists in France, where they were called Huguenots, although that country was split between Catholics and Protestants, who fought in the Wars of Religion of the second half of the 16th century. Spain, Portugal, and Italy remained Catholic.

In England, the seeds of reform were sown early. Many people objected to abuses such as the use of church funds to pay for clerics—including the Pope and foreign bishops—to lead a life of luxury. However, Protestant ideas were not yet widely enough held for the faith to take hold. Things changed when Henry VIII of England broke with Rome in 1534, rejecting papal authority and proclaiming himself head of the church in England. As supreme ecclesiastical leader, he exercised his sole right to authorize the publication of the English Bible, the Coverdale Bible, but English religious practice and doctrine remained Catholic. A moderate form of Protestantism was later established in England under Henry's daughter Elizabeth I.

Reformers risked their lives by speaking out at a time when heresy was punishable by death. Czech reformer Jan Hus had been burned at the stake in 1415, Zwingli died in a battle between Protestant and Catholic forces in 1531, and English Bible translator William Tyndale was executed in 1536. Luther, urged to recant by Pope Leo X in 1520, threw the written request on a bonfire, so church authorities handed him over to Frederick the Wise, Elector of Saxony and founder of the University of Wittenberg, for punishment. Frederick convened a formal inquiry or "Diet" at Worms, at which Emperor Charles V presided. The emperor rejected Luther's arguments and banned his views in the empire, but Luther refused to recant. He was outlawed and excommunicated, but Frederick saved him from execution by faking his abduction, then hiding him at the Wartburg castle. Luther continued to write and organize, garnering increasing support.

Powerful allies

Support from people in positions of power assisted the spread of the Reformation. Like Henry VIII in England, the princes of Germany resented church wealth, taxation, and its independent law courts, and were also eager to strengthen their own power. Throughout the Middle Ages, popes had made alliances with kings and emperors, and intervened in secular affairs. Many German princes wanted to prevent such alliances by cutting ties with Rome and removing bishops from their princedoms, so their support for the reformers was motivated by political expedience as well as personal piety.

In what would become the first in a long list of religiously motivated conflicts between Catholics and Protestants, the Holy Roman Emperor Charles V invaded Lutheran territory in an effort to stamp out the movement. Lutherans united against him and, despite his triumph at the Battle of Mühlberg in 1547, he was unable to suppress them. A temporary compromise was eventually reached at Augsburg in 1555 when the emperor conceded that each prince within the empire could choose how to worship in his own domain. The peace was not to last, however; bitter divisions drawn by the Reformation would cause people across Europe to take up arms again, and the continent was ravaged by more than a century of religiously-motivated conflict.

Cartoon images of the pope as a bestial monstrosity communicated to an international audience, literate and not, a common Protestant idea that the papacy was the institution of the devil.

Reform from within

Even before Luther wrote his 95 theses, a movement for reform had begun within the church. Inspired partly by Renaissance Humanism, it brought on a resurgence of scholarship and philosophy, and motivated churchmen such as Spaniard Francisco Ximenes, who produced a Bible with texts in Hebrew, Greek, Latin, and Aramaic. However, Luther's clear theological challenges prompted the papacy to prepare a more widely considered response. In 1545, Paul III called together the Council of Trent at which bishops and cardinals reaffirmed Catholic doctrines, from the importance of the priesthood and sacraments to the legitimacy of indulgences. But the council also introduced reforms: it forbade abuses such as the holding of multiple offices by one priest, set up training seminaries for priests, and, in an attempt to slow the spread of Protestant doctrine, established a commission to specify which books Catholics were forbidden to read. In addition, a number of popes from Paul III onward lived austerely, appointed like-minded bishops, and reviewed papal finances.

The Ecstasy of Saint Teresa, a white marble altarpiece and one of the masterpieces of High Roman Baroque, by Gian Lorenzo Bernini, the leading sculptor of his day.

Counter-Reformation

The council met periodically for 18 years, and provoked a renewal and resurgence of Catholicism from within the church that is usually called the Counter-Reformation. The new Society of Jesus (also known as the order of Jesuits), founded by Spanish knight Ignatius Loyola in 1534, was approved by the pope in 1540 as an answer to the Reformation, and it spread a powerful Counter-Reformation message across Europe. The contemporary revival of Christian art, which coincided with the flowering of the baroque style in Italy, added a vibrant emphasis. Baroque churches were imposing and ornate, filled with affecting sculptures, paintings, and strikingly posed biblical scenes. This potent propaganda served to underline the difference between Catholic churches and their Protestant counterparts, which were usually plain and undecorated. Baroque art, together with the zeal of reforming popes and Jesuit priests, helped ensure that the Catholic church survived and flourished in countries such as Italy and Spain, even while the Protestant movement was gathering strength elsewhere. Europe, which had once been united under the pope in the Roman Catholic Church, was now irrevocably split into Catholic and Protestant states. The seeds were sown for over a century of conflict as subjects took up arms against their rulers, kings and princes clashed, and nations attacked nations in the name of religion. ■

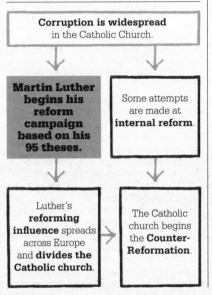

Corruption is widespread
in the Catholic Church.

Martin Luther begins his reform campaign based on his 95 theses.

Some attempts are made at **internal reform**.

Luther's **reforming influence** spreads across Europe and **divides the Catholic church**.

The Catholic church begins the **Counter-Reformation**.

THEY CHERISHED A GREAT HOPE AND INWARD ZEAL
THE VOYAGE OF THE *MAYFLOWER* (1620)

IN CONTEXT

FOCUS
North American colonization

BEFORE
1585 English settlers found Roanoke Island Colony in North Carolina, but within five years it is abandoned.

1607 The first permanent English settlement in North America is founded at Jamestown, Virginia.

1608 French settlers found Quebec in Canada.

AFTER
1629 English settlers found the Massachusetts Bay Colony on North America's east coast.

1681 English Quaker William Penn founds Pennsylvania to provide a refuge for fellow Quakers.

1732 English settlers found Georgia, the last of the 13 original colonies on the southeast coast.

English Protestants seeking religious freedom sail to North America on the *Mayflower*.

More **religious separatists** follow, swelling the **colony's population**.

Other English colonies are founded by **companies** granted **royal charters** from the **Crown**.

The colonists develop a **form of government** based on the **pursuit of religious freedom**, following the English **parliamentary model**.

I n 1620, a group of English people who could not legally worship as they wished to in England set sail across the Atlantic to begin a new life in America. This group later became known as the Pilgrims. They set off on two ships, but one proved unseaworthy so they had to continue in just one, the *Mayflower*. Winter storms ravaged the 66-day crossing and the ship's main beam fractured. While still aboard, the Pilgrims drew up the *Mayflower Compact*, which pledged their loyalty to the Crown but also asserted their right to make their own laws within the English legal framework. They settled at Plymouth and, although many died that first winter, their community endured.

Early colonization
At that time, England, like other countries, was competing to establish colonies in North America. Jamestown had been founded thirteen years before the Pilgrims landed at Plymouth, but it was not a religious community. The Colony of Virginia, centered around Jamestown,

The *Mayflower* **attempted** to depart England on three occasions: from Southampton and then Dartmouth in August, and finally from Plymouth on September 6, 1620.

had been established by English colonists in 1607 under a charter from the Crown, and was their first permanent settlement in the Americas. French explorers had established fur trading posts up the rivers of Canada, Dutch and Swedish colonists arrived in North America in the early 17th century, and in 1613 the Dutch established a trading post on the western shore of Manhattan Island.

Government and trade

Both Plymouth and Jamestown developed representative institutions in which colonists elected officials to govern their own affairs. Inspired by the English parliamentary model, and growing out of the assertion of rights articulated in the *Mayflower Compact*, these early developments established a model of self-rule that came to characterize English colonization in North America.

Each colony had a governor, appointed by the British monarch, and a legislature, elected by the colonists. There was often tension between the two, because the legislature had to work within the framework of existing English law. However, the king and government in London, working with the governor, saw the colonies as a resource, rich in raw materials, that they could exploit to their advantage.

To ensure America remained a ready market for British industry, colonial trade was restricted by the Navigation Acts, which required that all commodity trade take place in British ships crewed by British sailors. The colonists came to see these measures as a willful suppression of their trade and manufacturing. Tensions arose on both sides of the Atlantic as British and colonial merchants sought to protect their interests.

Colonial growth

Relations between the colonists and the indigenous peoples of the East Coast were also starting to strain. The increasing colonial population put pressure on land and resources, pushing people west to settle on land belonging to American Indians.

The groups struggled to coexist harmoniously. An uneasy peace, punctuated by violence, typified relations between settlers and Native Americans for many years. ∎

Religious persecution

In the early 17th century, the English were legally obliged to worship as prescribed by the Church of England. Although the English church had already broken from the Catholic Church, many people still felt that its hierarchical priesthood and set rituals, hymns, and prayers were Catholic features that should be swept away.

Puritans, so-called because of their desire for religious purity, hoped to reform the church from within. Other groups, known as Separatists, set up their own "separate" congregations, but when their leaders were imprisoned or even executed, they moved to the more tolerant Netherlands. Here they could adopt the simpler form of worship they preferred, but it was very hard to earn a living because the country's professional guilds were closed to them. This is part of the reason that the Pilgrims, and later others, decided to seek a new life in North America.

WE WILL CUT OFF HIS HEAD WITH THE CROWN UPON IT

THE EXECUTION OF CHARLES I (1649)

IN CONTEXT

FOCUS
English Civil War

BEFORE
1639 English and Scottish forces clash in the first "Bishops' War."

1642 The Civil War begins at Edgehill, Warwickshire.

1645 Oliver Cromwell's "New Model Army" scores victories at Naseby and Langport.

1646 Charles is forced to surrender to his opponents.

AFTER
1649 The Commonwealth of England (a republic) is formed.

1653 Cromwell takes the title Lord Protector for Life, giving him the power to call or dissolve parliaments.

1658 Cromwell dies and is succeeded as Protector by his son, Richard.

1660 The monarchy is restored: Charles II becomes King of England.

King Charles I asserts his **divine right to rule**.

The king needs to **raise taxes to** pay for wars.

Parliament attempts to **limit the king's authority**. A **civil war** erupts between Crown and parliament for the **right to rule**.

Parliamentary forces, led by Cromwell, **win the war.**

The king is executed and an English republic is instituted.

D uring the 1640s, England was plunged into a series of wars, fought to decide the future of the country and known collectively as the English Civil War. On one side were the Royalists—predominantly landed gentry and aristocrats who supported King Charles I and his right to rule independently of parliament. On the other were the Parliamentarians—mainly smaller landowners and tradesmen, many of whom held Puritan beliefs and disliked Charles's autocratic stance. By 1648, the Parliamentarians had beaten Charles on the battlefield and Oliver Cromwell, their leader, ejected from parliament all those who were prepared to negotiate with the king, leaving the remainder (known as the Rump Parliament) to vote to end the monarchy. Charles was tried for treason against England and was beheaded in 1649, after which England began an 11-year period as a republic.

The causes of war
King Charles I and parliament were natural opponents. Charles was sympathetic to Catholics while parliament was Protestant,

and he believed in the divine right of kings—the idea that the monarch's appointment is approved by God and so he or she has absolute power.

The clash first came to a head over the king's repeated attempts to raise money for a war in France. Parliament tried to curb his power to do so by introducing a Petition of Right in 1628, making it a necessity for its members to approve taxation. However, Charles got around this by levying taxes using antiquated medieval laws, selling trading monopolies to raise cash, and ruling without parliament. In 1640, the king was forced to call parliament for the first time in 11 years to raise money to quell a Scottish revolt. Once called, parliament tried to bring in further measures to limit his power, such as making it illegal for the king to dissolve parliament, but he responded by trying to arrest five MPs. The dispute escalated into the First Civil War in 1642.

The war and its effects

Initially, the Royalists gained the upper hand but in 1644 the Parliamentarians reorganized their troops under Oliver Cromwell. With their disciplined, professional approach, this "New Model Army" forced Charles to surrender in 1646. However, the king restarted the war two years later, and this Second Civil War—which ended in a Royalist defeat at the Battle of Preston in 1648—began the chain of events that led to his execution in 1649 and the formation of a republic under Cromwell called the Commonwealth of England.

Like Charles, Cromwell found relations with parliament difficult, but he tried to bring in reforms. He ruled with stern Puritan authority, imposing it ruthlessly on the Scots and the Irish. Soon after he died, the country—perhaps tired of Puritan austerity—welcomed Charles I's exiled son home to reign. Charles II agreed to limitations on royal power and to uphold the Protestant faith, but his heir—his Catholic brother James II—clashed with Anglican bishops and offended Protestants by offering prominent positions to Catholics.

Fears of having another Catholic king mounted until, in 1688, in what became known as the Glorious Revolution, James was deposed. The king was sent into exile and replaced by his Protestant daughter Mary, who ruled with her Dutch husband William of Orange. In 1689, William and Mary accepted a Bill of Rights, which ensured their subjects had basic civil liberties, such as trial by jury, and making the monarchy subject to the law of the land. Britain has remained a constitutional monarchy, in which no king or queen could defy Parliament as Charles I did, ever since. ∎

King Charles I of England

The son of Stuart King James I of England (King James VI of Scotland) and Anne of Denmark, Charles was born in 1600 and became king in 1625.

From the start, he alienated both subjects and parliament with his demands for taxation (mostly to fund wars in France) and his assertion of his divine right to rule. He also clashed with the church because of his sympathies with Catholicism (he was married to the French Catholic princess, Henrietta Maria). In addition, he was unpopular in Scotland, where he tried to replace the prevailing presbyterian system of church governance (without bishops) with the more hierarchical episcopal system (with bishops, following the Anglican model), which led to political and military conflict in 1639 and 1640 (known as the Bishops' War). During the English Civil War, he took an active part in leading the Royalist armies until he was captured; initially, he was put under house arrest, then he was imprisoned before his execution in 1649. He continued to assert his divine right to rule during his trial.

THERE IS NO CORNER WHERE ONE DOES NOT TALK OF SHARES

THE OPENING OF THE AMSTERDAM STOCK EXCHANGE (1602)

IN CONTEXT

FOCUS
The Dutch Golden Age

BEFORE
1585 The founding of the Dutch Republic; Protestants in the south move northward.

1595 Cornelis de Houtman leads an expedition to Asia, starting the Dutch spice trade.

AFTER
1609 The Bank of Amsterdam is founded.

1610–1630 Land is reclaimed; the Dutch Republic increases in area by one-third and agricultural output increases.

1637 A single tulip bulb sells for up to 10 times the annual income of a skilled craftsman.

1650 Half the Republic's population lives in urban areas; the Netherlands is the most urbanized region in Europe.

The Amsterdam Stock Exchange—the world's first permanent market for stocks and shares—opened in 1602 under the auspices of the Dutch East India Company (known in the Netherlands as VOC). The company was a vast enterprise—in effect, the first international corporation—and it was created to facilitate trading expeditions to Asia.

Unusually, the Dutch government had granted the company the power not only to trade, but also to build fortifications, establish settlements, raise armies, and enter into treaties with foreign rulers. Since the organization had a huge network of ships, ports, and personnel, it required considerable funding and many investors. The Amsterdam Stock Exchange was originally set up to enable investors to trade their shares in the Dutch East India Company, but it then developed to become a vibrant market in financial assets and one of the drivers of a growing capitalist economy in the Dutch Republic.

An expanding economy

In the 17th century, the Netherlands was growing economically despite being involved in a long war with Spain. The northern part of the region (the Dutch Republic, which was Protestant) had split from the southern half (Flanders, which was Catholic) in the late 16th century. The Republic consisted of seven separate northern provinces, each with a great deal of independence but under the umbrella of a federal government called the States-General. Protestant merchants who had lived in Catholic cities, such as Antwerp, moved north to escape persecution, taking with them their capital and trading links. Also, many Flemish artisans who were skilled in textile production (primarily weaving wool, silk, and linen) emigrated to the northern cities of Haarlem, Leiden, and Amsterdam, boosting the Dutch Republic's economy further.

The Dutch East India Company ran its own shipyards, the largest being in Amsterdam, shown here. Very powerful in the 17th century, the company went bankrupt and was dissolved in 1800.

As the 17th century progressed, the Republic really began to prosper. Various factors came together to make this small region successful. Most importantly, the nation had a strong tradition of seafaring, giving it a huge advantage over many other countries. In addition, its citizens had a strong work ethic—largely due to the Protestant belief that worldly work was a duty and a route to salvation—so productivity was high. There was also a growing population (especially of the urban middle classes) and an expanding major city—Amsterdam—which proved an ideal center for trade. All of these contributing factors resulted in the Dutch economy moving increasingly toward shipping, trading, and finance.

Exploration and trade

As a coastal nation, the Dutch Republic produced notable sailors and explorers, so long-distance trading was a natural consequence of the country's maritime history. In addition, advancements in ship-building technology in the Republic enabled the Dutch merchant fleet to expand rapidly; by 1670, the Dutch had more merchant ships than the rest of Europe put together.

The expanding merchant class saw large potential profits in the spice trade with Asia and, as in other maritime cultures such as Spain and Portugal, navigators sought new sea routes to the east. The Dutch traveled all over the globe and set up colonies, including one in North America: New Amsterdam, which they officially settled in 1624 and was renamed New York when the British took over. In 1596, the Dutch explorer Willem Barentsz tried to find a northern passage to Asia and in the process discovered Svalbard (Spitsbergen), which later became a destination for Dutch whalers.

Most importantly for their prosperity, from 1595 the Dutch began to make regular journeys to Southeast Asia to trade in spices, particularly pepper, nutmeg, cloves, and cinnamon. They established colonies in the region and founded the city of Batavia, later renamed Jakarta. With this permanent base, the Dutch had the ability to trade long-term, producing a massive boost to their economy.

A need for investment

While the wealth generated by exploration and trade was injected back into the Dutch »

Agricultural revolution

The expanding population of the Dutch Republic in the 17th century encouraged farmers to make agriculture much more productive. In large part, this was achieved through continued land reclamation—a process that was already well underway by the late Middle Ages. The Dutch also changed the way they used their land. Instead of growing grain one year and letting the land lie fallow the next, farmers began planting certain nitrogen-producing crops (such as peas, turnips, and clover, which they could use as animal feed), in order to improve the soil ready for the next corn crop. Growing more fodder meant that farmers could keep larger herds, thereby increasing production of meat and milk as well as manure, which could be used as fertilizer. This greater productivity helped sustain a growing population, although some wheat still had to be imported to make up the shortfall. It also freed up larger segments of the population to work in trade or finance rather than agriculture.

If one were to lead a
stranger through the streets
of Amsterdam and ask
him where he was,
he would answer
"among speculators."
Joseph Penso de la Vega
Confusion of Confusions (1688)

Birth of the Exchange

In 1602, these trading companies merged
to form the Dutch East India Company, and
shares in the enterprise were allocated at
the new Stock Exchange in Amsterdam.
It was established at the outset that the
owners could buy and sell these shares,
and very quickly other companies were
listing their own shares on the Stock
Exchange in order to raise money. The
ease of buying and selling shares meant
that the Stock Exchange became very
busy indeed, fueling the growth of
capitalism in this part of Europe; increased
investment resulted in more industry,
which then led to further investment
and the generation of greater wealth.

economy, at the same time investment was
required to cover the considerable costs of
overseas expeditions. A trading voyage to
Asia in the 17th century was a very risky
venture—the potential profits were high,
but storms at sea, pirates, warfare, or an
accident could lead to the loss of a ship,
crew, or cargo and wipe out all the profits.
It therefore made sense for many people to
invest in each voyage and spread the risk,
rather than one entity shouldering all the
costs and responsibilities. Private trading
companies were set up, each investing a
small amount in a larger whole, and all
being well they would then receive a
commensurate share of the profits.

A history of trading

The Amsterdam Stock Exchange did not
develop in a vacuum. Buying and selling
securities—tradable financial assets such
as shares—already had a long history in
Europe. By the 14th century, possibly
earlier, merchants in rich Italian trading

Batavia was the headquarters of the Dutch
East India Company in Asia. The port city was
founded by the Dutch in 1619, after razing the
existing city of Jayakarta to the ground.

cities, such as Venice and Genoa, had traded in securities. However, the prevailing conditions in the Netherlands in the 17th century meant that the market was especially buoyant. Since the 16th century, there had been a strong financial market in Amsterdam, where there was a tradition of trading in commodities and speculation in everything from whale oil to tulips. The idea of buying and selling shares therefore appealed in this entrepreneurial society, especially as there was a good prospect of healthy profits from the Asian trade. In addition, the unique way in which the exchange traded—opening for limited hours only—encouraged rapid buying and selling and produced a very fluid market.

Boosts to the economy

The opening of the Amsterdam Stock Exchange was followed in 1609 by the foundation of the Bank of Amsterdam—the forerunner of modern national banks. The bank provided a secure place to keep money and bullion, and it assured that local currency kept its value. It thus helped make the Dutch Republic more financially secure, underpinning the vigorous and often risky trading activity that went on in this burgeoning market.

In 1623, the market had a further boost when the Dutch East India Company negotiated a new charter, paying investors a regular dividend and permitting those who wanted to leave the company to sell their shares on the Stock Exchange. This action further increased trade on the Stock Market, which was also pioneering other lucrative activities such as futures trading.

The insurance business was also thriving in Amsterdam during this time—particularly marine insurance, which had been created in the 16th century to protect ship owners and investors against the risks of long-distance voyages. When the Stock Exchange opened, a special area was set aside for the buying and selling of insurance.

A flourishing culture

The very buoyant financial activity prevalent in Amsterdam in the 17th

Dutch explorers discover **new sea routes** and the **Dutch merchant fleet expands**.

↓

Trading voyages to the spice-producing countries of Asia yield **high profits** but pose a **high risk**.

↓

The **Dutch East India Company** is set up to share the **financial risk of voyages** between **multiple investors**.

↓

The Amsterdam Stock Exchange is formed to allow shares in the East India Company to be traded.

↓

Rapid **buying and selling** creates a fluid financial market, encouraging speculators to **take more risk**.

century encouraged the expanding middle classes to buy consumer goods, including fine furniture and oil paintings, further fueling the economy of this already successful region. A particularly strong art market developed, allowing major painters—such as Vermeer and Rembrandt, as well as numerous lesser followers—to flourish. Many artists were specialists, satisfying a growing demand for portraits, landscapes, seascapes, and still lifes, although great artists like Rembrandt excelled in all genres and art forms, including painting, drawing, and printmaking.

The increasing wealth also led to the expansion of towns, with new town halls, warehouses, and merchants' homes springing up. Numerous brick houses, owned by the middle classes, survive in cities such as Amsterdam and Delft, many of them set on the banks of the canals that were built during this period—a time of economic boom that combined elegance and artistic flair with success in trade. ∎

ASSEMBLE ALL THE KNOWLEDGE SCATTERED ON THE EARTH
DIDEROT PUBLISHES THE *ENCYCLOPÉDIE* (1751)

IN CONTEXT

FOCUS
The Enlightenment

BEFORE
1517 The Reformation begins, challenging the authority of the Catholic Church.

1610 Galileo Galilei publishes *Sidereus Nuncius* (*Starry Messenger*), containing his observations of the heavens.

1687 In *Principia*, Newton outlines a concept of the universe based on natural, rationally understandable laws.

AFTER
1767 American thinker and diplomat Benjamin Franklin visits Paris, and transmits Enlightenment ideas to the US.

1791 English writer Mary Wollstonecraft adds feminism to Enlightenment ideas in the pioneering *A Vindication of the Rights of Women*.

I n the mid 18th century, the French philosopher Denis Diderot invited some of his country's leading intellectuals—literary men, scientists, scholars, and philosophers to write articles for a huge "Classified Dictionary of Sciences, Arts, and Trades," for which he was both editor-in-chief and contributor. The first volumes of his *Encyclopédie* appeared in 1751, and the full work was completed 21 years later, made up of 17 volumes of text and another 11 volumes of illustrations.

The *Encyclopédie* was not the first large encyclopedia to be published, but it was the first to feature content by named authors, and to give close attention to the trades and crafts. Its most striking feature, however, was its critical approach to contemporary ideas and institutions: its authors were champions of scientific thought and secular values. They sought to apply reason and logic to explain the phenomena of the natural world, and humankind's existence, rather than religious or political dogma. As such, the work challenged both the Catholic Church and the French monarchy, which derived their authority from traditional ideas such as a divinely ordained, unchanging order.

A revolution in thought

The mission of the *Encyclopédie* was to catalog the collective knowledge of the Western world in the spirit of the Enlightenment. This was a multifaceted intellectual movement that took root around 1715, although its origins lay in work done by the pioneers of modern scientific and philosophical thought in the previous century. The work's multidisciplinary articles, which numbered around 72,000, distilled the ideas and theories of France's key Enlightenment thinkers—including the writers and philosophers Voltaire, Jean-Jacques Rousseau, and Montesquieu.

The articles were extremely wide-ranging, but centered on three main areas: the need to base society not on faith and the

| Scientists begin to make **systematic investigations** into natural phenomena. | → | Growing belief that **knowledge, freedom, and happiness** are achieved through the **use of reason**. | → | **Questioning of traditional** social, religious, and political **ideas**. |

The Enlightenment movement begins, spearheaded by the publication of the _Encyclopédie_.

doctrines of the Catholic Church but on rational thought; the importance of observations and experiments in science; and the search for a way of organizing states and governments around natural law and justice.

Diderot organized the _Encyclopédie's_ articles into three main categories: memory (subjects connected to history); reason (philosophy); and imagination (poetry). Controversially, there was no special category for God or the divine—religion, like magic and superstition, was treated as part of philosophy. This approach was groundbreaking, and contentious. Religion had been at the very heart of life and thought in Europe for centuries: the _Encyclopédie_, and the Enlightenment itself, denied it this key position.

In spite of repeated efforts by the authorities to censor some of its articles, and to intimidate and threaten its editors, the _Encyclopédie_ became the most influential and widely consulted work of the period. The ideas that it transmitted inspired the revolutions that exploded in France and the US at the end of the 18th century.

Science and reason
The Enlightenment movement was characterized by a focus on the power of human reason and skepticism of accepted knowledge. This marked a break from earlier generations in which beliefs about the world derived from religious teachings and the doctrines of the Church. These

governed everything from the laws of marriage to the way people understood the movement of the planets and the creation of the universe. For Enlightenment thinkers, however, the evidence of a person's senses and the use of one's reason was far more important than their blind adherence to a faith. They argued that "truths" about the tangible world, which had been set down in antiquity by Aristotle and others, and upheld by the Church, should be tested through experimentation and observation, checked, and then discussed in a rational way.

This radical mode of thinking had its origins in the scientific revolution of the 17th century. Scientists and philosophers including Francis Bacon, Johannes Kepler, Isaac Newton, and Galileo Galilei had transformed the study of nature and the physical universe, making it more observational. They conducted careful experiments and subjected their results to mathematical analysis; in the process they drastically updated and expanded the fields of physics, chemistry, biology, and astronomy. »

 Dare to know! Have courage to use your own reason!
Immanuel Kant
"What is Enlightenment?" (1784)

Enlightenment scientists took this investigation of reality further, making possible, for example, Swedish botanist Carl Linnaeus's development of a proper, rational biological classification in the early 18th century. The inquiring, reason-based approach of the Enlightenment also triggered dramatic technological advances. In the 1760s, the Scottish physician Joseph Black discovered carbon dioxide, while in 1769, Scotsman James Watt made improvements to the steam engine that increased its efficiency, thereby enabling the improvement of factories. The *Encyclopédie* helped to publicize these, and other, achievements of 18th-century scientists, as well as those of their precursors.

The work also found an audience in the learned societies, academies, and universities that flourished in the Enlightenment period. Although many teachers and scholars at Europe's older, Church-dominated universities remained deaf to the new scientific way of thought, more progressive ones helped teach and promote it.

Equality and freedom

The scientific revolution and the Enlightenment also encouraged the belief that reason could reveal natural laws in human affairs. Instead of drawing fact from faith, Enlightenment thinkers believed that politics should be separated from religion, that neither should curtail the rights of the individual, and that people should be free to express their opinions, worship in their own way, and read what they want to. This political doctrine, which is often labeled liberalism, had roots in the work of 17th-century philosophers such as Englishman John Locke—the father of liberalism. Locke asserted that there are certain intrinsic human rights that are not

EXPÉRIENCE AEROSTATIQUE A ANNONAY, le 4 Juin 1783

In 1783, France's Montgolfier brothers gave the first demonstration of their new invention, the hot-air balloon, bringing science to the forefront of public attention in a spectacular way.

dependent on law or custom—in other words, they exist quite separately from what the Church or monarch might decree. These rights could be expressed in different ways, but included the right to life, the right to liberty, and the freedom to own what one has produced. These ideas were central to Enlightenment thinkers, following Locke, who felt that such natural rights should form the basis of any system of government.

Liberal ideas also found expression in the work of Enlightenment writers. For example, Voltaire, in books such as the Philosophical Dictionary, highlighted the injustices and abuses of the Catholic Church, and espoused values such as tolerance, freedom of the press, and the promotion of reason over doctrine and religious revelation. In his Spirit of the Laws, Montesquieu advocated the separation of governmental powers (legislature, executive, judiciary) and pressed for an end to slavery. In The Social Contract, Jean-Jacques Rousseau rejected

> 66 In all the ages of the world, priests have been the enemies of liberty.
> **David Hume** 99

the power of the monarch in favor of that of the people, who, he said, must balance rights with duties, and should be able to decide the laws that govern their lives. The contributors to the *Encyclopédie* also promoted liberal values in economics. They were critical of fairs—where goods were sold by visiting dealers at the expense of local traders, who often had to close their businesses for the duration—and favored markets, which allowed local traders to meet the needs of the local population.

Ideas such as these spread across Europe. Conversations and debates on philosophical, political, and scientific subjects took place in the coffeehouses that had sprung up in English, French, German, and Dutch cities a century earlier. These coffeehouses now served as information-sharing hubs where men from all walks of life, including writers, politicians, philosophers, and scientists, could congregate to exchange views.

Into the light

In Europe, the Enlightenment movement, and the *Encyclopédie* itself, which helped promote its ideals, had a profound impact on social, political, and intellectual life. Its proponents believed that they were sweeping away an oppressive medieval worldview and ushering in a new era that they hoped would be characterized by freedom of thought, open-mindedness, and tolerance.

The Enlightenment's questioning, rational approach, and urgent demand for liberty, paved the way for the granting of new civil rights. The movement affected the policies of monarchical rulers, such as the freeing of serfs in the Holy Roman Empire in the 1780s. Monarchs who accepted Enlightenment values took on the movement's name, titling themselves Enlightened Despots. Enlightenment thought also provided the intellectual fuel for the French Revolution of 1789–1799—begun by citizens inspired by Enlightenment notions of individual freedom and equality—and the campaign to abolish the Atlantic slave trade in the 19th century.

Liberalism and other aspects of Enlightenment political philosophy began to influence leaders in many parts of the world when they came to draw up legal systems and establish rights for their citizens—most notably in the fledgling United States, whose Constitution (1787) adopted Montesquieu's idea of the separation of power into branches of government.

More generally, the movement promoted the pursuit of knowledge for its own sake and recognized that one person's quest for understanding could benefit the entire human race. ∎

Voltaire

François-Marie Arouet, who chose to be known publicly by the name Voltaire, was one of the greatest writers and social activists of the Enlightenment, renowned for his wit and intelligence. He was born in Paris in 1694, and spent much of his long life there, although he traveled widely and spoke several languages. He was a hugely prolific writer, producing works in almost every literary genre: novels, plays, poems, essays, historical studies, and philosophical books as well as countless pamphlets.

Voltaire was an outspoken supporter of social reform, including the defense of civil liberties and freedom of religion and speech; he also denounced the hypocrisy of the political and religious establishment. This led to the censorship of some of his work, and also to short spells of imprisonment and periods of exile in England—after which he converted his experiences into an influential book, *Philosophical Letters on the English*—and Geneva, Switzerland, where he wrote his most famous work, the philosophical novella *Candide*.

I BUILT ST. PETERSBURG AS A WINDOW TO LET IN THE LIGHT OF EUROPE
THE FOUNDING OF ST. PETERSBURG (1703)

IN CONTEXT

FOCUS
The rise of Russia

BEFORE
1584 The emperor Ivan the Terrible dies. The following succession of rulers bring greater unity to Russia.

1696 Peter the Great assumes sole rule of Russia.

AFTER
1709 Russia wins a decisive victory over Sweden at the Battle of Poltava.

1718 Peter's son Alexis, opposed to his father's reforms, dies under torture.

1721 Russia and Sweden sign the Treaty of Nystad, pledging mutual defense.

1725 Peter the Great dies, ushering in an era of less competent emperors.

1762 Catherine the Great becomes empress and continues Peter's work of reform and expansion.

St. Petersburg offered a new vision for the country. Its strategic location facilitated trade, its ethos encouraged education, and its architecture provided a showcase for Russian achievement.

Russian ruler Peter the Great founded St. Petersburg, on the estuary of the Neva River, on May 27, 1703. This new city, fortress, and port by the Baltic gave Russia direct sea access to Europe, opening new opportunities for both trade and military conquest. In 1712, Peter made his new city Russia's capital, stripping the title from the ancient seat of Moscow.

An admirer of Western palaces, Peter employed European architects to design the government buildings, palaces, university, and houses in the fashionable baroque style. He also pressed 30,000 peasants each year into construction gangs, along with Russian convict laborers and Swedish prisoners of war. The regimen was strict, and living conditions stark: more than 100,000 workers died, but those who survived could earn their freedom.

The lavish design and vast scale of Peter's architecture showed not only his appreciation of European culture, but also his determination to be an exalted, absolute ruler in the manner of Western despots such as Louis XIV. Peter used his power to make significant changes in Russia. He founded the Russian navy and reformed the army, which until then had relied on bands of men led by untrained village elders. He reorganized the army along European lines and developed new iron and munitions industries to equip it. By 1725, Russia had a professional army of 130,000 men.

A new and modern culture

Peter transformed his court, making his courtiers adopt French-style dress instead of traditional robes, and ordering them to cut off their long beards. He founded colleges, forced the nobility to educate their children, and promoted people to high rank according to their merit rather than their birth, as had previously been the case.

The emperor was also known for his harsh treatment of rebels, his aggressive foreign policy, and particularly for his successful war against Sweden, which gave him control of the Baltic Sea. This style of rule was continued under later monarchs, notably Catherine II, also "the Great," who extended the modernizing trend Peter had begun. Influenced by the ideas of the European Enlightenment, she promoted education and the arts, sponsored translations of foreign literary works, and wrote books herself. She, too, increased Russia's imperial strength, gaining military victories over the Ottoman Empire.

The rulers were also influenced by the example of Prussia, a north-German state that expanded in the 18th century due to

Peter I visits **Western Europe**, absorbing **ideas and influences**.

↓

Contemporary theories of rulership provide a **model of enlightened despotism**.

↓

Baroque western palaces and **cities demonstrate their rulers' power**.

↓

Peter founds St. Petersburg as the capital of a Westernized Russian empire.

an efficient bureaucracy, a powerful army, and strong leadership under kings such as Frederick II. Between Prussia and Russia lay Poland, whose territories these two powers and Austria carved up and took over in a series of partitions. This left Russia with influence over an area stretching from Eastern Europe to Siberia that it still largely retains today. ∎

Peter the Great

Peter (1672–1725) became ruler of Russia in 1682, at first jointly with his half-brother Ivan as co-czar and their mother

as regent, and then as sole monarch. Well-educated and constantly curious, Peter traveled to the Netherlands and England to learn about Western life, government, and architecture. He also studied disciplines such as shipbuilding and woodworking, and practiced many with distinction. His rule was greatly influenced by these travels and by Western advisers, leading him to carry out military reforms and adopt a dictatorial style of rule. The position and grand architecture of

his new city illustrated how his focus had been directed toward Western European culture and power.

Although Peter forged lasting diplomatic ties with Western Europe, he failed in his attempt to form a European alliance against the Ottomans. He was more successful in his war against Sweden, his reforms, and in establishing himself as emperor of a vast empire and monarchy that survived until the revolution in 1917.

CHANGING

1776–1914

F rom the late 18th century, history took on a perhaps delusory air of "progress." Change accelerated and seemed to have a clear direction. The world population exceeded 1 billion in 1804 and was approaching 2 billion by 1914. This growth was made possible by tremendous increases in economic output. Agriculture became more efficient and large areas of new land were put to productive use. The exploitation of new sources of energy—especially steam power—the application of new technology, and organized industrial production in factories revolutionized the manufacture of commodities. Railroads made it possible for humans to travel faster than a horse for the first time and cities expanded—for instance, the population in London increased from 1 million in 1800 to 7 million in 1910. Improvements in public health and medicine increased life expectancy in the most advanced countries.

Human rights and equality

Despite these advancements, it is debatable whether progress was detectable in the quality of life. At the start of this period, political revolutions in America and France enunciated principles of human rights and equal citizenship that radically challenged the existing order of society. By the early 20th century, liberals and democrats in Europe and North America could look with some complacency upon successes such as the widespread expansion of voting rights, the abolition of slavery, and freedom of speech. However, women remained mostly excluded from voting, and there was no economic equality. Extremes of wealth and poverty polarized the world's wealthiest and most advanced societies, and conditions of life for industrial workers were often very miserable. Artists and intellectuals of the Romantic movement criticized the impact of mechanized industry on people and the environment, while socialist movements looked forward to further revolutions that would end the exploitation of man by man and create egalitarian societies.

Western imperialism

The most obvious losers in the new world order created by industrial capitalism were the inhabitants of countries at the periphery of the global economy. The industrializing countries of the West, needing places to invest their excess

SOCIETIES

capital, raw materials for their factories, and markets for their new products, found them in Asia, Africa, and Latin America. They also sought land for their expanding populations to settle in thinly populated zones such as the North American plains and Australia. Peoples who stood in their way were swept aside. The Europeans started expanding the areas under their direct rule or control. The British takeover of the Indian subcontinent, more or less complete by the mid-19th century, was the most spectacular example of imperialism in action, and Sub-Saharan Africa was divided among the European powers as if the local population did not exist.

The world's response to Western imperialism was mixed. Resistance was widespread in the form of wars and uprisings against European dominance. On the other hand, the growing superiority of the West in technology, science, military power, and social organization led several non-European governments to try to modernize based on the Western model. In the Muslim world, Egypt, Turkey, and Iran attempted, with only partial success, to pursue a modernizing agenda. In East Asia, Japan successfully transformed itself into an efficient modern state, becoming an imperialist power in its own right. China, by contrast, experienced turmoil and invasion, and imperial rule collapsed in the early 20th century.

Rising nationalism

Most Europeans and people of European descent gloried in a false sense of their own racial and cultural superiority to the rest of the world, but Europe remained a deeply divided continent. Militant nationalism, unleashed by the French Revolution, was a threat to stability. By 1815, the Napoleonic Wars had generated battles of unprecedented scale. After the wars of the mid-19th century that created a unified Italy and Germany, the great powers maintained large conscript armies and formed mutually hostile alliance systems. These armies were equipped with high-explosive shells and rapid-fire weapons.

European military power, which was supported by highly organized state systems and economies, was certainly one of the key elements in European world domination. There would be disaster when European states turned this power against one another. ■

WE HOLD THESE TRUTHS TO BE SELF-EVIDENT, THAT ALL MEN ARE CREATED EQUAL
THE SIGNING OF THE DECLARATION OF INDEPENDENCE (1776)

IN CONTEXT

FOCUS
The American Revolution

BEFORE
1773 Boston Tea Party protests tax on tea imports.

1775 Armed clashes take place between patriot militia and British forces.

AFTER
1777 British defeat at Saratoga persuades France to support the American rebels.

1781 The British surrender at Yorktown, Virginia.

1783 Britain recognizes American independence.

1787 Drafting of the Constitution begins.

1789 George Washington is elected as the first president of the United States.

1790 The US Constitution is ratified.

There has been no more daring assertion of statehood than that proclaimed by the Declaration of Independence, adopted by the Second Continental Congress on July 4, 1776, and signed by all 56 delegates present. What would become the United States consisted of 13 British colonies, steadily established since the 17th century, and scattered along the east coast of North America. They were not just geographically remote from their mother country; most were also geographically remote from each other. Their economies were fragile, and they had no coherent political identity—citizens of Virginia considered themselves to be Virginians, for example, not Americans— beyond an increasingly strained loyalty to the British crown.

However, the colonies were also remarkably self-aware and acutely conscious of Enlightenment notions of political liberty, and they were concerned that their freedom would come under threat as a result of British rule. Unable to assert their own natural rights, and subjected to what they considered unreasonably imposed taxes, the colonists questioned why a distant parliament and a distant king should impose their will on them. Impelled by a series of exceptional leaders, in 1776 they not only rejected British authority, but they set about establishing an entirely new kind of state in which government would derive from "the consent of the governed." This explosively novel idea would lead to the creation of a new and enduring republican government.

Support for a formal assertion of American independence was far from universal in the colonies, however. Five states in particular—New York, New Jersey, Maryland, Delaware, and Pennsylvania—feared it would damage trade and, if unsuccessful, provoke harsh

France and Britain's **new ideals of political liberty** take hold in Britain's American colonies.

American colonists' **protests against taxes** imposed by Britain **lead to conflict** with the British government.

The Declaration of Independence is issued.

American victory in the war with the British government leads to the **recognition of independence**.

reprisals from Britain. In the same way, as many as 500,000 of a population of 2.5 million remained loyal to the British crown to the end of the conflict, many subsequently settling in Canada.

The conflict takes shape

It would take a drawn-out and bitterly fought war to make independence into reality. Britain was determined to assert what it saw as its legitimate rule, while the hastily assembled forces of the nascent United States were no less determined to assert what they saw as their right to independence. The two modest armies—Britain's, because of the difficulties of sending forces en masse to America; the colonists', because they consistently lacked the means to raise and equip any substantial fighting force—confronted each other in a series of minor engagements over six years.

At their peak, the American forces numbered scarcely 40,000 and had almost no navy at all. Britain deployed about the same number of soldiers but in addition had a vastly greater number of ships. In 1778, however, France declared support for the colonists and sent 5,000 troops and a substantial fleet. Facing certain defeat, in October 1781, the British surrendered at Yorktown, Virginia. The war would not formally end for another year, but in every important respect, the colonists—and their French allies—had dealt a huge blow to their British masters.

The French involvement in the creation of this new nation owed everything to a desire to reverse the humiliations of the Seven Years' War. But the debts incurred would, ironically, be among the many causes of the bankruptcy of the French crown that led to the French Revolution in 1789. There was a profound irony, too, in absolutist France seeking to win Americans the freedoms that it was unwilling to accord its own citizens.

Revolutionary ideals

At the heart of the American Revolution was the new political philosophy encapsulated by the Declaration of Independence. It was the work of a distinctly patrician Virginian, a haughty, wealthy slaveholder named Thomas Jefferson. He was one of a committee of five charged with writing the Declaration, yet the two drafts it went through in June 1776 were almost entirely his own. It is »

These United Colonies are, and of Right ought to be Free and Independent States.
Richard Henry Lee
Proposed resolution at the Second Continental Congress (June 1776)

In *Declaration of Independence*, by John Trumbull, the drafting committee is shown presenting its work to Congress. Thomas Jefferson can be seen standing in a red waistcoat.

hard to overstate the importance of the Declaration of Independence. It made, for the time, an astonishing claim: "that all men are created equal." It further claimed "that governments are instituted among men deriving their just powers from the consent of the governed."

These were actively seditious sentiments that neither George III of England nor Louis XVI of France could have any sympathy with. They nonetheless formed the bedrock of what would become the United States and, indeed, liberal political systems across the Western world. These political creeds, derived from the work of British and French Enlightenment thinkers, led to the creation of the first modern state and, in doing so, changed the world.

The destiny of America

Jefferson remains an enigma. He loathed monarchy yet loved pre-Revolutionary France, where he was the United States' first ambassador, delighting in its civilized elegance. He claimed to despise high office yet served two terms as President of the United States. And, as president, in 1803 he drove through the Louisiana Purchase, which saw a vast area west of the Mississippi transferred at a bargain price from France, its nominal ruler, to the United States. He understood that the destiny of the US lay in its colonization of the vast lands to the west, he assented to the notion that its indigenous inhabitants should be driven off, and he held enslaved people. "Blacks," he asserted, "are inferior to the whites in the endowments both of body and mind." Whereas Washington, also a patrician Virginian, freed his enslaved people, Jefferson opted not to.

None of this, though, can diminish Jefferson's significance in articulating notions of liberty that resonate today. And even though he felt slavery was wrong, his personal belief was that emancipation would be bad for both enslaved and white Americans—unless they were returned to Africa.

A new constitution

Although Jefferson can readily be considered the guiding spirit behind the Declaration of Independence, he played no formal role in the drawing up of the next great document that shaped the nation: its Constitution. The United States was legally able to assert its independence from Britain in 1783. But for the next four years, it existed in an increasingly unstable political vacuum, its fate decided by an ever-more divided Confederation Congress, meeting variously in Pennsylvania, New York, and New Jersey.

There were serious reasons to believe the new nation might fail, torn apart by those arguing for the primacy of the rights of the individual states over the central government, and those in favor of a strong central government or even the creation of an American monarchy. In the spring of 1787, a Constitutional Convention took place in Philadelphia. The written, formalized Constitution proposed would not be provisionally ratified until June the following year, and then only after prolonged disputes. The result was an assertion of a new form of government. It was both a bill of rights and a blueprint for an ideal government, whose three branches—executive, legislative, and

 The god who gave us life, gave us liberty at the same time.
Thomas Jefferson

judiciary—would keep each other in check. It would have a profound influence on that issued in Revolutionary France in 1791 and remains a model of its kind.

"Unfinished business"

The founding fathers were rightly optimistic about the United States' potential, but they had failed to resolve one crucial question. Jefferson's first draft of the Declaration of Independence called slavery "an execrable commerce" and "a cruel war against human nature itself." However, to placate the slave states of the South and the slave traders of the north, these radical statements were later dropped. Almost 90 years later, it would take a civil war and 620,000 dead to end the practice and complete what Abraham Lincoln saw as the "unfinished business" of the Declaration of Independence and the Constitution. ■

George Washington

Born in 1732, George Washington served the British crown with distinction during the Seven Years' War

(1756–1763) against France. He represented Virginia in the House of Burgesses and in the Continental Congresses of 1774 and 1775. With the outbreak of the American Revolution, he was the unanimous choice to lead the Continental Army, which he did with imagination and great fortitude, especially in the very difficult early years of the conflict: his "skeleton of an army," under-equipped and close to starving, was forced to endure an exceptionally harsh winter in 1777–1778 at Valley

Forge in Pennsylvania. From 1783, Washington sought to establish a constitutional government for the new nation. The nation's first president, he served two terms, retiring in 1797 in the face of increasing disputes between Jefferson's Democratic Republicans and the Federalists, who were led by the quick-tempered Alexander Hamilton. Washington died in 1799 and was buried at his Virginia plantation, Mount Vernon, overlooking the Potomac River.

SIRE, IT'S A REVOLUTION
THE STORMING OF THE BASTILLE (1789)

IN CONTEXT

FOCUS
The French Revolution

BEFORE
May 1789 Louis XVI summons the States General. In June, the commons forms the National Assembly, taking effective power in the name of the people.

AFTER
April 1792 The Legislative Assembly declares war on Austria and Prussia. The first French Republic is declared.

January 1793 Louis XVI is executed.

March 1794 The Terror is at its peak. In July, Robespierre, its prime exponent, is executed.

October 1795 Napoleon forcibly restores order to a turbulent Paris.

November 1799 Napoleon effectively becomes the ruler of France.

O n July 14, 1789, an enraged Parisian mob, seeking weapons to defend their city from a rumored royal attack, stormed the crumbling fortress known as the Bastille and murdered its governor and guards. This violent defiance of royal power has become the symbol of the French Revolution, a movement that not only engulfed France but also reverberated around the world. The ideas articulated in the revolution spelled the beginning of the end for Europe's absolute monarchies and inspired their eventual replacement by more democratic governments.

The French Revolution originally set out to sweep away aristocratic privilege and establish a new state based on the Enlightenment principles of *liberté*, *égalité*, and *fraternité*. But although it was introduced by a surge of optimism, the revolution soon degenerated into a violence that played out over several years and that would be brought to an end only by the dictatorship of Napoleon Bonaparte. It remains a story of confusion and chaos, of a collision between a privileged old order, the *ancien régime*, and a new world that struggled, often violently, to create a coherent new order.

A country in disarray

The French king, Louis XVI, well-meaning but indecisive, was hardly the man to confront any crisis, let alone one as grave as that facing France in 1789. In the previous century, his great-great-great-grandfather Louis XIV, the Sun King, had established France as an absolute monarchy, with all power concentrated in the king's hands, and his palace at Versailles as the most sophisticated court in Europe and a bastion of aristocratic privilege.

Louis XVI thus ruled over a country where nobles refused to surrender any privileges, and taxes were paid almost exclusively by an oppressed peasantry:

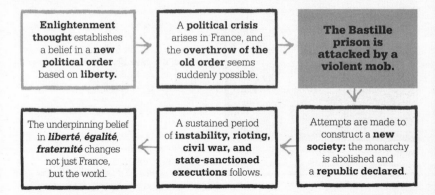

Enlightenment thought establishes a belief in a **new political order** based on **liberty.**

→

A **political crisis** arises in France, and the **overthrow of the old order** seems suddenly possible.

→

The Bastille prison is attacked by a violent mob.

↓

The underpinning belief in *liberté, égalité, fraternité* changes not just France, but the world.

←

A sustained period of **instability, rioting, civil war, and state-sanctioned executions** follows.

←

Attempts are made to construct a **new society:** the monarchy is abolished and a **republic declared**.

France was effectively bankrupt. In the late 18th century, France's population was expanding rapidly, but unlike England, France had not had an agricultural revolution and remained particularly vulnerable to any failure of the harvest, as happened in 1787 and, again, in 1788. These desperate summers were followed in 1788–1789 by a bitterly harsh winter, leading to mass starvation.

The king's response

The financial crisis critical, Louis was desperate to raise further funds while preserving his authority, so he summoned what was called the States General, a semi-parliamentary body that had last assembled in 1614. It consisted of clergy, the first estate; nobles, the second; and the commons (essentially a kind of bourgeoisie, lawyers predominating), the third. The States General met at Versailles on May 5, 1789. Almost instantly, the nobles and clerics tried to assert that their votes should be worth more than those of the commons. In response, on June 17, the commons declared itself a National Assembly, vesting power in itself instead of the crown. In August, with peasant uprisings across rural France, the Assembly abolished feudal taxes and aristocratic privileges and issued what it called the Declaration of the Rights of Man, a statement asserting fundamental freedoms.

In October 1789, events were suddenly accelerated when a vast crowd, outraged by the lack of bread in Paris, descended on Versailles and forcibly removed the royal family to Paris, ransacking the palace for good measure. In what would become an unnerving foretaste of the violence to come, the severed heads of the guards at Versailles were paraded on stakes as Louis and his family were escorted to the capital.

It had been comparatively easy to overthrow the existing royal government, but it would prove infinitely harder to establish a new government. It was presumed that a kind of constitutional monarchy would be the most obvious solution. In the end, France found itself wrenched between those arguing for this more or less moderate option, and those in favor of a much more radical republican alternative.

The First Republic

Although in most important respects Louis's reign seemed by now to be doomed, the king had not entirely abandoned hope of reasserting his authority. Large numbers of French aristocrats—émigrés—had already fled France, fearing the revolution had made it unsafe. In trying to persuade other European regimes—Austria above all, whose emperor was the brother of the French queen Marie-Antoinette—they stirred up opposition to the revolution, but their principal impact was to reinforce a determination in France to see the revolution succeed.

In June 1791, Louis attempted to escape, but was intercepted near the border with the Low Countries and brought back to Paris to the jeers of the »

Louis XVI was executed in 1793. Using the guillotine as the only means of execution for all people—royals and paupers alike—was meant to reinforce the revolutionary principle of equality.

increasingly violent, politicized common folk, the sans-culottes—their name a reference to their striped, baggy trousers. There was an increasingly hostile stand-off between political factions in Paris, such as the Girondins and more extremist Jacobins, which attracted the support of the sans-culottes, and the French government.

An external threat

Whatever the obvious instability, progress toward a new social order was being made. In September 1791, a constitutional monarchy was proclaimed. Similarly, the church's privileged position was forcibly ended, though this, too, provoked lasting upheaval and violence. Equally critically, the freedom of the press was asserted.

At the same time, revolutionary France faced an external threat from Austria and Prussia, both determined to reassert the primacy of hereditary monarchy and to forestall revolutionary tendencies in their own countries. In April 1792, France declared war on both, a war that would continue, in different guises, for 23 years. By August, the combined Austrian and Prussian forces were within 100 miles (160 km) of Paris.

A kind of hysteria gripped the city. A mob stormed the Tuileries, where the royal family was held, slaughtering its Swiss Guards. The following month, a further round of killings, the September Massacres, was unleashed against anyone suspected of royalist sympathies. September 1792 also marked the establishment of the directly

elected National Convention and of the First French Republic. Almost its first act was to put Louis XVI on trial as a traitor. In January 1793, he was executed, an early victim of the guillotine, championed as a humane and egalitarian means of death.

The sense of crisis continued to grow. In April 1793, the Committee of Public Safety was created to safeguard the revolution. For a year or more, under the chairmanship of a provincial lawyer, Maximilien Robespierre, the most influential of the now-dominant Jacobins, it would effectively become the government of France. Its impact on France, however short-lived, was devastating. This was the Terror. Counterrevolutionary movements across the country were ruthlessly suppressed, most obviously in the Vendée region of the southwest, where up to 300,000 died. Churches proved particularly rich targets. The Terror's victims were less likely to be remaining aristocrats and more anyone Robespierre suspected of impure thoughts, including almost all of his political opponents.

Robespierre's single-minded pursuit of revolutionary purity reached an improbable climax with his creation in 1794 of a new religion, the Cult of the Supreme Being. It was intended as a focus of, and spur to, patriotic and revolutionary virtues, the superstition of the Catholic Church replaced by a belief dedicated to reason celebrating the natural laws of the universe. The megalomania it suggested contributed significantly to his sudden downfall, and at the end of July 1794, Robespierre was put to the guillotine.

Order restored

With the end of the killings—more particularly with the establishment of yet another government, the Directory, at the end of 1795—order of a sort was restored. Tellingly, it was achieved in part by the Directory's willingness to use force against the Paris mob, ordered by Napoleon Bonaparte, then a young general in the revolutionary army.

Furthermore, France's armies, boosted by mass conscription, were reversing early

The French Revolution set out with the idea of building a new state that would take the Enlightenment principles of liberty, equality, and brotherhood as its foundation.

> ### Liberté
> A new understanding of liberty suggested that all were free to behave as they chose if they did no harm to others.

> ### Égalité
> This idea asserted that all people were equal under the law and ended aristocratic privilege.

> ### Fraternité
> This was the hope that the revolution would usher in a newfound, rational spirit of brotherhood.

defeats, apparently poised to carry the revolution into new territories. Emboldened, France reinforced its assertion of what it claimed were its "natural frontiers" on the Rhine, which in reality meant an audacious extension of French rule into Germany. By 1797, it had inflicted crushing defeats over Austria in the Low Countries and in northern Italy. France was ready to reassert what it saw as its natural primacy in Europe.

Historical significance

Whatever the importance of the French Revolution, it remains the subject of continuing and intense historical debate. Its notional goals were clear: the ending of repressive monarchy and entrenched privilege; the establishment of representative government; and the championing of universal rights. But the reality was confused and often violent.

Furthermore, by 1804 Napoleon had effectively swapped one form of absolutism for his own, albeit one vastly more effective than any France had known since Louis XIV. Yet the revolution's consequences reverberated well into the 20th century. It remains a pivotal moment in the belief that freedom should underpin the civilized world. ■

Maximilien Robespierre

Robespierre (1758–1794), a lawyer and a member of the third estate in 1789, was the chief architect of the Terror that gripped France between September 1793 and July 1794. He was a consistent champion of the dispossessed, as well as a remarkable orator, capable of astonishingly intense speeches that electrified his supporters and opponents alike. He was also a fierce opponent of the Revolutionary Wars, believing that a strengthened army risked becoming a source of counterrevolutionary fervor. Initially, at least, he was also opposed to the death penalty. His change of mind was startlingly absolute. When persuaded that terror was the most effective means of preserving the revolution, he embraced it implacably, arguing that it was the natural handmaiden of the virtue he felt should drive the revolution. He remains the original, chilling model for all those who have since championed state violence in the interests of a supposed greater good.

I MUST MAKE OF ALL THE PEOPLES OF EUROPE ONE PEOPLE, AND OF PARIS THE CAPITAL OF THE WORLD

THE BATTLE OF WATERLOO (1815)

IN CONTEXT

FOCUS
Revolutionary and Napoleonic Wars

BEFORE
1792 The Revolutionary Wars against Republican France begin.

1799 Napoleon seizes power in a military coup.

1804 Napoleon names himself Emperor of the French.

1805 The British are victorious against France and Spain in the naval Battle of Trafalgar.

1807 France invades Portugal.

1809 Austria is defeated in Napoleon's last major victory.

1814 A series of defeats lead to Napoleon's abdication.

AFTER
1815 Napoleon is exiled for the final time, and the Bourbon monarchy is restored.

1830 The Bourbon monarchy is overthrown.

France institutes **mass conscription**, creating armies of an unprecedented size.

↓

Napoleon becomes emperor and vows to **restore France's dominant role** in Europe.

↓

Sweeping conquests create the largest **European empire** since Charlemagne's time.

↓

The invasion of Russia leaves **Napoleon overextended** and French manpower depleted.

↓

The rate of Napoleonic conquest becomes **unsustainable**.

↓

Napoleon is finally defeated at Waterloo.

Napoleon's defeat at the Battle of Waterloo, south of Brussels, on June 18, 1815, marked his final overthrow as Emperor of the French, ending 23 years of European warfare. It was an epic encounter, fought on rain-soaked ground, in which 118,000 British, Dutch, and Prussian forces finally prevailed over a French army of 73,000, hastily assembled by Napoleon.

France's Revolutionary Wars, which began in 1792, had been launched to extend Revolutionary principles to neighboring states and to defend France against its enemies. Under Napoleon, they became, in effect, wars of conquest, despite being waged in the name of the Revolution.

A continent reshaped

During the Revolutionary Wars, France had established sister republics in northern Italy and the Low Countries; under Napoleon, many of these were reformed into kingdoms, whose monarchs came from the Emperor's family. States across Germany were carved up, at the expense of Prussia, to become a French puppet state, while the 800-year-old Holy Roman Empire was abolished. From 1807, much of Poland was controlled by the French as the Grand Duchy of Warsaw. These were states recast on French lines: clerical power was reduced, serfdom abolished, and aristocratic privilege ended. But such reforms provoked inevitable resentments.

Napoleon's conquests were the result not just of military genius but also of greatly enlarged French armies. Conscription, introduced in 1793, swelled the French army from 160,000 men to 1.5 million.

Only Britain, protected by the English Channel, remained undefeated, its position as the world's leading maritime power underscored by victory at Trafalgar, off southern Spain, in 1805. But maritime muscle alone was not enough to beat Napoleon. Britain's most significant role was financing the endlessly shifting alliances confronting the French.

In response, Napoleon imposed the Continental System, which forbade trade between continental Europe and Britain. However, Portugal and Russia continued to trade with Britain, prompting Napoleonic invasions in 1807 and 1812 respectively.

Resistance to Napoleonic rule was mounting; the Spanish began a brutal guerrilla war that drained French resources and came to be referred to by Napoleon as the "Spanish ulcer."

The final defeat

Napoleon had bred a sense of French invincibility, and this made his eventual defeat all the more traumatic for the nation. Of the 450,000 men he led against Russia in 1812, barely 40,000 survived.

Napoleon had overreached himself. At Leipzig, Germany, in 1813, outnumbered three to one by forces from Austria, Prussia, Russia, and Sweden, he suffered his first major defeat. By Waterloo, his forces had recovered slightly, and the ratio was only two to one, but Napoleon's military genius failed to redress the balance and his imperial ambition ended in the Waterloo mud. ∎

Napoleon Bonaparte

Born in Ajaccio, on the island of Corsica, to a family with claims to minor Italian nobility, Napoleon Bonaparte (1769–1821) was commissioned in the French army in 1785 and was an enthusiastic supporter of the Revolution. In 1796, at the age of 26, he was appointed to command the Army of Italy, winning a series of impressive victories. Two years later, Napoleon led an unsuccessful French invasion of Egypt.

Increasingly convinced of his destiny, by 1800, having staged a coup d'état, he dominated France as he would subsequently dominate Europe. He was as brilliant and tireless an administrator as he was a soldier. His most enduring reform was the introduction, in 1804, of the Napoleonic Code, which is still the basis of French law. Forced to resign in 1814, Napoleon was exiled to the island of Elba in the Mediterranean, from where he escaped before his final defeat at Waterloo. In 1815, he was dispatched to St. Helena in the South Atlantic, where he died six years later.

LET US LAY THE CORNERSTONE OF AMERICAN FREEDOM WITHOUT FEAR. TO HESITATE IS TO PERISH
BOLÍVAR ESTABLISHES GRAN COLOMBIA (1819)

IN CONTEXT

FOCUS
Latin American independence

BEFORE
1807–1808 Napoleonic invasion of Iberia leads to governmental crisis in the Iberian colonies of South America.

1819 Spain is expelled from its former province of New Granada, and the Republic of Colombia is declared.

AFTER
1822 Portugal assents to Brazil becoming a constitutional monarchy under Pedro I.

1824 The Spanish capitulate in Peru, and their New World empire ends.

1830 Break up of the Republic of Colombia. Ecuador, Colombia, and Venezuela emerge as independent states.

The establishment in 1819 of the Republic of Colombia, or Gran Colombia as it came to be known, by Simón Bolívar, the self-styled *Libertador*, marked a pivotal moment in the emergence of an independent Latin America.

By 1825, the continent had successfully ended almost 300 years of Spanish and Portuguese rule. In Brazil, which won its independence in 1822, the process was relatively easy and also largely bloodless. Elsewhere, it was complex, long, drawn out, and violent. It was a reflection of societies comprising a teeming range of classes and races—ruling Europeans, native peoples, black people, and those of mixed race—that were never likely to produce coherent political wholes. Plagued by bitter disputes, the short-lived republic of Gran Colombia would break up in 1830.

Brazilian independence

Though partly influenced by the liberal doctrines of the American and French revolutions, the drive to independence in South America was seldom the product of a desire for social justice or representative government. Aside from two abortive Mexican revolutions in 1810 and 1813, it was a struggle for supremacy between ruling elites, none of which had much interest in the kind of social change—society recast on liberal principles—that underpinned the French Revolution. That said, this drive was also significantly affected by the Napoleonic Wars. Napoleon's invasion of Portugal in 1807 forced the Portuguese king, João VI, and his court to flee to safety in its Brazilian colony. João remained there even after the fall of Napoleon in 1815, returning to Portugal only in 1821. However, his son and heir, Pedro, stayed in Brazil.

As in Spain's Latin American colonies, Brazil was dominated by a land-owning elite, a great many of whom, over many generations, had been born in South America. They came to resent the fact that ultimate authority was exercised by a distant monarchy, and saw no reason why they should submit to it.

Notions of **political liberation** spread across the territories colonized by the Spanish and Portuguese in **South America**.

These ideas **destabilize the Spanish administration** on the continent.

Bitter wars against colonial powers in South America lead to the creation of a newly independent Gran Colombia.

The new state faces **divisions and instabilities**. Hopes of unity are undermined by political infighting.

South America, racially and socially **dislocated**, consistently **struggles to assert itself** economically and politically.

There are clear parallels with the American Revolution. But while in North America it was the fundamental liberties of free-born men that were disputed, in Brazil the issue was narrower— it was simply a question of who would govern.

In 1822, to protect the interests of the native-born elite, Pedro declared Brazil an independent constitutional monarchy and himself its emperor. This was a revolution only in the sense that it produced Brazilian independence in the interests of those already ruling it. One of the more obvious consequences was that, with no change to the social or economic order, slavery remained legal in Brazil until 1888, later than anywhere else in the Western world.

Governing Spain's colonies

In Spain's colonies, the drive for independence stemmed partly from the desire of the native-born »

Simón Bolívar

Born in Caracas, Venezuela, in 1783, Simón Bolívar came from one of the oldest and wealthiest noble families in the city. His education was completed in Europe, where he absorbed the republican ideals of the American and French revolutions. The idea of independence for Hispanic America accordingly took root in his imagination.

His revolutionary career began with an abortive uprising in Caracas in 1810. In 1814, the charismatic Bolívar declared himself "liberator" and head of state of the new republic of Venezuela. In 1817, he staged a daring invasion of Colombia and went on to complete the conquests of Ecuador and Peru in 1824. Bolívar's dream was to unite all of South America—except Argentina, Brazil, and Chile—in a single great republic. However, his dictatorial tendencies and the brutality of his armies eventually led to dissent and the fracturing of Gran Colombia in 1830, the year of his death.

ruling class—the creoles—to assert their interests, not least in the face of Spain's restrictive control of South American trade and punitive taxation policies, both to the disadvantage of the colonies. In the short term, however, it was a reaction to Napoleon's invasion of Spain in 1808 and his deposition of the Spanish king, Ferdinand VII, in favor of Napoleon's brother, Joseph. In effect, Spain's colonies no longer had a legitimate ruler of their own, so it was their plain duty to become rulers themselves, at least until the monarchy could be restored.

While South American liberals saw Joseph as the harbinger of a new, more just social order in place of the absolutism of Ferdinand VII, monarchists in the colonies saw any such liberalizing tendencies as inherently destabilizing. The seeds of internal conflict were being sown.

Social revolution in Mexico
At the time, Mexico, which was known as the Vice-Royalty of New Spain, encompassed an immense area that extended almost from present-day Wyoming to Panama and that included most of Texas. Events there took a different turn. In 1810, a priest, Miguel Hidalgo, appalled at the obvious inequalities of Mexico, led a popular revolution that ended the following year in its brutal suppression and Hidalgo's execution. Another popular

Pedro I of Brazil, whose coronation is illustrated in this painting by Jean-Baptiste Debret, was the son of the king of Portugal. He had been left in Brazil to rule as regent.

uprising led by a second Catholic priest, José Morelos, between 1813 and 1815 was similarly put down. When, in 1821, Mexico did gain independence, it was by force against more or less token Spanish resistance, and under the leadership of Agustín de Iturbide, a Mexican general who proclaimed himself emperor of Mexico the following year. His rule lasted less than a year. By 1838, Mexico had lost all its Central American territories, and by 1848, it had lost all its North American territories.

Gran Colombia
Events in Spanish South America—which included the triple Vice-Royalties of New Granada, Peru, and Rio de la Plata—followed a very different course. The key figure here was Simón Bolívar. Born in modern-day Venezuela, he was a creole, aristocratic, and highly educated. He had visited Europe several times and was an enthusiastic supporter of modern nation-building on the model established by the French Revolution. He believed, in particular, that the diverse peoples and interests of South America could be brought together by the

assertion of a shared South American identity, expressed by the creation of a vast new South American state. This was to be Gran Colombia, which embraced an immense area of northern South America, essentially the modern states of Ecuador, Colombia, Venezuela, and Panama.

Bolívar's vision of an independent South America consistently fell foul of a series of political realities. His military successes—for example, in 1824, the routing of the remaining Spanish strongholds in Peru, when his armies attacked from the north and the south in a pincer movement in the Central Andes—proved impossible to translate into enduring and stable states.

Bolívar was an idealist and a passionate opponent of slavery. He considered that so disparate a land and a people could only be ruled by a strong central government. Seeing himself as its natural leader, he proposed himself as the lifelong president of Gran Colombia. This provoked predictably bitter opposition.

Gran Colombia breaks up

By 1830—the year Bolívar died, aged 47, of tuberculosis—Gran Colombia had already broken up. Arguably, it was the result of the kind of nationalism already surfacing in Europe, with the independence of Greece and, the following year, of Belgium. More particularly, it was due to a failure to agree on the future of Gran Colombia. There were disputes over

 May slavery be banished forever together with the distinction between castes.
José Morelos
Leader of the failed
Mexican Revolt of 1813–1815

whether its government was to be liberal, conservative, or authoritarian. Venezuela, in particular, was subjected to bitter wars throughout the 19th century that cost the lives of an estimated 1 million people.

This lack of direction resulted in instability and a social inequality that would persist for a century or more. It would also produce a series of authoritarian military leaders acting in the interests of the landowners. An inevitable consequence was a persistently oppressed underclass, urban and agricultural, black and white. The *hacienda*—vast acres inefficiently worked by armies of peasants in the interests of a complacently cruel, land-owning elite—dominated.

In 1910, Mexico descended into another revolution. This was partly a result of being wrenched between ineffectual liberal regimes that sought to alleviate the obvious suffering of the poor but did little to address fundamental economic weaknesses, and self-serving authoritarian regimes that cared more for bombast than real reform.

Bolívar's visions of a recast, independent South America could never contend with the reality of an unequal society that shared no common belief in its own destiny and that was consistently the victim of competing, mostly violent efforts to assert special interests. ∎

The Battle of Ayacucho (1824) saw the defeat of the Spanish army at the hands of the South American liberation troops. It marked the end of Spanish rule in Peru and in South America.

LIFE WITHOUT INDUSTRY IS GUILT

STEPHENSON'S *ROCKET* ENTERS SERVICE (1830)

IN CONTEXT

FOCUS
The Industrial Revolution

BEFORE
1776 Adam Smith's *The Wealth of Nations* is published.

1781 Watt's first rotating steam engine is invented; the world's first iron bridge is built at Coalbrookdale, England.

1805 The Grand Junction Canal, between Birmingham and London, is completed.

1825 The world's first commercial steam-powered railroad, linking Stockton and Darlington, opens.

AFTER
1855 The Bessemer furnace is introduced.

1869 The first transcontinental railroad is completed in the US.

1885 The first practical gasoline-driven internal-combustion engine is installed in a motor vehicle, in Germany.

A **scientific revolution** in the West creates a sense that the world can be **better understood** and better exploited.

⬇

The development of steam-powered machinery encourages the growth of **factory-based mass production**.

⬇

Stephenson's *Rocket* heralds a new form of faster, more reliable transportation.

⬇

The West imposes itself across the rest of the globe, creating **interlocked global markets**.

⬇

Industrial societies' **dependence on fossil fuels** leads to a strain on the **natural environment**.

O n September 15, 1830, the world's first commercial passenger rail service to be powered by a steam engine—George Stephenson's *Rocket*—was opened. This was the Liverpool and Manchester Railway, which was 35 miles (56 km) long and served by locomotives, also designed by Stephenson, that were capable of reaching speeds approaching 30 mph (48 km/h).

Stephenson's *Rocket* symbolized what remains the key development in world history over the past 250 years: the transformation from an agricultural society that relied on windmills, watermills, horses, and other beasts of burden, to an industrial one, in which steam engines were capable of generating reliable power on a scale that was previously unimaginable.

The background

The industrialization process that started in Britain around the mid- to late 18th century was initiated by the scientific revolution in Europe in the late 17th century. Of similar importance were financial changes pioneered in the Netherlands, then imported to Britain: more readily available credit helped boost entrepreneurial activities. It had never been easier for members of the increasingly wealthy middle class, looking for ways to invest their money, to support new inventions and technologies.

A third factor was an agricultural revolution, which began in the Netherlands and Britain, where farmers realized that crop rotation made it unnecessary to leave land fallow every third year. In both of these countries, land reclamation increased the acreage available for farming. Crop yields were thus boosted, just as selective breeding produced larger and more profitable domesticated animals—sources of food and wool alike. With any likelihood of famine now receding, the population of Britain grew, between 1750 and 1800, from 6.5 million to over 9 million. This, in turn, meant new markets and an expanded workforce.

In Britain, an improved transportation network allowed goods, produced on an ever-larger scale, to be transported faster and more reliably. Between 1760 and 1800, as many as 4,250 miles (6,840 km) of canals were built in England.

Thinkers sought to understand the impulses behind these societal changes. The publication in 1776 of *The Wealth of Nations* by the Scottish philosopher Adam Smith underpinned what was becoming known as political economy, and the central role of the profit motive and of competition in increasing efficiencies and lowering prices.

This economic transformation also contributed to and was, in turn, boosted by the emergence of global markets—a consequence of burgeoning European colonial empires, which offered greater access to raw materials and also provided markets for finished goods. A better-mapped world, and improvements in ship types and position-finding at sea, also facilitated global trade.

Steam power

The overriding force behind the economic transformation, though, was the development of the steam engine. In an astonishingly short time, it would revolutionize Britain, making it the world's first industrial power, and ultimately transform the world. Even so, it might never have had its dramatic global impact had Britain not had huge reserves of the fuel needed to make it work: coal. The replacement of wood as the prime source of fuel was critical to industrial development. In exactly the same way, the development of coke (processed coal that burns at much higher temperatures than coal) at the beginning of the 18th century would make the production of iron—the indispensable core material of the new technologies—faster and simpler.

Steam engines of varying degrees of reliability had been developed as early as 1712, when Thomas Newcomen built an "atmospheric engine." But it was only with James Watt's first rotating steam engine in 1781 that the extraordinary potential of machine power became clear. The earliest steam engines had been used mainly as pumps. Watt's rotating engine, on the other hand, could power machinery. The engineering company he and Matthew Boulton established in Birmingham in 1775 produced over 500 steam engines.

When Watt's patents expired in 1800, others started producing their own steam engines. The textile industries in the northwest benefited in particular from the increased availability of steam power, and large-scale, almost entirely mechanized, factory production soon replaced small, home-based manufacturing. By 1835, there were more than 120,000 power looms in textile mills. No longer dependent on rivers as power sources, factories could be built » anywhere, and they came to be concentrated in towns in the north and Midlands of England that rapidly grew into major industrial centers as the century progressed.

Social changes

Huge numbers of workers were drawn to these new cities, which became synonymous with poor living and working conditions for the workforce, many of whom were children. This influx led to the creation of an urban underclass. It took a long time before the workers saw any improvement in their lives, and the realization that they should share in the rewards of this social and economic transformation, rather than simply be exploited as mere drudges, came very slowly. In the meantime, however, the increasingly wealthy factory owners emerged as a significant political voice.

The wider world

As late as 1860, Britain was, by some margin, still the world's leading industrial and mercantile power, but other Western nations were quick to see how they could benefit. In continental Europe, industrialization was initially uncertain, inhibited by the kind of political instability Britain had managed to avoid, such as the revolutions of 1848. Later, the pace of its development would rival Britain's. In 1840, Germany and France each had around 300 miles (480 km) of railroad lines; in 1870, both had 10,000 miles (16,000 km). Similarly, pig-iron output

from each rose from about 125,000 tons in 1840 to 1 million in 1870.

However, the most startling developments came in the United States, where there were around 3,300 miles (5,300 km) of railroad in 1840, almost all in the northeast. By 1860, this had increased to 32,000 miles (51,500 km), and by 1900 it had soared to 193,000 miles (310,600 km) of rail track. The production of pig iron rose similarly: in 1810, it was a little less than 100,000 tons a year; in 1850, it was approaching 700,000 tons; in 1900, it was over 13 million.

The role of steel

By about 1870, in both Europe and the United States, a second wave of industrialization began, in which oil, chemicals, electricity, and steel became increasingly important. The production of steel had been transformed after 1855, when English engineer Henry Bessemer devised a way to make the metal lighter, stronger, and more versatile; from that point forward, steel would prove the linchpin for industry. In 1870, total world steel production was 540,000 tons, but within 25 years it had risen to 14 million tons, and railroads, armament production, and the shipbuilding industry all benefited from its ready availability.

While Germany was beginning to threaten Britain's preeminent industrial position in Europe, quadrupling its industrial output between 1870 and 1914, the United

Isambard Kingdom Brunel

No figure better encapsulates the determination, ambition, and vision that drove the first phase of the Industrial Revolution in Britain than the prodigiously hard-working Isambard Kingdom Brunel (1806–1859). He was responsible for an extraordinary series of firsts: the world's

longest bridge (the Clifton Suspension Bridge), the world's longest tunnel (Box Tunnel in Wiltshire), and the world's largest ship (the *Great Eastern*). In 1827, still only 21, he was appointed chief engineer of the Thames Tunnel. In 1833, he became engineer to the newly formed Great Western Railway, which by 1841 linked London directly with Bristol, whose docks he had rebuilt from 1832. Believing it should be

possible to travel directly from London to New York, Brunel also designed the world's first practical ocean-going steamship, the *Great Western*. He followed this with the screw-driven iron-built *Great Britain*. Despite his great vision, delays and cost overruns dogged many of Brunel's projects, but his works include some of the grandest feats of engineering the world had yet seen.

States was rapidly becoming the world's largest industrial power. In 1880, Britain was still producing more steel than the United States, but by 1900 the United States was producing more steel than Britain and Germany together.

At the same time, steam-powered ships were also being introduced. Sailing times, no longer dependent on the vagaries of the wind, became more controllable, and journey times were shortened. The ships were significantly larger, too. While the largest wooden ships rarely exceeded 200 ft (60 m) in length, the *Great Eastern*, launched in 1858, was 689 ft (210 m) long. Total world steamship tonnage in 1870 was 1.4 million. By 1910, it had reached 19 million.

Winners and losers

The benefits of industrialization were unevenly spread. Southern Europe was slow to react to it, and Russia also struggled to catch up. The Chinese and Indian empires proved unwilling or unable to industrialize,

Latin America did so only intermittently, and Africa was dominated by technologically superior powers. By contrast, after 1868, Japan's single-minded pursuit of industrialization made it a world power.

Industrialization also made possible a new kind of warfare, one capable of bringing death on a scale never seen before. An enduring irony of industrialization is that the nations that benefited most from it turned it against themselves in two world wars, deploying weapons of extraordinarily destructive power.

The Industrial Revolution laid the foundations for the modern world. Fueled by an enormous sense of new possibilities, in some places it raised living standards across all sections of society in ways unimaginable in earlier ages. However, in the wealthy West, it also produced a sense that material superiority was equivalent to a kind of moral superiority, one that not merely made it possible for the West to dominate the world, but demanded that it do so. ∎

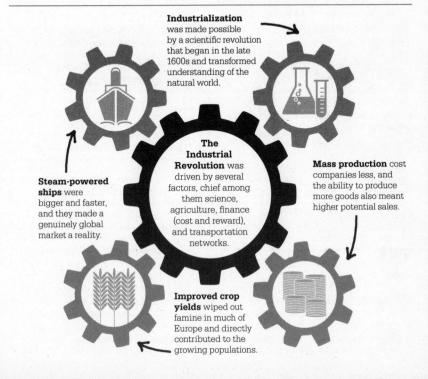

Industrialization was made possible by a scientific revolution that began in the late 1600s and transformed understanding of the natural world.

The Industrial Revolution was driven by several factors, chief among them science, agriculture, finance (cost and reward), and transportation networks.

Mass production cost companies less, and the ability to produce more goods also meant higher potential sales.

Steam-powered ships were bigger and faster, and they made a genuinely global market a reality.

Improved crop yields wiped out famine in much of Europe and directly contributed to the growing populations.

YOU MAY CHOOSE TO LOOK THE OTHER WAY, BUT YOU CAN NEVER AGAIN SAY YOU DID NOT KNOW
THE SLAVE TRADE ABOLITION ACT (1807)

IN CONTEXT

FOCUS
Abolitionism

BEFORE
1787 The Society for the Abolition of the Slave Trade is founded in London.

1791 Enslaved people revolt in the French Caribbean island of Haiti (St. Domingue). Independence is successfully declared in 1804.

AFTER
1823 The Anti-Slavery Society is founded. It campaigns to abolish slavery throughout the British Empire.

1833 Slavery is outlawed throughout the British Empire.

1848 Slavery is abolished in France's colonies.

1865 The Thirteenth Amendment outlaws slavery in the United States.

1888 Brazil abolishes slavery, the last country in the Americas to do so.

Radical notions of freedom in Britain combine with the religious belief that **slavery** is an **abomination.**

Merchants and **plantation owners** resist calls for an end to slavery.

After several parliamentary defeats, the Slave Trade Abolition Act is passed by an overwhelming majority.

Britain campaigns vigorously to persuade other nations to **oppose the shipping of enslaved people.**

⬇

Slavery is abolished in the British Empire in 1833. It does not finally end in the US until 1865.

The passing in 1807 of the Act Prohibiting Importation of Slaves in the United States and the Abolition of the Slave Trade Act in Britain marked a radical shift in Western thinking. Even as late as the 1780s, the trade in enslaved people was still regarded as a "natural" economic activity. Both the newly created United States, "conceived in liberty," and the European

colonies in the Caribbean depended on enslaved labor that was obtained in West Africa. Portuguese-ruled Brazil was even more dependent on the enslaved. Yet Britain in particular found itself in an uncomfortably anomalous position. Not only had slavery never been legal there—a point critically reinforced in 1772 in what was called the Somersett case, which ruled that any

William Wilberforce, portrayed here by Karl Anton Hickel, was a fervent Christian and the British politician who campaigned most vociferously against the slave trade.

enslaved person was free once on British soil—but Britons prided themselves on their defense of fundamental freedoms.

Even so, Britain was also, by some margin, the West's leading slave-trading nation. It was this contradiction that offended both religious and Enlightenment political sensibilities alike.

Global changes

To a number of high-minded and unusually active campaigners such as William Wilberforce and Thomas Clarkson, the abolition of slavery became an imperative. A remarkably effective campaign was launched that, despite entrenched opposition, rapidly won wide public and parliamentary support. For much of the 19th century, the Royal Navy would be at the forefront of the campaign to intercept those still engaged in slave trading.

While Britain took the lead, the movement had important supporters elsewhere. The revolutionary French National Convention outlawed slavery in 1794 (though this would partially be overturned by Napoleon in 1802). Brazil aside, where slavery would not be banned until 1888, all the newly independent states that emerged in Latin America after 1810 likewise outlawed slavery.

It wasn't until 1833 that slavery itself, as opposed to the trade, was made illegal in the British Empire. Whatever the efforts of a new set of campaigners, not least Elizabeth Heyrick, the motive was not entirely humanitarian. The Haitian slave revolt, which began in 1791 and led to the emergence of an independent Haiti in 1804, had left the West uncomfortably aware that any such uprisings might prove difficult to suppress. A slave revolt in British-ruled Jamaica in 1831 reinforced the point: in the longer term, freeing the enslaved might prove less trouble than enslaving them.

The United States, forward-looking and expansive, remained the great troubling sore. The more abolitionists in its industrializing northern states denounced slavery, the more its southern states, their agrarian economies dependent on enslaved labor, were determined to retain it. It would take a four-year civil war and 670,000 dead to settle the question. ■

The Haitian Revolt

Few uprisings illustrate the contradictions of the revolutions that swept across the late 18th-century Western world better than that in Haiti (1791–1804). This French Caribbean colony, known as St. Domingue, owed its enormous prosperity to enslaved labor. The revolt, led by a formerly enslaved man, Toussaint L'Ouverture, was inspired by the American and French revolutions. Yet neither country supported it: The US was concerned it might inspire similar revolts in its slave states; France, despite its pledge to abolish slavery, was wary of the damage to its trade. Spain, which ruled the eastern half of the island, also opposed it, as did Britain, fearing it would spread to its own colonies. Even the South American colonies seeking independence refused to back it, fearful of its impact among their substantial enslaved populations. Yet the occasional combined resources of all these states were unable to quell the uprising. This was the only slave revolt to result in the emergence of an independent state.

THIS ENTERPRISE WILL RETURN IMMENSE REWARDS
THE CONSTRUCTION OF THE SUEZ CANAL (1859–1869)

IN CONTEXT

FOCUS
Imperial economies

BEFORE
1838 The first Atlantic crossing under steam power alone is made.

1858 The first transatlantic telegraph cable is laid.

AFTER
1869 The Suez Canal opens, slashing sailing times between Europe and the East.

1878 The Gold Standard is adopted in Europe; the US follows suit in 1900.

1891 The Trans-Siberian railroad is begun. It is completed in 1905.

1899–1902 Britain aims to secure control of South Africa in the Second Boer War.

1914 The Panama Canal, linking the Atlantic and Pacific oceans, opens.

The **Industrial Revolution** allows the **rapid development** of Western economies.

New industries are hungry for **more resources**.

New classes of workers hanker for **consumer goods**.

Developed countries **build empires** and use their **colonial muscle** to feed their industries.

Technology and transport develop to support this new global economy.

The Suez Canal is constructed, facilitating global trade by shortening shipping routes substantially.

The ceremonial opening, on November 17, 1869, of the Suez Canal, linking the Mediterranean and the Red seas, was an emphatic declaration of European—specifically, French—technological and financial means. It was also a significant illustration of a rapidly emerging and increasingly interdependent global economy, featuring goods from all parts of the world being traded on an ever-larger scale. This was a process dominated by Europe's colonial powers and the United States, overwhelmingly its principal beneficiaries. It was simultaneously a further boost to Europe's imperial ambitions.

The Suez Canal reduced the route between London and Mumbai (Bombay) by 41 percent, and the route between London and Hong Kong by 26 percent. The impact on trade was plain to see. However, reduced sailing times also greatly simplified the defense of India and its crucial markets, Britain's key imperial goal. By the end of the 19th century, trade in the Indian Ocean, protected by no fewer than 21 Royal Navy bases, had become almost a British monopoly, a point further underlined when Britain gained control of the Suez Canal in 1888 after having invaded and occupied Egypt six years earlier. This "gunboat diplomacy" proved a remarkably effective means of protecting British interests.

The Panama Canal

The Suez Canal was just one of a number of similar massive engineering undertakings in the interest of imperial trade. An even more challenging project was the construction, begun in 1881, of the Panama Canal in Central America, linking the Atlantic and Pacific oceans. It, too, was a French initiative, but one dogged by controversy and a consistently hostile climate that cost the lives of 22,000 laborers. The United States eventually completed the Panama Canal in August 1914, stepping in when the French finally admitted defeat. It was the largest and most expensive engineering project in the world. It, too, dramatically reduced sailing times, shortening the Liverpool to San Francisco route by 42 percent, and the New York to San Francisco route by 60 percent.

US involvement

The fact that the United States took over the construction of the Panama Canal

The Suez Canal opened in 1869 and dramatically cut sailing times between Europe and Asia. This provided a massive boost for trade, which, in turn, spurred technological advances.

underlines a crucial shift in US attitudes: they were committing not just to expanding trade but also to advancing US overseas interests. This had begun in 1898, when the US itself became a colonial power, taking over the Philippines from Spain.

The process began to accelerate under the presidency of Theodore Roosevelt (1901–1909). He actively advocated US military involvement, above all, in Latin America, to ensure stability as a means of advancing American interests. One consequence of this was his strengthening of the US Navy, the Great White Fleet.

Roosevelt's successor, William Taft, pursued a more legalistic variant of the policy—Dollar Diplomacy—by which American commercial interests, chiefly in Latin America and East Asia, were to be secured by the full backing of the US government, and huge overseas investments encouraged.

Trains and telegraphs

At the same time, major new railroads were constructed in both the US and Europe. The east and west coasts of the US were first linked by rail in 1869, with the opening of the 1,907-mile (3,070-km) Central Pacific Railroad. By 1905, there were eight more transcontinental rail lines across the United States and one in Canada.

The building of the Trans-Siberian Railroad in Russia, between 1891 and 1905, was undertaken in the same spirit. A remarkable 4,600 miles (7,400 km) long and spanning seven time zones, it remains the longest continuous railroad in the world. It played a key role not just in the settlement of Russia's vast Siberian territories, but in Russia's encroachment on parts of northern China, too.

The impact of the telegraph was just as significant, allowing messages to be communicated along electrical lines. Samuel Morse devised the system in the United States in the 1830s, and the first telegraph line was inaugurated in May 1844. Within a decade, there were 20,000 miles (32,200 km) of telegraph cable in the US.

The first telegraph cable across the Atlantic, laid in 1858, worked for only two » weeks. But by 1866, a new cable had been installed, capable of transmitting 120 words per minute. By 1870, a telegraph link had been established between London and Mumbai; this was then extended to Australia in 1872 and New Zealand in 1876. By 1902, the United States was linked to Hawaii. This was the first near-instant international communications system.

The *Great Eastern*
The ship responsible for laying the transatlantic cable in 1866 was the *Great Eastern*, designed by the most visionary engineer of the first phase of the Industrial Revolution, Isambard Kingdom Brunel. Designed to carry 4,000 passengers from England to Australia nonstop (and to return to England without refueling), the ship was overly ambitious in concept and a commercial failure.

However, it was indicative of a trend toward larger, faster, and safer ships. Unlike the *Great Eastern*, which was built of iron, later, steel-built, propeller-driven ships would prove more versatile. Their introduction coincided with the development of more powerful and efficient steam engines.

Steamships and trade
The decline of the sailing ship further transformed imperial trade. One notable

The RMS *Mauretania*, built at Wallsend, Tyne and Wear, UK, was the largest and fastest ship in the world. In 1909, it set a record, sailing across the Atlantic in less than five days.

result was the introduction of a series of ever-larger passenger ships. The transatlantic route saw the most obvious developments. In 1874, the British steamer *Britannic*, capable of generating 5,500 horsepower, set a new east–west Atlantic record of just under eight days. In 1909, the *Mauretania*, which generated 70,000 horsepower and carried over 2,000 passengers, set a new record of four days and 10 hours, cruising at an average speed of 26 knots, or 30 mph (48 km/h).

The Great Mineral Rush

The search for new sources of minerals, both precious and industrial, reached new heights toward the close of the 19th century. Discoveries of diamonds and gold in the US, Canada, Australia, and—most significantly of all—South Africa sparked a frenzy of development. Diamonds were discovered in South Africa's Orange Free State in 1867, and gold in the Transvaal in 1886. Both were independent Boer republics, established by the descendants of the original Dutch settlers of what had become British Cape Colony. Their heightened economic importance reinforced Britain's determination to annex them, which they could do only after the bitter Boer War (1899–1902), which stretched Britain's military resources to their limits. The exploitation, both before and after the conflict, of the mineral resources of what in 1910 became the Union of South Africa by armies of underpaid black workers would later prove to be critical in the institutionalizing of Apartheid.

Working conditions in South Africa's gold mines were harsh, and the work force—mainly young black men—was exploited and underpaid.

The Suez Canal greatly shortened travel times—and eased journeys—between parts of the British Empire, such as England and India. That distance of 10,800 nautical miles was cut by more than 40 percent, to just 6,200 nautical miles.

⊢ Suez Canal
••• Route via Suez Canal
••• Previous route
▬ Countries ruled by British Empire

production increased from 100,000 bales in 1800 to 4 million in 1860. During the American Civil War, the southern, Confederate states restricted exports of cotton in an attempt to force European intervention in the war. However, the ploy failed, since Britain merely increased its imports of raw cotton from India. After weaving the cotton, it then exported it back to India at substantial profits.

New types of merchant ships—mainly refrigerated vessels—were also being built. Such developments show how technology helped drive trade, making it possible to reach global markets. The cattle and sheep farms in South America (especially Argentina), Australia, and New Zealand were growing in size in line with their own populations. At the same time, the number of people in Europe was also increasing—for example, Britain swelled from 28 million to 35 million between 1850 and 1880. Feeding and clothing the populations were important priorities. Wool could be easily transported, but lamb and beef could not be shipped because it would rot en route—until 1877, when 80 tons of frozen beef were shipped from Argentina to France on board the world's first refrigerated ship. By 1881, regular shipments of frozen meat were traveling between Australia and Britain. The first shipment of lamb from New Zealand was made the following year. There was a vast increase in the export of meat from all three countries—New Zealand, for example, exported 2.3 million frozen sheep in 1895, 3.3 million in 1900, and 5.8 million in 1910.

The demand for cotton—above all in the great textile mills of the northwest of England, which by 1850 were producing up to 50 percent of the world's cloth—led to an enormous surge in cotton growing. In the southern states of the US, raw cotton

Global finance

This complex trading network could not have grown without developments in banking and financing. Throughout the late 19th century, new banks were established, their capital used to support enterprises around the world. At the same time, London emerged as the world's financial capital. By the end of the 19th century, the British pound sterling, its value pegged at 113 grains of gold, was the currency against which all others were measured.

Western overseas investments dramatically increased. By 1914, the United States had overseas assets worth $3.5 billion, Germany $6 billion, France $8 billion, and Britain almost $20 billion. Between them, North America and northern Europe's share of world income in 1860 was about $4.3 billion a year, 35 percent of the world's total. In 1914, it was $18.5 billion, 60 percent of the world's total.

Patterns of imperialism varied over the 19th century. In the British Empire, for example, clear and increasing distinctions were drawn between those colonies—in Africa and Asia, above all—whose native populations were governed by Europeans, and those—such as Canada, South Africa, Australia, and New Zealand—deemed capable of self-government. By 1907, all four had been granted dominion status. It was not a privilege extended to a single British African colony or to India. ■

ENDLESS FORMS MOST BEAUTIFUL AND MOST WONDERFUL HAVE BEEN, AND ARE BEING, EVOLVED

DARWIN PUBLISHES *ON THE ORIGIN OF SPECIES* (1859)

IN CONTEXT

FOCUS
Scientific advance

BEFORE
1831–1836 The voyage of the HMS *Beagle* takes the young naturalist Charles Darwin around the world.

AFTER
1860 Thomas Huxley defends Darwin from an attack by the established Anglican church.

1863 Gregor Mendel demonstrates how genetics influence all plant life.

1871 Darwin's *The Descent of Man* advances the view of sexual selection, whereby the most successful members of a species are naturally attracted to perpetuate the species.

1953 Discovery of DNA demonstrates how traits are passed on genetically.

Geologists begin to understand that **the Earth has existed** for previously unimaginable **eons of time**.

↓

It became clear to scientists that the Earth had undergone a series of **immense changes and extinctions**.

↓

Charles Darwin publishes *On the Origin of Species.*

↓

Darwin's book explains the **diversity of animal species** and posits that all life on Earth is **related to a common ancestor**.

↓

Modern science decisively **reinforces the evidence and conclusions** presented in **Darwin's landmark text**.

Perhaps the most important scientist of the 19th century, Charles Darwin originally intended to follow his father into medicine and was subsequently sent to Cambridge to train as an Anglican cleric. Endlessly curious, he was interested in almost any scientific question.

The publication of his book *On the Origin of Species* (1859) introduced a new scientific understanding of what gradually came to be known as evolution. In the book, Darwin asked a fundamental question. The world teems with plant and animal life: where and what had it come from? How had it been created?

Darwin was far from the first to propose that a process of change over vast periods had produced this diversity, but he was the first to suggest an explanatory theme, which he called "natural selection."

The finches on the Galapagos Islands were key to Darwin's work. The 13 species he found there all had different types of beaks, which evolved to deal with the food available to the birds.

Natural selection

At the heart of Darwin's idea was his contention that all animal life was derived from a single, common ancestor—that the ancestors of all mammals, humans included, for example, were fish. And in a natural world that was never less than relentlessly violent, only those most able to adapt would survive, in the process evolving into new species.

These views were largely formed by the around-the-world voyage he made as the naturalist on the British survey vessel HMS *Beagle* between 1831 and 1836, most of it spent in South America. It would take him 10 years to work up his voluminous notes and to go through all the samples he collected on his voyage.

Darwin's book inevitably generated controversy, outraging Christian views that the world had been created intact and unchanging by a benevolent deity. Yet however heated the initial debate, quite rapidly there was widespread acceptance of Darwin's views and a realization that he had made a decisive contribution to the understanding of the world. In the process, the status of science generally was immensely boosted.

The primacy of science

Despite everything, it was possible for Darwinism to be warped. What came to be called "the survival of the fittest" would later prove to be influential in justifying imperialism, racism, and eugenics.

On the Origin of Species was published at a time when a growing understanding of the natural world and rapid technological progress meant scientific study had a greater practical worth than ever before. Darwin was one of the last amateur gentleman scientists in a discipline that was becoming professionalized as society came to view science more highly. Partly as a result of Darwin's work, but also because of these changing attitudes, science began to have a more central place in public life. By the end of Darwin's life, continual progress in scientific knowledge had become an almost standard expectation. ∎

Charles Darwin

Charles Darwin (1809–1882) was only the fifth choice for the position of naturalist on the voyage of the HMS

Beagle in 1831. However fortuitous his selection, it would transform his life. Although he was constantly seasick during his time aboard the craft, Darwin proved himself an assiduous observer of the world around him. He would take as much amazed delight in the jungles of Brazil as he would in the pampas of Argentina or in the arid wastes of the Galapagos Islands. Upon returning to England, he settled into a life of persistent hard work—the model high-Victorian scientist, aided by considerable private means and a notably happy family life, despite the deaths of three of his ten children. Although his own health may effectively have been severely damaged by the time he spent on the *Beagle*, his output remained prodigious, as did his level of intrigue at almost any subject in the natural world. In the absence of the exotic, he was as fascinated by pigeons as by parasites, barnacles as much as earthworms.

LET US ARM. LET US FIGHT FOR OUR BROTHERS

THE EXPEDITION OF THE THOUSAND (1860)

IN CONTEXT

FOCUS
Nationalism

BEFORE
1830 Greece obtains its independence from the Ottomans.

1848 Nationalist revolutions sweeping across Central Europe and Italy are crushed.

1859 Austria is driven out of Lombardy, which is then annexed by Piedmont.

AFTER
1861 The Italian kingdom is established.

1866 Austria is forced to cede Venetia in northeast Italy to the new Italian kingdom.

1870 The Papal States are incorporated within Italy.

1871 Germany is united under Prussian control. Rome is declared the capital of Italy.

Ideas of **national self-determination**, inspired by the **French Revolution**, begin to proliferate across Europe.

↓

The **Greek War of Independence** epitomizes the struggles necessary to free nations from **foreign domination**.

↓

The **failed revolutions of 1848** illustrate the **ruling elites' resistance** to notions of national independence.

↓

Garibaldi lands in Sicily and overthrows the Kingdom of the Two Sicilies, but Italy remains a constitutional monarchy.

↓

German unification under Prussia reinforces **conservative nationalism** at the expense of **republican liberties**.

O n May 11, 1860, the Italian patriot and guerrilla fighter Giuseppe Garibaldi landed in Sicily, then part of the Bourbon-ruled Kingdom of the Two Sicilies, in southern Italy, leading a force of volunteers drawn from across Italy and just over 1,000 strong, hence their name, *I Mille* (The Thousand). Their goal was to overthrow the Bourbons, but there was much uncertainty as to what government would replace the ruling family.

Like the other great 19th-century stalwart of Italian liberty, Giuseppe Mazzini, who in 1849 had briefly established a Roman republic, Garibaldi was committed to ending royal, clerical, and aristocratic privilege.

Giuseppe Garibaldi, in the red shirt that symbolized his makeshift army, managed to overthrow Bourbon rule in the Kingdom of the Two Sicilies but had to compromise on governmental form.

He was also driven by the goal of ending Austrian rule in the north of the country and by the idea of a united Italy. The desire to form new political entities based on common national elements such as geography and history came to be known as nationalism.

Reaching a compromise

In 1859, much of Italy had already been united under the state of Piedmont-Sardinia, in the northwest of Italy, a process directed by its shrewd and pragmatic prime minister Camillo Benso, Count of Cavour, and critically boosted by French military assistance in expelling the Austrians.

For Cavour, unification meant the creation not of a republican Italy, but of a centralized state under a constitutional monarchy. He believed this was the only way that Italy could realize its potential—above all, to press ahead with industrialization and compete with the leading powers of Europe.

The Redshirts' forces, swelled by locals flocking to join them, soon overcame the ineptly led armies of the Kingdom of the Two Sicilies.

When it came to deciding upon a government for the newly united Italy—Venice and Rome excepted, though both would subsequently be incorporated, in 1866 and 1870 respectively—Garibaldi recognized the inevitability of Piedmontese domination. In November 1860, with Garibaldi at his side, Victor Emmanuel II of Sardinia entered Naples. In March 1861, he was crowned king of Italy.

Divided goals

The difference between Garibaldi's and Cavour's goals illustrates the contradictions at the heart of nationalism in 19th-century Europe. Prompted by the notions of liberty and equal rights promised by the French Revolution, nationalism developed an idealistic view of a more just society. National groups oppressed by alien rule believed they should be able to assert their independence as a natural right.

Nationalism was furthermore characterized by a romantic view of the right of peoples to lay claim to their historic destinies and rule themselves: independence. In place of loyalty to an established ruling dynasty, new loyalties to national groups defined by language, culture, history, and self-identity were formulated. The idea of the nation-state became increasingly common, and likewise a belief in the right to national self-determination.

The failure of the revolutions of 1848 in central Europe and Italy, intended to advance these very goals, made plain the resolve of Europe's ruling elites to oppose such initiatives and to preserve the Europe created by the Congress of Vienna in 1814–1815, after the defeat of Napoleon—a Europe of monarchs, multinational empires, and pre–French Revolution frontiers.

Metternich's failures

The new Europe was far from stable, and the principal architect of the Congress of Vienna, the Austrian Prince Metternich, would later admit: "I have spent my life in shoring up rotten buildings." By 1830, Belgium had revolted against the Kingdom of the Netherlands, of which it was a province; the next year, it secured its independence with British support. Similar nationalist uprisings followed in Poland in 1831 and in 1846, both savagely repressed by Russia.

German nationalism

Rising nationalism had momentous consequences, especially in the various states across Germany. The country's unification under the chancellorship of Otto von Bismarck of Prussia in 1871 and »

The Ottoman army's brutality in suppressing Greek revolts—as seen in Eugène Delacroix's painting *The Massacre at Chios*—led to increased support for the Greek cause.

the declaration of a German empire jolted Europe into a new era. For Bismarck, much as they had been for Cavour, the benefits of unification were clear. It would be the means by which a common German nationality could be expressed, allowing the country to fill the need to underline an overarching German character that the philosopher Georg Hegel had identified. It would also break the dominance of Hapsburg Austria over the German-speaking world—in particular, to lever the southern Catholic German states, Bavaria above all, away from Austrian influence.

In the interests of building this great German state, Bismarck pressed into service a kind of conservative nationalism. The goal was not social or democratic reform to establish a more just or liberal state; it was the creation of a country to challenge the world. German nationalism under Bismarck translated into a determined adoption of industrialization and the creation of ever larger and more efficient armed forces.

And it was military means that Bismarck single-mindedly deployed to create this new Germany. He mounted three major campaigns. The first, against Denmark in 1864, saw Prussia subsuming the southern Danish territories of Schleswig and Holstein, with Austrian support. In 1866, Prussian troops routed Austria itself; finally, in 1870–1871, an army from across Germany comprehensively and humiliatingly defeated France, toppling Napoleon III's government, and starving Paris into submission. These military victories underlined a seemingly irresistible German destiny whose logical consequence was a unified German empire under the Prussian king, now emperor, Wilhelm I.

The proclamation of Wilhelm I as Emperor of Germany took place in Versailles in 1871. It was heralded by a series of military campaigns, including one against France.

Nationalist aspirations

Nowhere were the conflicting impulses of nationalism more tangled than in the Hapsburg Austrian Empire, an immense patchwork of ethnic groups across Central Europe under the nominal rule of Vienna. In 1867, following Austria's defeat by Prussia the previous year, Hungary was able to secure almost complete independence from Austria. The "dual-monarchy" that resulted—the Austrian Empire, now the Austro-Hungarian Empire—not only greatly boosted an assertive sense of Hungarian self-identity but also secured Hungary significant territorial concessions from Vienna, notably in Transylvania and Croatia. Yet whatever the continuing tensions between Austria and Hungary, the two warily preferred to remain united precisely for fear of further nationalist agitations from their own splintered ethnic populations. The Hungarians, for example, were notably reluctant to concede the kind of political rights they demanded for themselves to their substantial Slovak, Romanian, and Serb populations. At the same time, waning Ottoman control of the Balkans also encouraged nationalist aspirations—Serbia, for example, had emerged as a more or less independent state as early as 1817. Wallachia and Moldavia, essentially modern Romania, could lay similar claims to independence by 1829. The Greeks, portraying themselves as the legatees of ancient Greek civilization, a role that won them support from liberals across Europe, had secured their independence by 1830 after a nine-year war.

Both Austria and Russia competed to fill the void left by the Ottomans. Austria's provocative occupation of Bosnia in 1878, which it peremptorily annexed in 1908, would create tensions that led directly to the outbreak of World War I in 1914. The Balkan Wars of 1912–1913—in effect a bitter squabble for supremacy between Serbia, Bulgaria, and Greece—were further evidence of the destabilizing effect of nationalist-driven state building.

The consequences

The notion that social justice could be secured by peoples pursuing the right to self-determination would rarely be realized in the 1800s—Vienna would continue to rule over its multi-ethnic empire until its defeat at the end of World War I in 1918, for example. Likewise, the people of Poland were denied any means of exercising such nationalistic rights to self-determination. And the Jews of Europe remained persistently oppressed, whatever the promise of Zionism from the 1890s to create a Jewish nation in the Holy Land. ∎

Otto von Bismarck

Minister-president of Prussia from 1862 and chancellor of Germany 1871–1890, Otto von Bismarck (1815–1898), also known as the Iron Chancellor, towered over continental Europe after engineering the unification of Germany. Bismarck's main goals were to ensure Prussian leadership of the German world at the expense of Austria and to contain the threat of renewed French hostility. A supreme opportunist, despite starting three wars, in 1864, 1866, and 1870, Bismarck thereafter worked tirelessly to maintain the balance of power in Europe, a task in which, juggling competing interests, he was remarkably successful. He committed Germany to a huge program of industrialization, oversaw the further growth of the German armed forces, and launched a program of colonization. Despite being socially conservative, Bismarck also introduced the world's first welfare system, though his motive was as much to outflank his socialist opponents as to protect the interests of German workers.

GOVERNMENT OF THE PEOPLE, BY THE PEOPLE, FOR THE PEOPLE, SHALL NOT PERISH FROM THE EARTH
THE GETTYSBURG ADDRESS (1863)

IN CONTEXT

FOCUS
The American Civil War

BEFORE
1820 An attempt is made, in the Missouri Compromise statute, to restrict slavery in the new states to a line south of the Missouri border.

1854 The Kansas-Nebraska Act sparks violence in Kansas.

1857 The Dred Scott Decision rules that even in non-slave states enslaved people cannot be freed.

1861 The Confederate States are declared (February); in April, the Civil War begins.

1863 In July, the Confederates are defeated at Gettysburg and Vicksburg.

AFTER
1864 Lincoln is reelected.

1865 General Lee surrenders; Lincoln is assassinated.

On November 19, 1863, little more than halfway through the American Civil War, in Gettysburg, Pennsylvania, US President Abraham Lincoln gave what came to be known as the Gettysburg Address. In it, he characterized the Civil War as a struggle both for national unity and to guarantee equality for all people.

Lincoln was talking at the dedication of the Soldiers' National Cemetery, which commemorated the 7,058 soldiers killed at the Battle of Gettysburg, an encounter fought between July 1–3 the same year that had left 27,224 more wounded. Gettysburg had been the bloodiest battle of the American Civil War, as well as a turning point in which the outnumbered, outgunned, yet improbably successful Southern army led by Robert E. Lee, the Army of Northern Virginia, suffered its first major defeat.

The causes of the war
The American Civil War was not simply a war about slavery; it was a war about whether so divisive an issue could be allowed to break up the United States. The United States, as Lincoln said, was a nation "conceived in liberty and dedicated to the proposition that all men are created equal," yet its Southern states had a population of almost 4 million enslaved black people. Under the US constitution, they were legally owned property. For the abolitionists of the rapidly industrializing north—always a minority, but still exceedingly vocal— slavery was morally repugnant and an outrage against their Christian sensibilities.

However, slavery was not just the backbone of the agricultural prosperity of the Southern states; for slave-owning Southerners, it was a right. For them, "liberty" had an additional meaning: the liberty to possess enslaved people.

The disagreement underlined the question over States' Rights—the extent to which the rights of individual states

The Battle of Gettysburg took place in 1863. After three days of fighting and the death of more than 7,000 soldiers, the Confederate army was forced to retreat.

trumped the authority of the federal, or central, government in Washington. This question repeatedly resurfaced as territories in the west were settled and sought admission to the Union: would they be slave or "free" states?

The 1820 Missouri Compromise stated that slavery would be allowed only in new states south of a line extending westward from the southern border of Missouri. It was later agreed that the settlers of new states should decide for themselves whether theirs would be free or slave states—a decision that was reinforced by the Kansas-Nebraska Act of 1854. Since

both Kansas and Nebraska were to the north of Missouri's southern border, what followed, in Kansas above all, was a sudden inrush of pro- and anti-slavery settlers, each desperate to prevail. The two sides clashed repeatedly and violently.

The South breaks away

This conflict led to the founding of a new anti-slavery party, the Republicans, on whose ticket Abraham Lincoln, with practically no support from any slave state, was voted into office in November 1860. Lincoln's victory prompted the almost immediate decision by South Carolina to secede, to leave the Union. By February, a further six Southern states had broken away, and the seven declared themselves a new nation: the Confederate States of America. By May, when Richmond in Virginia was made the capital of the new country, four more states had joined them. However, five slave states, the so-called Border States, opted to remain within the original Union.

The Confederacy argued that the Constitution had been freely adopted, and as such any state could legitimately break away from the Union if it felt oppressed. As free-born men, the citizens of the South had an "inalienable" right to shape their own destinies, just as the founding fathers had when they rejected the tyranny of »

Abraham Lincoln

When he arrived in Washington in February 1861 for his presidential inauguration, Abraham Lincoln (1809–1865) was widely dismissed in political circles as an ignorant, socially awkward backwoodsman. By the time of his assassination just four years later, he had come to dominate America. Lincoln had not just won the Civil War, but he had also established himself as a kind of irresistible political oracle.

Born in a log cabin in Kentucky, Lincoln qualified as a lawyer by his late 20s. He became an increasingly articulate champion of what would emerge as the anti-slavery Republican party. Despite having no military experience, Lincoln proved an increasingly shrewd judge of how the Civil War should best be fought, actively arguing in favor of General Grant. He never lost sight of his wider aims: the maintenance of American liberties and the essential dignity of humanity. He pushed on with the war with unflinching determination, yet he understood precisely what loss of life on the scale of the Civil War meant.

The United States is born as a **beacon of liberty** in which **slavery** is nonetheless permitted.

↓ ↓

The **Southern states** increasingly see slavery as a key part of their **agrarian society**.

The **industrial Northern states** are **opposed** to any extension of slavery into any new states.

↓ ↓

These differences of opinion help spark the **Civil War**, bringing **destruction on an unforeseen scale**, with neither the North nor the South able to best the other.

↓

The Gettysburg Address is Lincoln's most eloquent attempt to justify the war as the means to a more just United States.

↓

The **South's defeat** results in **political paralysis** and **institutionalized discrimination** against its black population that persists **to this day**.

---

slavery while preserving the Union. On the second point, Lincoln was immovable; he felt the authority of the federal government overrode that of individual states.

The United States, the only fully democratic country on Earth, had been created as what Lincoln called "a great promise to the world," so ensuring its survival was an absolute moral duty. By the time of his Emancipation Proclamation in January 1863, Lincoln felt politically secure enough to order the freeing of all enslaved people in the South. But in the short term, the Civil War was fought to keep this "great promise" intact.

Eventual Northern victory

The outcome of the American Civil War was dictated ultimately by the human and material discrepancies between the North and the South. There were 21 Union states with a population of 20 million, and 11 Southern states with a population of 9 million, 4 million of whom were enslaved, and therefore not allowed to bear arms. Despite the fact that by 1864, 44 percent of males in the North aged 18 to 60 were in military service, versus 90 percent in the Southern states, the North was still able to enlist 2.2 million men over the whole war, compared to the South's 800,000.

The North was three times richer than the South. It had 2.4 miles (3.8 km) of railroad to every 1 mile (1.6 km) in the South. Its factories manufactured 10 times more goods. It produced 20 times more iron than the South, 38 times as much coal, and 32 times as many firearms. The only area in which the South exceeded the North was in cotton production, at 24 to 1.

In the face of this superiority, the fact that the South was not only able to resist the Union forces for four years but also to

---

British rule. In the minds of many Southerners, the US government was guilty of precisely the same kind of tyranny in seeking to limit these freedoms.

It was a deeply held position. As Alexander Stephens, vice-president of the Confederacy, asserted, the cornerstone of this new state "rest[ed] upon the great truth that the negro is not equal to the white man; that slavery … is his natural and normal condition …."

As a supreme political operator, Lincoln realized the need to proceed with caution. Initially at any rate, his position was that he sought only to restrict the expansion of

 I cannot raise my hand against my birthplace, my home, my children.
Robert E. Lee
On his resignation (April 1861)

Grant stood by me when I was crazy, and I stood by him when he was drunk, and now we stand by each other.
William Sherman

come close to victory in 1862 and 1863 was a reflection of the Southern soldiers' profound belief in their cause. It was also the result of its plainly superior generals—the Virginian Robert E. Lee above all. By contrast, at least until the emergence of Ulysses S. Grant and William Sherman as the two leading commanders of the Union forces, the North had been able to muster only a succession of timid and inept generals who frittered away the advantages they so abundantly possessed.

Reinvigorated by Grant and Sherman, the North prevailed. The razing of Atlanta in September 1864 was followed by Sherman's "march to the sea" at Savannah, Georgia. Completed in December, it left a 60-mile- (96.5-km-) wide swathe of destruction, deliberately targeting civilian property. "War is cruelty," Sherman asserted. "The crueler it is, the sooner it will be over."

A new freedom

The US Civil War was the world's first major industrial war, the first to make widespread use of railroads, and the first widely reported in a new kind of popular press. There was concentrated death on a scale never seen before: around 670,000 dead, 50,000 of them civilians, in little more than four years.

For Abraham Lincoln, the war represented what in the Gettysburg Address he called "unfinished business." The Constitution had left unresolved the question of how slavery could exist in a nation "conceived in liberty." Despite the destruction and the huge death toll, the war brought a chance at "a new birth of freedom." The end of slavery, confirmed by the Thirteenth Amendment in 1865, represented an opportunity for the US to be recast as a genuinely free land for all its citizens, black and white. ∎

This Thomas Nast illustration shows life for black Americans before and after emancipation. Abraham Lincoln is also portrayed.

AMERICA IS GOD'S CRUCIBLE, THE GREAT MELTING POT
THE OPENING OF ELLIS ISLAND (1892)

IN CONTEXT

FOCUS
Mass migration and population growth

BEFORE
1840s The Irish potato famine leads to mass emigration.

1848 The failure of liberal revolutions sparks large-scale German emigration.

c. 1870 Major emigration of Jews from Russia begins as they flee persecution.

1882 Restrictions are placed on the entry of Chinese into the United States.

1880s Mass emigration from Italy begins.

AFTER
1900 The population of Europe reaches 408 million; the United States, 76 million.

1907 The largest number of immigrants in a single year enters the United States: more than 1 million.

1954 Ellis Island closes.

Industrialization, urban growth, and lower infant mortality **boost European populations**.

↓

Political and religious freedoms and **economic opportunities** in young countries such as the US attract **millions of immigrants**.

↓

Steamships make **ocean voyages** to distant lands **safer, faster, and cheaper**.

↓

An immigration station on Ellis Island opens to process arrivals to the United States.

B y the mid-19th century, the world was experiencing an unprecedented boom in population, particularly in Europe. This increase would continue into the 20th century and beyond. It was partly due to improvements in health, backed by more ready access to food as a consequence of improved agricultural methods. It was also a result of industrialization and urban growth, as well as the affluence and improved living standards that both produced. Political stability played a role, too. After the defeat of Napoleon in 1815, Europe enjoyed almost 100 years of largely unbroken peace.

Nature also had a hand in the increase in migration. The Irish potato famine of the 1840s, resulting from a failed crop, may have been the last major European famine, but it brought suffering on a startling scale: up to 1 million people died. It provoked among survivors a vast wave of emigration of over 1 million, almost all to the US. The population of Ireland in 1841 was 6.5 million; by 1871, it had dipped to 4 million.

Urban underclass

Industrialization produced a similar paradox. Whatever the civic pride and bombast of the immense new urban centers of the Industrial Revolution, especially in Britain, a new urban underclass was being created, desperately impoverished and living in extreme squalor.

For the citizens of continental Europe, the lure of new lands in which to be free and prosper would prove irresistible. Substantial numbers of Germans, Czechs, and Hungarians left central Europe after the suppression of the nationalist revolts of 1848. From 1870, huge numbers of Russian and Polish Jews—1.5 million in 1901–1910 alone—similarly emigrated, fleeing anti-Semitic pogroms.

The numbers involved in this huge transfer of populations were remarkable. From the mid-19th century to 1924, 18 million people emigrated from Britain; 9.5 million from Italy, mostly from its deprived south; 8 million from Russia; 5 million from Austria-Hungary; and 4.5 million from Germany. Between 1820 and 1920, the US attracted 33.6 million

 I had always hoped that this land might become a safe and agreeable asylum to the virtuous and persecuted part of mankind, to whatever nation they might belong.
George Washington

immigrants, where they often found themselves in poor living conditions in rapidly expanding cities such as Chicago and New York, aiding the growth of American industry with their cheap labor. Over the same period, 3.6 million Europeans settled in South America, and 2 million in Australia and New Zealand.

Unwelcome guests

This process of relocation was not exclusively European. Indians settled in South Africa, Chinese migrants spread across the East Indies, and Japanese migrants settled in California; many found themselves unwelcome.

By 1910, more than one in seven of the US population had been born outside of the United States. ∎

Ellis Island

Opened on January 1, 1892, Ellis Island, along with the Statue of Liberty, became a symbol of the vast stream of immigrants that poured into the United States. This immigration center processed perhaps 12 million people, and it is claimed that as much as 40 percent of the immigrant population of the United States has at least one relative who was fed through this immense bureaucratic machine. Built on nothing more than a nondescript sandy island, close to the New Jersey shore in New York Harbor, Ellis Island had at its heart a vast, echoing hall. Here, shuffling forward, the newly arrived immigrants, speaking a dazzling array of languages, would be processed. They were examined medically before being subjected to a series of simple questions to establish their eligibility. The great majority would then become accepted as citizens of the United States, with scarcely 2 percent turned away. Ellis Island finally closed its doors on November 12, 1954.

In its first 30 years, Ellis Island saw 80 percent of United States' immigrants passing through—almost 12 million people.

ENRICH THE COUNTRY, STRENGTHEN THE MILITARY
THE MEIJI RESTORATION (1868)

IN CONTEXT

FOCUS
Modernizing Japan

BEFORE
1853 A US naval force arrives in Japan and demands trading links.

1854–1855 The US, Britain, the Netherlands, and Russia force trading treaties on Japan.

1866 The rulers of the Choshu and Satsuma regions form a secret alliance against the ruling Tokugawa shogunate.

1867 The Tokugawa shogunate ends.

AFTER
1868–1869 Defenders of the shogunate are defeated.

1871 Feudalism is abolished, and Japan launches a far-reaching program of reform.

1894–1895 The Sino-Japanese War underlines expansionist Japanese aims in the region.

1904–1905 The Russo-Japanese War ends in Japanese victory.

Aggressive Western demands for trading rights in Japan highlight the **weakness of its ruling elite**.

↓

Leading feudal barons reassert the authority of the boy emperor Meiji and oust the shogunate.

↓ ↓

The barons see the adoption of Western political and social methods as the best way to **strengthen Japan**.

Military might is seen as an essential way of fulfilling Japanese ambitions.

↓ ↓

Modernization and Westernization encapsulate the Meiji period, and Japan emerges as an **imperial power**.

The overthrow in 1868 of the Tokugawa shogunate, rulers of Japan for 250 years, was led by feudal barons from the southern provinces of Choshu and Satsuma and was the direct consequence of its weakness in the face of aggressive demands by the United States, Britain, Russia, and the Netherlands to establish trading links. In place of the shoguns, the pliant 14-year-old Meiji emperor would "exercise supreme authority." The goal of the barons was not to take over and maintain Japan as it had existed under the shogunate—rigidly hierarchical and deliberately isolated from the wider world. Rather, it was that they felt Japan's clear destiny could only be established by the adoption not just of Western technological means but of Western political and financial systems, too.

Japan transformed

There followed a transformation of a kind no society had seen before or has seen since. Modeling itself on the West, in 30 years Japan became one of the most dynamic industrial powers in the world and the leading military power in East Asia.

Almost no aspect of Japanese society was left untouched by this whirlwind of change. In 1871, Japan abolished feudalism and established the yen as its currency. By 1872, the first railroad was under construction; within 15 years, there was 1,000 miles (1,600km) of track. In 1873, Japan introduced conscription, along with Western weapons and uniforms. The same year saw an overhaul of the education system, and in 1877 Japan's first university was established in Tokyo. Japan also introduced a new legal code in 1882, and a new constitution seven years later. As industry boomed, so exports grew. Cities similarly expanded, as did the population, swelling from 39.5 million in 1888 to 55 million by 1918.

The spur to modernization had largely been the fear that Japan, like China, would become another Western colonial pawn. In fact, the opposite occurred.

This image of Yokohama in 1874 depicts the modernity of Meiji-era Japan in the form of steam-powered trains and ships, which also served to open up the country to trade.

Military expansion

By the 1890s, Japan was a colonial power. In 1894, Korea had asked both Japan and China to help curb an insurrection there. When both countries later sought to take over Korea, the Japanese swept the Chinese aside, and then demanded and received possession of Taiwan, as well as rights in Manchuria. Here they came into conflict with Russia. The Japanese victory in 1905 over a disorganized Russian fleet at the Battle of Tsushima Strait was the first time an industrial European power had been defeated by an Asian power. Japan had the world's attention. ■

Emperor Meiji

Important not as a statesman or as the ruler of Japan in the sense of exercising actual power,

Emperor Meiji (1852–1912)—whose personal name, never used, was Mutsuhito—was instead the symbol of the reborn Japan. Until the restoration of Meiji in January 1868, the emperors of Japan were little more than a symbol. Under the shogunate, they were obliged to remain invisibly at the royal palace in Kyoto more or less permanently. Strictly speaking, the "restoration" never happened: Meiji had already become emperor in February 1867, following the sudden death of his father, Emperor Komei.

For those ambitious *daimyo*, or feudal barons, who were determined to drive Japan into the modern world, elevating the emperor to a higher profile bestowed legitimacy on what was otherwise an act of usurpation. It is telling that one of their first acts was to force the emperor to move to Edo, which was renamed Tokyo in 1868, the former residence of the shogun. Meiji himself remained an impenetrable cypher to the end.

DEEDS NOT WORDS

THE DEATH OF EMILY DAVISON (1913)

IN CONTEXT

FOCUS
Women's suffrage

BEFORE

1869 In the US, the National Woman Suffrage Association and American Woman Suffrage Association are formed.

1893 New Zealand is the first country to grant women the vote.

1897 The National Union of Women's Suffrage Societies is formed in Britain. It campaigns peacefully for the right to vote.

1903 Emmeline Pankhurst forms the Women's Social and Political Union in Britain. Vote campaigns grow violent.

AFTER

1917 The National Women's Party begins a 30-month protest at the White House.

1918 All women 30 or over are granted the vote in Britain.

1920 The vote is granted to all American women 21 and over.

More women are educated and hold professional posts, **raising expectations** for them to have the right to vote.

Societies are established to **campaign for women's suffrage**, particularly in Britain and the United States.

Militant campaigners from Britain's Women's Social and Political Union are **arrested and imprisoned**.

Emily Davison's death raises the profile of women's suffrage across the world.

Women's war work **emphasizes their capabilities**. British **women win the vote** in 1918; American women, in 1920.

O n June 4, 1913, Emily Davison stepped onto the course at the Derby, England's premier horse race, and was knocked to the ground by a horse owned by King George V. She died four days later. It is unclear if this was a protest that went wrong or an active attempt at martyrdom. However, the intended disruption was typical of the Women's Social and Political Union (WSPU), which Davison had joined in 1906.

Britain: the suffragettes

Women in the West had begun to feel that they, and by extension those elsewhere, should no longer be regarded as second-class citizens. Extension of the right to vote to increasing numbers of men in countries such as Britain and the United States had left them asking why women should not be entitled to vote. In 1903, Emmeline Pankhurst founded the WSPU with the aim of using militant tactics to further this cause. Its slogan declared "Deeds not words," and the tactics of the suffragettes, as the vote-seeking women were by now mockingly known, became increasingly violent. Chaining themselves to public buildings and the disruption of meetings escalated into the smashing of shop windows, acts of arson, and bombings.

The more active members of the WSPU were repeatedly arrested and imprisoned: Pankhurst received seven prison sentences; Davison, nine. In 1909, the WSPU began to stage hunger strikes in prison; in response they were force-fed—a painful and degrading process.

The US: the suffragists

The experience of what in the US were known as the suffragists had clear parallels. The Women's Christian Temperance Union campaigned peacefully for women's rights, arguing that women could not influence political decisions—in this case, Prohibition—without having the right to vote.

However, the National Women's Party (NWP), established in 1916, imitated the militant tactics of Britain's WSPU. This was no surprise, given that its founder, Alice Paul, had been a member of the WSPU from 1907 to 1910 and had been sent to prison three times. The NWP's so-called Silent Sentinels, protesting outside the White House from January 1917, were also arrested and force-fed.

Success at last

At the outbreak of World War I, the WSPU stopped campaigning, mobilizing itself instead in support of the war effort. The contribution made by women during the war plainly demonstrated just how much wider their role could be than that traditionally expected of them as wives and mothers. In 1918, all British women aged 30 or over were granted the right to vote. In 1928, suffrage in Britain was extended to women aged 21 or over.

Meanwhile, in the United States, the NWP continued its protest into 1919, when Congress approved the Nineteenth Amendment, which was ratified the following year, granting women the same voting rights as men. ■

Emmeline Pankhurst

The best known of all the suffragettes, Emmeline Pankhurst (1858–1928) epitomized a new breed of politically active women in the early 20th century. She was born into—and later remained in by marriage—an eminently respectable, somewhat left-leaning, middle-class world in the north of England, which only served to cement her desire to further the cause of women's rights. This decision would prove explosive. She was single-minded, exceptionally active, and wholly unflinching in her refusal to compromise. Her leadership of the WSPU exhibited a determination to take the fight for women's suffrage into the heart of what she saw as the enemy camp. Her increasing readiness to use more violent methods to secure suffragette goals alienated many who may otherwise have been her natural supporters— women as much as men. Nonetheless, her absolute refusal to back down, coupled with the fervor she inspired in her followers, introduced a new mood of feminist militancy into a complacent masculine political world.

THE MODE

WORLD

1914–PRESENT

Historical perspectives on events close to the present day are inevitably shifting and uncertain. A historian writing in the mid-20th century might have characterized the modern era as a period of catastrophe, in which all the economic and political gains of liberal civilization had been squandered. However, by the early 21st century it was tempting to see continuity with the pre-1914 world, as a globalized capitalist economy and great technological innovation were combined with rapidly rising population and productivity.

The two world wars

The convulsions of the period from 1914 to 1950 were on an epic scale. Two world wars between them caused the deaths of between 70 and 100 million people, making them by far the most destructive conflicts in history. Both European civilization and science—the twin pillars of the traditional 19th-century idea of "progress"—were tarnished by association with this slaughter. Germany, often considered one of Europe's most "civilized" countries, descended into dictatorship and genocidal massacre. Science was used to create

weapons of mass destruction, from poison gas to the atom bomb. Even in the interlude of relative peace between the world wars, global capitalism failed to function effectively, the economic misery of the Great Depression driving a retreat from democratic government and free markets.

To revolutionaries inspired by a Marxist vision, these upheavals seemed the death throes of the capitalist order. But the building of alternative "communist" societies, based on the model of a single-party state and a state-controlled economy, proved to be a costly experiment. In Russia, followed by China, communism succeeded in transforming relatively undeveloped countries into major industrial and military powers, but millions died as victims of the state, and citizens were denied fundamental freedoms.

A battle of ideology

World War II was followed by the Cold War confrontation between the "free world," led by the United States, and the communist bloc. Instead of disarmament, there was a potentially disastrous nuclear arms race. Meanwhile, the main European powers, economically weakened and demoralized, found themselves in no position to sustain their empires against colonized populations eager for freedom. The newly independent nations became an ideological and even, at times, military battleground between the capitalist and communist systems.

In the end, the issue was settled by economics. Capitalism showed its ability to generate economic growth on a vast scale, creating a booming consumer society in more advanced countries. In contrast, by the 1980s communist countries confronted economic stagnation and rising popular discontent. With great rapidity, communist regimes collapsed in the Soviet bloc, while communist China later became a powerhouse of capitalism.

In the wake of communism, the political scientist Francis Fukuyama coined the expression the "end of history" and argued that Western liberal democracy was "the only game in town." Certainly, by the end of the 20th century liberalism was surfing a wave: in 1950, only a few nations in Europe were democracies; 50 years later, all of them were.

Progress and pessimism

From the 1960s, hotly contested campaigns for civil rights had progressed liberal ideals in areas such as racial equality and gender politics. Growing prosperity was also impressive. In Latin America and much of Asia, living standards had risen dramatically by the early 21st century. Despite the world's population increasing on a huge scale—from under 2 billion in 1914 to over 7 billion one century later—food supplies had not run out, as had once been predicted by many. Restricting environmental damage was recognized as a major challenge for the future, a problem generated by humanity's growth and success.

Indeed, human progress in the 20th century was remarkable, from rising literacy and life expectancy to the development of air and space travel and computers. Yet there was no outbreak of general optimism. Environmental issues aside, it was all too evident that the future held potential dangers: the unsettled politics of the Middle East, sucking major powers into wars; brutal acts of terrorism; economic inequality generating mass migration; financial instability and market breakdown; epidemics spread by global travel—all provided plenty of material for pessimists. History offered no solid ground for predictions, suggesting only that the unexpected was to be expected. ∎

YOU OFTEN WISH YOU WERE DEAD

BATTLE OF PASSCHENDAELE (1917)

IN CONTEXT

FOCUS
World War I

BEFORE
1870–1871 Defeat for France in the war against Prussia leads to the creation of a powerful German Empire.

1887 Germany orders large shipbuilding initiatives.

1912 The Balkan Wars erupt, hardening Austro-Hungarian attitudes to Serbia.

1916 Secret meetings between Britain and France produce the Sykes–Picot Agreement, splitting the Ottoman Empire.

AFTER
November 9, 1918 Kaiser Wilhelm abdicates, and his imperial government collapses.

1919 At the Paris Peace Conference, stiff terms are imposed on Germany by the victors in the Treaty of Versailles.

Soldiers at Passchendaele fought in appalling conditions. In the absence of anything better, these machine-gunners are using bomb indentations as makeshift shelter.

P asschendaele, officially known as the Third Battle of Ypres, was a large-scale attack against the German front line around Ypres, Belgium, during World War I. The Allies' aim was to advance into Belgium and free the German-held ports on the Belgian coast, which the Germans had been using to attack British shipping. The biggest challenge was to break through the defensive positions taken by the Germans on the West Flanders Ridge. Key to the breakthrough was seizing the village of Passchendaele.

Preparations for the battle began on June 7, 1917, with a heavy two-week bombardment of German positions. The infantry offensive began on July 31, 1917. Within days, the Allied forces were stuck in mud as torrential rain turned the area into a quagmire. By the time the Allies—made up of British, French, Canadian, and Australian troops—captured Passchendaele on November 6, the village was in ruins. The conflict cost 300,000 Allied lives, with a gain of 5 miles (8 km), while the Germans lost 260,000 of their troops. It was hailed as a victory by the British government but became a byword for the utter futility of war.

Secret diplomacy

Two main disputes led to World War I: one between Germany and France, and the other between Russia and Austria-Hungary. The long history of mutual antipathy between Germany and France came to a head in 1870 with France's humiliating defeat by Germany in the Franco-Prussian war, which led to the annexation of most of the French provinces of Alsace and Lorraine.

In Eastern Europe, the Austro-Hungarian and Russian empires had a long-standing dispute over which of them had the strongest claim to power in the Balkans. Both depended on the area for access to the Mediterranean, and each eyed the movements of the other with intense suspicion.

Each state needed allies, and in 1882 Austria-Hungary, Germany, and Italy signed a Triple Alliance promising to give each other military support in case of war. Then, in the 1890s, Russia and France signed an agreement to protect one another in the event of a war against Germany. By the turn of the century, Kaiser Wilhelm II's provocative nationalistic speeches and naval expansion pushed Britain into closer ties with France. In 1904, Britain and France agreed an *entente cordiale*, or friendly alliance, which was broadened into a triple entente, embracing Russia, in 1907. The triple entente would become known as the Allied Powers. The atmosphere generated by this international jostling led to an increase in military spending by European governments and the expansion of armies and navies.

War erupts

A spark was all that was needed to ignite the flame of enmity between these two alliances. It came on June 28, 1914, when a Bosnian Serb assassinated Archduke Franz Ferdinand, heir to the Hapsburg throne, in Sarajevo. The Austrians suspected Serbia, their principal enemy in the Balkans, of the attack. After securing support from its ally Germany, Austria-Hungary presented Serbia with an ultimatum on July 23, demanding that the Serbs stop all anti–Austria-Hungary activities. Serbia accepted most of the demands, but Austria-Hungary declared war on Serbia on July 28. Britain called for international mediation, but the crisis quickly escalated into European war. When Russia mobilized against Austria-Hungary, Germany

---

European powers are bound together in a **complex web of alliances**.

A European arms race leads to **larger armies** and more **destructive weapons**.

↓

War breaks out, eventually drawing in all the major powers and causing **death on a scale previously unimaginable**.

↓

The **relative equality of the armies** means that neither side can score a decisive victory.

↓

The fighting on the Western Front becomes a bitter stalemate despite the enormous cost of battles like Passchendaele.

↓

With both sides exhausted, **US entry into the war** on the side of the Allies facilitates a **breakthrough in the conflict**.

---

declared war on Russia on August 1, and on France two days later. Britain joined the war on August 4, after the Germans invaded neutral Belgium. The British Expeditionary Force (BEF), a small professional troop led by Sir Douglas Haig, had arrived in France by August 22. It was deployed near the Franco-Belgian border, in line with pre-war military plans agreed with the French government.

Germany had to fight a war on two fronts. On the Western Front, in the first weeks of the conflict, the Germans invaded Belgium and France, but their advance was halted by the French and British at the Battle of the Marne. By the end of fall, the two sides had reached a stalemate. Meanwhile, on the Eastern Front, the fighting remained fluid. Germany dominated, scoring a great victory against the Russians at »

Huge artillery guns such as the Howitzer cannon were transported by horses and tractors. High-explosive shells fired in massive quantities were key to the war's high casualty rates.

Tannenberg, but its Austrian allies suffered several defeats. On the Western Front, however, a 400-mile (645-km) trench line stretched from the Belgian coast in the north, down through eastern France to the Swiss border. The two sides faced each other across the open space between their front lines. This area—no-man's-land—had barbed wire fronting the trenches to slow the opposition. Continuous fighting from the trenches, punctuated by appallingly bloody battles, failed to break the deadlock. More than 600,000 Allied troops were killed or wounded in the Battle of the Somme alone.

Total war

At the start of the conflict, both sides had been convinced it would be a short, decisive battle. No one had anticipated a war of attrition. New mechanized weapons added to the high casualty rates. Tanks were used for the first time, and machine guns such

as the German MG 08 Maxim could fire up to 600 bullets a minute. Aircraft, first employed for reconnaissance, were later used for bombing. Both sides used poison gas. Horses were the backbone of logistical operations, but as the war progressed, railroads and motor trucks were used to transport goods to the front.

Civilians were brought into the front line by the bombing of London and Paris by airships and bomber aircraft. By 1917, German submarines were sinking one in four merchant ships headed for Britain to try to starve the British into submission. Britain's naval blockade of Germany also led to acute food shortages. This was the first "total war," meaning not just soldiers but also civilian populations were involved.

Britain was forced to introduce conscription for the first time in its history. From January 1916, all single men aged 18 to 41 could be called up. Britain and France also assembled armies from their overseas colonies, such as India and Africa, and from the British dominions of Australia, New Zealand and Canada. War brought many social changes, notably for women, who filled positions in factories and offices. Women were also increasingly employed in the munitions industry as governments switched to large-scale production.

Life in the trenches

At the outbreak of World War I, both sides anticipated fast-moving battles that would cover hundreds of miles. None expected a static fight

with their forces deep in defensive trenches.

Early trenches were small furrows, but they grew more elaborate, fortified with wooden frames and sandbags. German trenches were more sophisticated and had electricity and toilets. Soldiers spent daylight hours avoiding enemy fire and endured periods of boredom and daily chores, broken up with spells in reserve and short rest periods.

The trenches sometimes filled up with

rats and lice, as well as water, which turned to ice. Life in such conditions was exhausting, and soldiers had a repetitive diet of canned food and few comforts.

Snipers shot at any heads that appeared over the parapet, and raiding parties throwing grenades were a constant danger. The trenches were bombarded with shells, bullets, and poisonous gas. It was a relentless war of attrition—smelly, dirty, and riddled with disease.

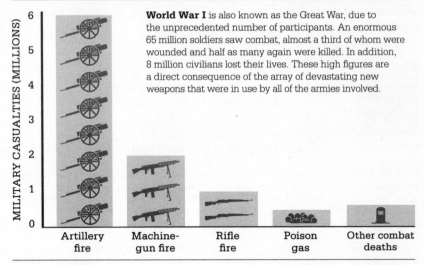

World War I is also known as the Great War, due to the unprecedented number of participants. An enormous 65 million soldiers saw combat, almost a third of whom were wounded and half as many again were killed. In addition, 8 million civilians lost their lives. These high figures are a direct consequence of the array of devastating new weapons that were in use by all of the armies involved.

MILITARY CASUALTIES (MILLIONS)

| Artillery fire | Machine-gun fire | Rifle fire | Poison gas | Other combat deaths |

Global conflict

The key belligerent states brought their vast empires into war with them, and the conflict soon became a world war. German colonies in China and the Pacific were invaded by Japan, which entered the war on the side of the Allies. Germany's colonies in Africa were overrun by British, French, and South African troops. In May 1915, Italy joined the Allies, fighting Austria-Hungary and Germany in the Alps.

In early November 1914, the Ottoman Empire, an Islamic power, abandoned its neutrality and declared a military *jihad* (holy war) against France, Russia, and Britain. The US was drawn into the war by German submarine attacks on commercial ships at sea, such as the one on British liner *Lusitania* in 1915, with 128 Americans on board. After a German plot to persuade Mexico into an anti-US alliance was discovered, Congress declared war in April 1917.

When the Bolsheviks in Russia negotiated a peace treaty with Germany at Brest-Litovsk on December 22, 1917, it seemed Germany had won a significant victory. They also made gains on the Western Front in 1918, but then, in July and August, the Allies counterattacked, beginning an advance that would continue until November. Four million fresh US troops helped defeat the Central Powers and bring the Germans to the peace table.

When the conflict ended, at 11 am on November 11, 1918, the alliance led by France and Britain emerged victorious. More than 65 million troops had been involved in the war, of which at least half were killed or injured. The Russian, Austrian, and German empires had collapsed. After the war, the Treaty of Versailles redrew the map of Europe, leaving nations, particularly Germany, embittered. A public assembly of countries, the League of Nations, was founded to help maintain peace. However, the League proved toothless in the face of countries that chose to ignore it. When fascist Benito Mussolini came to power in Italy in 1922, he denounced the Treaty. In Germany, where the response to the Treaty was one of deep resentment, the Nazi Party began to gain momentum. Far from being "the war to end all wars," World War I had instead sown the seeds of future conflict. ∎

One of the social changes brought on by World War I concerned the role of women. The female population joined the war effort by working in places like munitions factories.

HISTORY WILL NOT FORGIVE US IF WE DO NOT ASSUME POWER NOW

THE OCTOBER REVOLUTION (1917)

IN CONTEXT

FOCUS
Russian Revolution

BEFORE
1898 The Russian Socialist Democratic Labor Party is formed.

1905 Russia suffers a crushing defeat in a war against Japan, which leads to an uprising.

1914 Russia enters World War I and quickly suffers heavy losses in defeats to Germany on the Eastern Front.

AFTER
1918 Czar Nicholas II and his family are executed.

1922 Lenin creates the Union of Soviet Socialist Republics (USSR) under the control of the Communist Party.

1929 Stalin becomes leader of the USSR and establishes a dictatorship.

The Russian Revolution of 1905 forces a **range of reforms** from the autocratic Czar Nicholas II.

↓

Dissatisfaction persists among the people.

↓

Russia suffers defeats in World War I.

↓

Economic hardship leads to **food riots**.

↓

In February 1917, the **monarchy is overthrown** and replaced by the Provisional Government. **The Czar abdicates** in March.

↓

Lenin and the Bolsheviks demand total power for the proletariat, launching the October Revolution.

I n October 1917, Russia was in turmoil after suffering huge losses in World War I. There were food shortages, and workers in the cities faced low wages and appalling conditions. The February Revolution had ousted the Czar, but the Provisional Government that replaced him faced imminent collapse.

Vladimir Lenin, a member of the revolutionary Bolshevik Party, took full advantage. He was committed to

a workers' (proletarian) revolution and set out a series of proposals to overthrow the government in what became known as his April Theses. His simple slogan "Peace, land, and bread!" became a revolutionary rallying cry. On October 24 (November 6, Gregorian calendar [GC]), there were attempts by the government to curb the activities of the Bolsheviks to prevent a coup. Orders were issued for the arrest of leading party members, and their newspaper, *Pravda* (The Truth), was closed down. Lenin, keeping a low profile in his apartment, urged action. "We must not wait! We may lose everything! The government is tottering. To delay action is the same as death," he wrote.

On October 25 (November 7, GC), the government tried without success to find armed support. The Petrograd Soviet of Workers and Soldiers party, of which the Bolsheviks were a faction, could rely on the support of troops in Petrograd (later St. Petersburg). The Bolshevik paramilitary Red Guards occupied the main telegraph office, post office, and power stations. Only the Winter Palace, the seat of the government, remained. The small unit of military cadets guarding it willingly surrendered to the revolutionary soldiers. The regime was overthrown, and power had passed to Lenin and his Bolsheviks.

Laying the groundwork

The October Revolution was the culmination of the civil unrest that had rumbled on for months. On February 23, 1917 (March 8, GC), in Petrograd, a riot had started, led by women frustrated at waiting hours for bread. They marched through the city, gathering support as they went. This grew into a general strike, and the demonstrations took on a more political nature. Red flags began to appear, and statues of Czar Nicholas II were toppled. Soldiers refused to obey orders to fire on the crowd, but police shot and killed 50 people. »

Vladimir Lenin addresses his troops in Moscow's Red Square in 1919, during the civil war that followed the October Revolution.

Vladimir Ilyich Lenin

Born Vladimir Ilyich Ulyanov on April 10, 1870 (April 22, GC), the founder of the Bolsheviks and first leader of Soviet Russia was a bold theorist and tireless organizer. Lenin became an active Marxist revolutionary after his brother Alexander was executed in 1887 for conspiring to assassinate Czar Alexander III, an event that caused Lenin to lose faith in God and religion. In 1895, he was arrested and exiled for three years to Siberia.

Lenin's chief aim was to organize the opposition to the Czar into a single coherent movement. Following the Russian Revolution of March 1917, he returned to Russia believing his moment had come. In October, Lenin led the Bolsheviks against the government then, suppressing all opposition, became dictator of the world's first communist state.

Lenin's main challenge was civil war (1918–1920). The Communists won, but Russia was brought to its knees. The strain of leadership also broke his health. After two strokes, one of which deprived him of speech, he died on January 21, 1924.

Rise of revolutionary parties

With violence erupting on city streets, the Czar abdicated in March, having relinquished power to the Provisional Government in February, with Prince Georgi Y. Lvov as its head. The government still represented only the middle classes and continued to back Russia's involvement in World War I. Groups such as the Petrograd Soviet of Workers and Soldiers, a council made up of workers and peasants agitating for change, grew stronger and gained power within the Provisional Government. Lenin, in exile for revolutionary activities, was anxious to return to Petrograd, convinced that the collapse of world capitalism was imminent. He received the help of the German government, which hoped that he could further destabilize the political situation in Russia for their war effort, and arrived secretly in a sealed train. Full of revolutionary zeal, he was determined to shape a new Russian government according to his ideas, and he accused his associates of not doing enough to overthrow the current regime.

Prime Minister Lvov resigned after the disastrous July Offensive on the Eastern Front. His successor, Alexander Kerensky, formed a new socialist government with the Petrograd Soviet, but he, too, insisted on keeping Russia in the war. After mass demonstrations in Petrograd encouraged by the Bolsheviks, Kerensky banned them and arrested many of their leaders. Lenin fled to Finland.

Revolution is nigh

In August, Kerensky faced a new threat. General Lavr Kornilov, Russia's army commander-in-chief, ordered troops into Petrograd. Kerensky believed that Kornilov was plotting to seize power. In desperation, he released the Bolsheviks, who armed those who wanted to prevent a counterrevolution. This was a massive boost for their cause. They were able to represent themselves to the people as defenders of Petrograd. By September, the Bolsheviks had taken control of the Petrograd Soviet. Lenin seized the moment, returned to Russia, and renewed calls for revolution. He handed responsibility for military tactics to Leon Trotsky, a fellow Marxist. Peasants and farmers were revolting in rural areas, workers in the cities. Lenin decided the time was ripe for a Bolshevik seizure of power. The Bolsheviks took government buildings and the Winter Palace, where Kerensky's cabinet had sought refuge.

On the night of October 25 (November 7, GC), Lenin issued a brief address to the Russian people: "The Provisional

This painting of the storming of the Winter Palace portrays the dramatic moment in the October Revolution when the Bolsheviks seized the government building.

Government has been overthrown. Long live the workers, soldiers, and peasant revolution!" After this initial triumph, Lenin was compelled to hold democratic elections, but the Bolsheviks received only a quarter of the vote. Lenin dissolved the elected government and sent armed guards to prevent it meeting again. In February 1918, he signed a peace treaty with Germany, but the terms were extremely harsh. Russia ceded the Baltic States to Germany, while Ukraine, Finland, and Estonia were transformed into independent states. Russia was also forced to pay six billion German marks in reparations. This move freed the Bolsheviks from the German threat, but the terms of the treaty were deeply unpopular. Many regarded it as a betrayal of their country.

Civil war

The Bolsheviks had gained power, but now they had to keep it. Lenin established a highly centralized government system, banned all opposition, and started the Red Terror, a campaign of intimidation, executions, and arrests against anybody perceived to be a threat to the Bolsheviks.

The Bolsheviks were a minority in Russia, and their opponents marshalled their forces against them, primarily the Whites, made up of former czarists, army officers, and democrats. The Bolsheviks were known as the Reds.

As various factions fought over the future of the country, a civil war characterized by extreme violence erupted in Russia and ran from 1918 to 1921. The Whites received help from Russia's former allies—Britain, France, the US, and Japan—which feared the spread of communism. At first, they made significant gains. However, they were badly coordinated, and Trotsky proved to be a brilliant military tactician.

In 1920, Lenin ordered a war against Poland to liberate the workers of eastern and central Europe, but at the Battle of Warsaw, after a magnificent counterattack, the Red Army was driven back.

A country in ruins

By 1921, the Whites had been defeated, and Lenin could finally turn his attention to rebuilding the Russian economy.

 The execution of the Czar and his family was needed not only to ... instill a sense of hopelessness in the enemy, but also to show that ahead lay total victory or total doom.
Leon Trotsky

He faced a country on the verge of collapse. In the countryside, around 6 million peasants had died of starvation, and there was rioting in the cities. The Kronstadt naval rebellion in March 1921 further undermined the regime. Kronstadt was a naval town on an island off the coast of Petrograd. In 1921, 16,000 soldiers and workers signed a petition calling for "Soviets without Bolsheviks": freely elected Soviets and freedoms of speech and press. The Reds reacted ruthlessly, executing several hundred ringleaders and expelling over 15,000 sailors from the fleet.

In May 1922, Lenin suffered a stroke. In December, the Soviet government declared the establishment of the Union of Soviet Socialist Republics (USSR), a federal union consisting of Soviet Russia and neighboring areas that were ruled by branches of the communist movement. From its inception, the USSR was based on a premise of one-party rule, prohibiting all other political organizations.

Lenin was disheartened by political infighting and worried about how the USSR would be run after his death. In late 1922 and early 1923, he dictated what became known as his "testament," in which he expressed regret at the direction the Soviet government had taken. He was especially critical of Joseph Stalin, then general secretary of the Communist Party. Stalin's aggressive behavior had brought him into conflict with Lenin.

Lenin died in 1924, but his legacy lives on. The Bolshevik Party's establishment of the world's first socialist state in the largest nation affected every country in the world. The victorious socialist revolution inspired workers with an alternative to capitalism and old imperialist regimes. ∎

ANY LACK OF CONFIDENCE IN THE ECONOMIC FUTURE OF THE UNITED STATES IS FOOLISH
THE WALL STREET CRASH (1929)

IN CONTEXT

FOCUS
The Great Depression

BEFORE
1918 The global economy struggles to recover its stability after the disruption of World War I.

1922 The US economy starts to grow rapidly as factories mass produce goods.

1923 Prices in Germany spiral out of control in hyperinflation that destroys people's savings.

AFTER
1930 Mass unemployment hits the US, Britain, Germany, and other countries.

1939 The advent of World War II sees an increase in employment and government spending, speeding recovery.

1944 World leaders agree to set up the International Monetary Fund (IMF) and World Bank to finance economic development.

O ver six desperate days in October 1929, shares on the New York Stock Exchange crashed. The downturn began on October 23rd, when stocks from car manufacturer General Motors were sold at a loss and the market started to collapse. Panic set in, and the next day the market nose-dived.

On Tuesday October 29, which became known as Black Tuesday, stock prices plunged even lower. In total, $25 billion, approximately $319 billion in today's market, was lost. It was the biggest financial catastrophe ever, and it plunged the world into the Great Depression.

Roaring Twenties
The US had recovered quickly after World War I, and factories that had made supplies for the war effort switched to producing consumer goods such as cars and radios. The growth of new technologies and mass production saw economic output increase by 50 percent; the age of prosperity and consumerism that resulted became known as the Roaring Twenties.

Newspapers and magazines were filled with stories of people becoming rich overnight by dabbling in the stock market, and thousands of ordinary Americans bought shares, increasing the demand for them and inflating their value. Between 1920 and 1929, the number of shareholders rose from 4 million to 20 million.

By late 1929, there were signs of trouble within the American economy: unemployment was on the rise, steel production was declining, construction was slowing, and car sales had dipped. Still confident they could make a fortune, some people continued to invest on the stock market. However, when the stock prices began to drop in October 1929, panic set in. The ensuing crash triggered a worldwide recession known as the Great Depression.

Prosperity in the US leads to **overconfidence** and **reckless investment**.

⬇

The US stock market crashes in 1929.

⬇

A **worldwide recession** sets in.

⬇ ⬇ ⬇

Mass unemployment in the US results from overproduction and inadequate demand.

Discontent in Europe leads to the fall of governments and the **rise of dictatorships**.

US President Roosevelt introduces the **New Deal** to **stimulate the economy**.

Franklin D Roosevelt

Franklin Delano Roosevelt (1882–1945) was the only president ever elected to serve four terms in office. He achieved this success despite suffering from polio in 1921, which crippled both legs and almost led him to give up on his political career.

Roosevelt won the election to be the governor of New York in 1929, and in 1932 was nominated as Democratic candidate for the presidency. Pledging a New Deal for the American people, he won a landslide victory. In his first 100 days, he introduced a program of social and economic reform to combat the Great Depression. These immensely popular measures won him a second landslide victory in 1936.

In 1941, the US was propelled into World War II, and Roosevelt took his place as one of the allied war leaders. He was one of the principal movers in the plans for a United Nations but died in March 1945, just before the UN's first meeting was convened in San Francisco.

The Great Depression

In the US, factories were closed and workers fired. In the spring of 1933, the agricultural sector was on the verge of disaster: 25 percent of farmers were without work, and many even lost their farms. Unemployment went from 1.5 million in 1929 to 12.8 million, or 24.75 percent of the workforce, by 1933, a pattern seen around the world.

Unemployment in Britain rose to 2.5 million, 25 percent of the workforce, with heavy industry, such as shipbuilding, particularly badly hit. Germany suffered greatly, since its post-war economy was supported by huge American loans which it was unable to pay back.

A New Deal

The crash helped bring Democrat Franklin D. Roosevelt into the White House in 1932. His policy, the New Deal, introduced a program of social welfare for the poor and government expenditure on huge public projects that created new jobs.

The Great Depression marked the end of the United States' post-war boom. In Europe, many turned to right-wing parties, such as Adolf Hitler's National Socialist Party in Germany, with its promise to restore the economy. In many countries, recovery came only with the increase in employment brought about by World War II. ■

THE TRUTH IS THAT MEN ARE TIRED OF LIBERTY
THE REICHSTAG FIRE (1933)

IN CONTEXT

FOCUS
Rise of fascism

BEFORE
1918 World War I leaves Europe politically and economically unstable.

1920 The National Socialist (or Nazi) Party is founded in Germany, with racism a central tenet.

1922 Benito Mussolini is made Italian premier by King Victor Emmanuel III.

AFTER
1935 Mussolini invades Abyssinia (Ethiopia) as part of his ambitious foreign policy.

1936–1939 The Spanish Civil War is fought.

1938 Adolf Hitler invades Austria. The Munich Pact grants Hitler control of the Sudetenland.

1939 Hitler orders the invasion of Poland, which triggers World War II.

Slowing European economies make everyday life harder.

German resentment festers over the terms of the **Treaty of Versailles**.

↓

Extremist fascist and communist ideologies seem to offer easy solutions to **national problems**.

↓

The Reichstag Fire is blamed on the communists and is used as a pretext to curb civil liberties and jail dissenters.

↓

The **disintegration of formal structures** of government clears the way for **Adolf Hitler** to become dictator.

When fire broke out at the Reichstag, the German parliament building, just after 9 pm on February 27, 1933, Chancellor Adolf Hitler claimed it was a communist plot to bring down the government—a cynical ploy that gave Hitler an excuse to decimate his communist rivals.

The timing was perfect: elections were due to take place in March 1933. While Hitler's National Socialist, or "Nazi," Party was the largest party in parliament, he lacked a working majority because the two next-largest parties (the Social Democrats and Communists) were both on the left, and he feared his party would not fare well in the elections. Hitler rushed to blame the fire on a lone Dutch communist, which prompted suspicions that the Nazis were behind the arson, given that they had so much to gain from discrediting the communists.

The next day, the Reichstag Fire Decree banned the Communist Party. Hitler's response fed on fears of a communist takeover, and many Germans believed that Hitler's decisive action had saved the nation. By April, under pressure from the Nazis, the Enabling Act was passed by the Reichstag. This granted Hitler the right to make his own laws without involving the Reichstag, and it solidified his place as a fascist dictator with complete control over Germany.

The Reichstag Fire is said to have burned so fiercely that flames could be seen for miles around. Hitler blamed the communists in an attempt to build support for his Nazi Party.

Dictators seize power

Fascism emerged across Europe in the 1920s and '30s. As governments struggled with post-war economic hardship and the fear of communist revolutions, extreme right-wing movements—fascism in Italy and Nazism in Germany—were set up as defenders against communism. They used paramilitary groups to intimidate opponents, and spread propaganda to gain popularity. In Italy, Benito Mussolini was seen as the only man able to restore order. Once appointed prime minister in 1922, Mussolini gradually assumed dictatorial powers, becoming *Il Duce*, the leader. By 1928, Italy was a totalitarian state.

In Germany, Hitler worked ceaselessly to transform the Nazis into a major political force. Relying on a mix of nationalist rhetoric, anti-communism, vicious anti-Semitism, and an unceasing call to reverse the peace terms made at Versailles in 1919, Hitler rode a wave of popularity. In 1933 he became Chancellor, then, shortly after, dictator, calling himself *Führer*.

Fascists united

In 1936, Hitler and Mussolini began to send military support to aid General Franco in the Spanish Civil War, which pitted right-wing nationalists against left-wing republicans. Franco's victory against the left-wing Popular Front government emboldened the dictators and emphasized the weakness of Western democracies.

The Reichstag Fire was a key moment in Nazi history. It led to the absolute dictatorship of Adolf Hitler and the growth of fascism, setting Europe on the path to world war. ∎

Fascism across Europe

European fascism blossomed in a climate of economic disarray in the 1920s and '30s. Democracies lost legitimacy with their people, and fascist parties, offering a form of extreme right-wing nationalism, boasted that they would provide strength where weakness had prevailed.

In the 1930s, no European country, with the exception of the Soviet Union, was without a form of fascist party. Britain had Sir Oswald Mosley's British Union of Fascists (BUF). Ireland had the Blueshirts; France, Le Faisceau; and Denmark and Norway had many far-right parties. Engelbert Dollfuss's Fatherland Front was installed in Austria in 1934, while Greece was under the rule of General Ioannis Metaxas between 1936 and 1941. Portugal and Bulgaria also came under right-wing dictatorships, as did Romania.

By the end of the 1930s, authoritarian governments had assumed power in virtually every corner of central and Eastern Europe, and democracy was in decline.

IN STARTING AND WAGING A WAR, IT IS NOT RIGHT THAT MATTERS BUT VICTORY

NAZI INVASION OF POLAND (1939–1945)

IN CONTEXT

FOCUS
World War II

BEFORE
1919 The Treaty of Versailles at the end of World War I humiliates Germany and sows the seeds for future conflict.

1922 The Union of Soviet Socialist Republics (USSR) is founded.

1933 The Enabling Act gives Adolf Hitler dictatorial power in Germany.

AFTER
1942–1943 The Soviets defeat the Germans at Stalingrad.

1944 The June 6 D-Day Landings, which were the largest amphibious military operation in history, begin the liberation of Western Europe.

1945 As Russian troops win the Battle of Berlin, Hitler commits suicide. The Germans surrender unconditionally.

In August 1939, Nazi Germany and the Soviet Union signed a nonaggression pact, also secretly agreeing to invade and then divide Poland between them. Russian leader Joseph Stalin had decided that in the event of war, Germany offered the best hope of Soviet security. One week later, on September 1, 1939, more than a million German troops invaded Poland from the west. Soon after, on September 17, Russian troops attacked Poland from the east. The context for this unprovoked assault, as declared by the German *Führer*, Adolf Hitler, was the pursuit of *Lebensraum*, "living space" deemed necessary for the expansion of the German people, whom Hitler saw as a superior "Aryan master race," with the right to displace inferior races.

The invasion lasted just over a month. Trapped between two huge, well-armed powers, the Polish air force and army fought valiantly, but they lacked modern aircraft and tanks. The German Luftwaffe was quickly able to gain command of the skies. In the end, Poland's aviators and soldiers, fighting on two fronts, were overwhelmed.

The invasion ended in a resounding victory, and it added to Hitler's increasing belief that he was a military genius. Some areas in western Poland were absorbed into Germany, while territory east of the Bug River was annexed by the Soviet Union.

The Nazi regime in Poland
The Nazis imposed a brutal regime on the German part of Poland. Hitler was bent on the elimination of anyone who stood in the way of German domination.

As part of Hitler's plan for ethnic cleansing, around 5 million Polish Jews were rounded up and herded into ghettos. The invasion of Poland gave some forewarning of the violence that would soon be visited upon scores of countries and countless people around the globe.

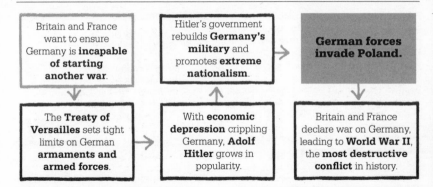

Britain and France want to ensure Germany is **incapable of starting another war**.

↓

The **Treaty of Versailles** sets tight limits on German **armaments and armed forces**.

→ With **economic depression** crippling Germany, **Adolf Hitler** grows in popularity.

↑

Hitler's government rebuilds **Germany's military** and promotes **extreme nationalism**.

→ **German forces invade Poland.**

↓

Britain and France declare war on Germany, leading to **World War II**, the **most destructive conflict** in history.

The rise of the Nazi Party

Although World War II was triggered by Hitler's invasion of Poland, its origins can be traced back to Germany's defeat in World War I and the demand for reparation payments. The defeated nations lost land and prestige, causing deep resentment. Germany was forced to return Alsace and Lorraine to France, and all of its overseas colonies were annexed by the Allies.

Germany's Weimar Republic began its economic recovery in the 1920s, but it could not survive the blow that was inflicted by the US economic crash of 1929. This financial crisis aided the rise of the National Socialist (Nazi) Party, led by Hitler, who promised the German people he would make the nation great again.

Hitler had fought in World War I, and the experience of trench warfare, the shock of defeat, and the terms of the Versailles Treaty were to influence the rest of his life. He developed extremist views based on

Adolf Hitler watches a victory parade in Warsaw following the invasion of Poland. He and Soviet leader Joseph Stalin agreed to the invasion and division of the country.

far-right nationalism; and by the time he became chancellor of Germany's coalition government in 1933, and dictator of the country the next year, he ruthlessly pursued his policies of nationalism, anti-Semitism, and anti-communism.

Hitler's *Lebensraum*

Under this creed, Hitler embarked on an ambitious foreign policy. In 1935, openly going against the terms of the Versailles Treaty, he began a massive program of rearmament. In 1936, he occupied the demilitarized Rhineland, but none of the major powers intervened. In March 1938, Hitler annexed Austria to Germany, before setting his sights on the German-speaking part of Czechoslovakia, the Sudetenland. British and French politicians wanted to avoid a repeat of the horrors of World War I and felt that the Sudetenland was not worth fighting for. In the Munich Agreement of September 29, 1938, the Sudetenland was handed to Hitler in exchange for his promise to end his land-grabs. British prime minister Neville Chamberlain declared that he had secured "peace for our time," only for the Nazis to invade the remainder of Czechoslovakia in March 1939.

Fascism in Europe

Italy's Fascist dictator Benito Mussolini also had aspirations for foreign glory. In October 1935, he invaded Abyssinia (Ethiopia) in retaliation for the defeat the Italians had suffered there in 1896. By May 1936, Mussolini had conquered the country, facing no opposition from the Western powers. »

Further evidence of Western democracies' weakness in facing up to the Fascist challenge was provided the same year, when both Mussolini and Hitler sent "volunteers" to fight in the Spanish Civil War, to aid nationalist General Franco in his campaign against left-wing supporters of the Spanish Republic. Britain and France took no action, and Franco's victory in 1939 bolstered the Fascist cause.

The West intervenes

Hitler's invasion of Poland, which began on September 1, 1939, finally forced Britain and France into a war they had been trying desperately to avoid. Deciding that they needed to take a tougher stance against Hitler after his takeover of Czechoslovakia, the two nations had guaranteed Poland support in the event of German aggression. Honoring this promise, they declared war on Germany on September 3, which meant British and French colonies were also drawn into conflict: Britain's dominions Australia and New Zealand declared war immediately, the Union of South Africa followed on September 6, and Canada on September 10.

Germany quickly overran Poland with its tactic of *blitzkrieg* ("lightning war"), which utilized tank divisions supported by the Luftwaffe, the German air force. The British sent an Expeditionary Force (BEF) to France, but neither Britain nor France attempted an offensive against Germany. They were not ready for a large-scale attack, and some politicians still believed that peace terms could be negotiated.

Operation Dynamo, in June 1940, focused on the evacuation of Allied soldiers from the port of Dunkirk, in France, after they had become surrounded by German troops.

 We shall defend our island whatever the cost may be. We shall fight on beaches, landing grounds, in fields, in streets, and on the hills. We shall never surrender.
Winston Churchill

This period became known as the "Phony War." Expecting to be bombed, Britain began to evacuate its children from major cities. Air-raid shelters were built, and gas masks handed out. The Phony War ended in April 1940, when Germany attacked and conquered Denmark and Norway. A month later, they turned on France, Belgium, and the Netherlands. The French army was poorly led and badly equipped. France had relied on the Maginot Line, a chain of fortresses along the frontier with Germany, to halt any attack. But the fortification did not extend along the Franco-Belgian border, and the Germans simply bypassed it at the north end. Within the space of six weeks, France had fallen to the German onslaught.

The Battle of Britain

Only a hesitation by Hitler, who may have wanted to rest his troops and spare them from a possible counterattack, prevented the destruction of British forces before they could be evacuated by sea from Dunkirk. Thousands of Allied soldiers were transferred across the Channel in all kinds of vessels in Operation Dynamo. Winston Churchill, the First Lord of the Admiralty and later Britain's wartime prime minister, told the British parliament, "The Battle of France is over. I expect the Battle of Britain is about to begin."

However, Hitler's attempts to invade Britain in Operation Sea Lion had to be abandoned after the Luftwaffe failed to win the battle of the skies. With the Luftwaffe triumphant in both Poland and France, the Germans had hoped that Britain could be beaten by air power alone. However, German crews were exhausted,

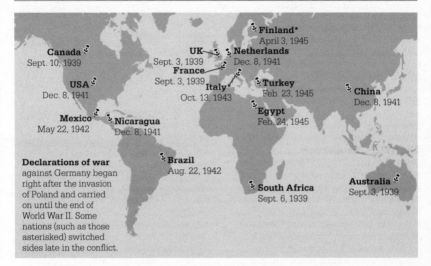

Finland*
April 3, 1945

Canada
Sept. 10, 1939

UK
Sept. 3, 1939

Netherlands
Dec. 8, 1941

France
Sept. 3, 1939

USA
Dec. 8, 1941

Italy*
Oct. 13, 1943

Turkey
Feb. 23, 1945

China
Dec. 8, 1941

Mexico
May 22, 1942

Nicaragua
Dec. 8, 1941

Egypt
Feb. 24, 1945

Declarations of war
against Germany began
right after the invasion
of Poland and carried
on until the end of
World War II. Some
nations (such as those
asterisked) switched
sides late in the conflict.

Brazil
Aug. 22, 1942

South Africa
Sept. 6, 1939

Australia
Sept. 3, 1939

intelligence was poor, and Britain's use of radar enabled the Royal Air Force (RAF) to track incoming planes and take off in time to meet an attack. The Battle of Britain in the summer of 1940 was the first real check on Hitler's progress, but Britain alone could not fight a power that now had control of almost the entire continent.

The world at war

What started as a European war gradually became a world war. In June 1940, Italy, emboldened by German successes, declared war on Britain and France, fulfilling the terms of the Axis agreement made between Hitler and Mussolini on May 22, 1939. But Italy's failures in Greece and North Africa forced Hitler to send German armies into these areas, as well as Yugoslavia.

On September 7, 1940 Germany began its first major air raid on London. The Blitz, as the bombing of the English capital became known, thrust civilians into the war and put relentless pressure on industry, ports, and British morale. With men joining the army, women were required to work in factories and on farms. Food rationing was introduced in Britain in January 1940, and people were urged to grow their own food. Nazi-occupied Europe also experienced food shortages, which weighed most heavily on the conquered populations.

Collaboration or exile

In some locations, the Germans worked with existing governments and fully supported puppet administrations, such as the pro-Nazi Vidkun Quisling in Norway and the Vichy regime in southern France. Led by Marshal Philippe Pétain, Vichy was officially neutral, but it collaborated closely with Germany, fighting the French resistance, and implementing anti-Semitic legislation.

Germany had total control in Poland and eventual control of the Baltic states. Monarchs and politicians of more than a dozen occupied countries escaped to Britain. Polish ministers set up headquarters in London, and Belgium's government operations were transferred there. The Dutch royal family, under Queen Wilhelmina, also sought refuge in London. When France fell to Germany, Charles de Gaulle, who opposed the newly installed Vichy government, became the voice of French opposition to the Nazi occupation.

In 1940 the biggest threat facing Britain was from German U-boats. As an island, Britain was dependent on its merchant ships to bring in vital supplies but also to export equipment to its fighting forces abroad, and German U-boats were sinking dozens of Allied ships each » month. Merchant ships traveled in convoy to increase the chances of supplies getting through on each journey, but casualties were high.

Fighting the USSR

In June 1941, Britain gained a new ally when Germany invaded the USSR in Operation Barbarossa. Hitler had looked to the Soviet Union for new territory for the German people. It would also remove any future threat from the east but fundamentally followed through on Hitler's plan to destroy communism. At first it looked as if Germany and its allies would be as successful against the Russians as it had been against the French. By winter, Germany had advanced to within 1 mile (1.5 km) of Moscow, and Leningrad, the USSR's second city, was under siege.

Another powerful rationale for war in the east was one based on racist ideology and Hitler's hatred of Slavs and Jews. As German troops swept into Russia, they inflicted a terrible campaign of genocide against communists and Jews. Russian troops endured extreme hardships. German tanks plowed through the Red Army defenses. Prisoners of war were shot or left to starve. Fleeing civilians were butchered without a moment's hesitation. The harshness of the Russian winter slowed the Germans, and Russian counterattacks drove back their front line by several hundred miles. In the Battle of Moscow, from early October 1941 to January 1942, an estimated 650,000 soldiers from the Soviet Army lost their lives. In the spring of 1942, the Germans

General Dwight D. Eisenhower led the Allied forces during the Normandy landings of June 1944. The invasion was a decisive step toward taking Europe back from the Nazis.

resumed their offensive in the USSR, driving the Red Army back and coming close to taking the Russian oilfields.

The Pacific and Africa

In December 1941, Japan entered the war by attacking the US fleet at Pearl Harbor, in the Hawaiian Islands, as part of its plan to drive American forces out of the Pacific. Germany—which had a tripartite agreement with Japan and Italy to provide mutual military assistance in the event any one of them was attacked by a nation not already involved in the war—immediately declared war on the United States. Britain now had two strong allies, the USSR under Joseph Stalin, and the US, led by President Franklin D. Roosevelt. Both were decisive in bringing about the defeat of the Axis powers. American industry became a triumph of wartime production, giving Americans in combat in Europe and Asia the tools they needed to fight the Axis.

Japan won quick victories in the Pacific. It successfully captured the Philippines, Malaya, Burma, Indonesia, and Singapore, Britain's main naval base in East Asia.

In North Africa, meanwhile, a renewed Axis offensive led by General Erwin Rommel brought the German and Italian armies within striking distance of Cairo and the Suez Canal. The first major Allied victory came in Egypt. In July 1942, Rommel was halted at El Alamein; in October, he was forced into retreat by the British 8th Army, led by Field Marshal Montgomery.

Operation Barbarossa, launched in June 1941, saw the invasion of the Soviet Union by Germany, in breach of the nonaggression pact the two countries had signed two years earlier.

That same winter, the Red Army defeated the Nazis at Stalingrad. The Soviets encircled the Germans, forcing a surrender in February 1943.

The turn of the tide

In a conference at Tehran in November 1943, the Allied leaders agreed on a strategy to liberate Europe. While the Russians drove the Germans back in the east, and the British and Americans advanced slowly through Italy, a huge Allied invasion force arrived in Normandy in June 1944. Eleven months later, it had reached the Elbe River in northern Germany, while Russian troops were advancing block by block through Berlin. Germany was being hit repeatedly by British Lancaster bomber aircraft from Bomber Command and the US Eighth Air Force. Staring at defeat, Hitler committed suicide on April 30, and Germany surrendered unconditionally a week later.

The last act of the war came in August 1945, when the US, after fighting island by island through the Pacific, put an end to Japanese resistance by dropping atomic bombs on Hiroshima and Nagasaki. The effects of the bombs were cataclysmic, inflicting unprecedented horror on the two Japanese cities.

Nations united

Hitler's invasion of Poland marked the start of World War II, the largest and most destructive war in history, by the end of which an estimated 60 million people had been killed. Like their predecessors in 1918, the Allies were determined that this should be the last war of its kind.

Representatives of 50 nations met in 1945 to set up the United Nations. There was hope that this would mark the start of a new era of international understanding. ∎

The Battle of Iwo Jima saw US troops fight against Japan's Imperial Army for possession of the tiny island in the Pacific Ocean, resulting in 100,000 Japanese casualties.

Hiroshima and Nagasaki

American planes dropped atomic bombs on the Japanese cities of Hiroshima and Nagasaki to force Japan to surrender and end World War II. On August 6, 1945, "Little Boy" was dropped on Hiroshima. The inhabitants below had no idea what was about to happen. People, animals, and buildings were incinerated in the searing heat. Some 70,000 died immediately. Despite this terrible event, Japan did not surrender.

Japan had cause to reconsider its position when the Soviets entered the war against them by crossing into Manchuria on August 9. When, that same afternoon, the US dropped "Fat Man" on Nagasaki, instantly killing 50,000, Japan was brought to its knees and agreed to the Allies' terms of surrender. These unprecedented attacks avoided a bloody ground assault by the Allies on the Japanese mainland, but many thousands lost their lives as a result of the long-term effects of radiation sickness.

THE FINAL SOLUTION OF THE JEWISH QUESTION

THE WANNSEE CONFERENCE (1942)

IN CONTEXT

FOCUS
The Holocaust

BEFORE
1933 The first concentration camp is built in Dachau, near Munich. Its first inmates are communists, socialists, and trade unionists.

September 1935 As a result of the new Nuremberg Laws, Jews lose their civil rights.

1938 During Kristallnacht, the "Night of Broken Glass," the Nazis terrorize Jews across Germany and Austria.

June 1941 The German invasion of the Soviet Union is accompanied by the mass killing of Jews.

AFTER
May 1942 Gassings start at Auschwitz, in Poland.

1945–1946 At the Nuremberg trials, 24 Nazi members are indicted and 12 sentenced to death.

Hitler becomes ruler of Germany and **introduces legislation** discriminating against Jews.

↓

Hitler's takeover of Austria is followed by **widespread attacks on Jews**.

↓

Germany conquers Poland, and Polish Jews are forced to move into **overcrowded ghettos**.

↓

The Nazis look for **efficient ways** to kill millions after the **invasion of Russia**.

↓

The Wannsee Conference organizes the Final Solution.

↓

More than **6 million Jews** are killed in **the Holocaust**.

On January 20, 1942, 15 members of the Nazi Party and German officials met in the Berlin suburb of Wannsee to discuss the implementation of the "Final Solution of the Jewish Question"—the code name for the systematic annihilation of European Jews. During the conference, a tabulation of all the Jews in Europe was presented, country by country, as well as a target number for extermination: 11 million. The meeting lasted two hours and was matter-of-fact and dispassionate. After approving the "Final Solution" and the slaughter of the Jews, the men called for brandy and cigars.

The Wannsee Conference was far from the start of Nazi brutality against Jews. Adolf Hitler had come to power in 1933, spreading his belief that Germans were the Aryan master race, superior to all others, and that their blood should not be contaminated. He identified Jews as a race of people, not just a religious group. German Jews were banned from marrying non-Jewish Germans and subjected to increasing discrimination and segregation. From the time of the German takeover of Austria in 1938, Nazi brutality against Jews worsened. Jews wanting to flee German rule found other countries unwilling to accept them.

Gathering momentum

After Germany's invasion of Poland in 1939, the Nazi campaign against the Jews reached a terrifying new level. Herded into ghettos, Polish Jews began to die in large numbers of starvation and ill-treatment.

When Germany invaded Russia in 1941, paramilitary death squads carried out mass killings of Jews in the conquered areas. To start with, victims were shot, up to 30,000 at a time, but the SS then began gassing Jews in the backs of vans. Poison gas was found to be a more efficient way to commit mass murder.

Until 1941, the Nazi leadership had envisaged solving the "Jewish problem" by deporting Jews to a distant location. By the time of the Wannsee Conference, however, they were committed to systematically killing Europe's Jewish population. Six dedicated death camps were built in Poland. Adolf Eichmann of the Nazi paramilitary corps, the SS, arranged the transportation of Jews to the camps from right across Europe, including France, Greece, Hungary, and Italy. The Jews from the Polish ghettos were also taken there to be exterminated. Prisoners arrived at these huge killing factories by train and were gassed in shower rooms, their corpses burned in large crematoria. At the Belzec camp, about half a million Jews were killed, and only seven prisoners are known to have survived. The death camp at Auschwitz, however, also had a labor camp attached, where those who were not killed on arrival were made to work. The Germans needed slave labor to support their war effort, and this offered Jews their best chance of survival. Along with other prisoners—including socialists, homosexuals, Roma, and prisoners of war—many Jews were sent to concentration camps. Their heads were shaved, and they were given a uniform to strip them of their identity. When the Allies liberated the camps in 1945, they found a vision of hell. The survivors were skeletal and traumatized.

State-sanctioned genocide

The Wannsee Protocol, the minutes of the conference, represents the unimaginable. For the first time, a modern state had committed itself to the murder of an entire people. As many as 6 million Jews lost their lives, and an estimated 5.5 million others—Slavs, homosexuals, communists—were also killed. ∎

The Nuremberg Trials

After the end of World War II, the Allies sought to bring the Nazis to justice. An international tribunal was held at Nuremberg, Germany, beginning in 1945. Newsreels captured from the Nazis revealed the gas chambers, the massacre of civilians, and the ill-treatment of prisoners. The trials were televised, showing to the world—and, in particular the German people— evidence of the horrors that had taken place in the concentration camps.

Adolf Hitler; Heinrich Himmler, head of the SS; and Joseph Goebbels, head of propaganda, had committed suicide, leaving 24 defendants facing four counts: crimes against peace, planning and waging wars of aggression, war crimes, and crimes against humanity. Most said they were "only obeying orders." Albert Speer, head of war production, was jailed for 20 years, while 12 of the other defendants were sentenced to death; the trials led to the setting up of a permanent international criminal court in The Hague, in the Netherlands.

AT THE STROKE OF THE MIDNIGHT HOUR, WHEN THE WORLD SLEEPS, INDIA WILL AWAKE TO LIFE AND FREEDOM

INDIAN INDEPENDENCE AND PARTITION (1947)

IN CONTEXT

FOCUS
End of empires

BEFORE
1885 The Indian National Congress (INC) is founded and campaigns for Indian rights.

1901 Australian colonies are united to form the Commonwealth of Australia.

1921 The Irish Free State (four-fifths of Ireland) gains independence from Britain.

1922 Egypt is given limited independence by Britain, but British troops remain to protect imperial interests.

AFTER
1947 The Commonwealth of Nations is formed—all former British colonies can take part.

1960 The Declaration of Decolonization asserts the rights of all peoples to self-determination.

For more than a century, India had been the crown jewel of the British Empire, but on the last stroke of midnight on August 14, 1947, it became an independent nation. In India's Constituent Assembly, Delhi, a special midnight gathering of parliament was convened. Jawaharlal Nehru, the first prime minister of India, rose to his feet to declare India's freedom. However, this independence also opened a social and geographic wound that has yet to heal.

The new Indian state was split into two independent nation states: Muslim-majority Pakistan and Hindu-majority India. Pakistan itself was split between northwest and northeast, because both wings had a Muslim majority. Immediately, millions of Muslims trekked to West and East Pakistan (the latter now known as Bangladesh), while millions of Hindus and Sikhs headed toward the newly independent India. Thousands never reached it, and many died from malnutrition and disease. Across India there were outbreaks of sectarian violence, with Hindus and Sikhs on one side and Muslims on the other.

By 1948, as the great migration drew to a close, more than 15 million people had been uprooted, and between 1 million and 2 million were dead. India was independent and India's Muslims had their own independent state, but freedom came at a great cost.

The road to independence

The spirit of nationalism in India gained ground in the mid-19th century and was strengthened in 1885 by the formation of the Indian National Congress (INC). During World War I, expectations for greater self-governance were raised when Britain promised to deliver self-rule in return for India's contribution to the war effort. But Britain envisaged a gradual progress toward self-government, beginning with

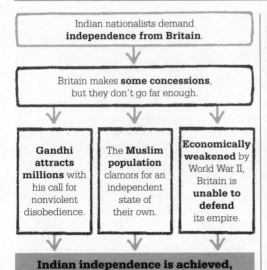

Indian nationalists demand **independence from Britain**.

⬇

Britain makes **some concessions**, but they don't go far enough.

⬇ ⬇ ⬇

Gandhi attracts millions with his call for nonviolent disobedience.	The **Muslim population** clamors for an independent state of their own.	**Economically weakened** by World War II, Britain is **unable to defend** its empire.

⬇ ⬇ ⬇

Indian independence is achieved, and the country is split in two.

Mohandas Gandhi

The Indian national leader known as Mahatma, meaning "great soul," Mohandas Gandhi (1869–1948) led his country to independence from Great Britain. He came from a Hindu family and studied law in England before spending 20 years in South Africa trying to secure rights for the Indians living there.

Gandhi's involvement in Indian politics began in 1919, and he soon became the unquestioned leader of the independence movement. He preached the doctrine of Satyagraha (soul force, or passive resistance) which he applied against the British with great effect. He adopted a simple life, believing in the virtue of small communities, and campaigned against Indian industrialization.

Gandhi's life work was crowned in 1947, when India finally won independence, but the concessions he had made to the Muslims led to his assassination the following year by a Hindu fanatic, who blamed him for the partition of India, although Gandhi himself bitterly opposed the dismemberment of the subcontinent.

the Government of India Act (1919), which created an Indian parliament where power was shared between Indians and British officials. This did not satisfy Indian nationalists, and the British responded to their protests with sometimes brutal repression.

The push for independence from the 1920s to the 1940s was galvanized by the work of Mohandas Karamchand Gandhi. Gandhi not only launched the Satyagraha campaign, promoting nonviolent protest, but also became an influential figure for millions of followers. In 1942 Gandhi led the "Quit India" campaign, calling for civil disobedience to disrupt Britain's efforts in World War II. The British immediately jailed Gandhi and other nationalist leaders.

By the end of World War II, it was clear that Britain lacked the means to defeat the nationalist campaign. Britain's officials in India were utterly exhausted, and Britain itself was almost bankrupt. Britain agreed to a fully independent India. While Gandhi and Nehru advocated Indian unity, the Muslim League, founded in 1906 to safeguard the rights of Muslims, demanded a completely separate Muslim state. Its leader, Mohammed Ali Jinnah, feared that Muslims could not protect their minority rights if left to live under Hindu rule. Congress rejected the proposal and violence on the streets between Hindus and Muslims began to escalate. »

Pakistan is born

In 1947, Lord Louis Mountbatten flew into Delhi as Britain's final Viceroy of India. Faced with irreconcilable differences over the demand for a separate state for India's Muslims, he persuaded all parties to agree to partitioning the country into Hindu India and Muslim Pakistan.

From its birth, Pakistan faced many challenges. It had limited resources and a huge refugee problem. There were different traditions, cultures, and languages, and Jinnah, its first governor general, died the following year. In 1948, India and Pakistan fought over Kashmir, the only Muslim-majority area to remain within India.

Colonies gain freedom

After World War II, the European colonial powers—mainly Britain, France, the Netherlands, and Portugal—recognized that change was inevitable. Some colonies won independence by peaceful means, such as in Burma (Myanmar) and Ceylon (Sri Lanka) in 1948, but often European powers tried to hold on to their colonies.

During World War II, Japan, itself a significant imperial power, drove the European powers out of Asia. After

India's independence was finally declared by Jawaharlal Nehru and Lord Louis Mountbatten at Delhi's Constituent Assembly, just seconds into August 15, 1947.

the Japanese surrender in 1945, nationalist movements in the former Asian colonies campaigned for independence rather than a return to European colonial rule. Dr. Ahmed Sukarno, leader of Indonesia's nationalist movement, declared the Independent Republic of Indonesia in 1945. The Dutch sent troops to restore their authority, and in two military campaigns that followed, an estimated 150,000 Indonesians and 5,000 Dutch soldiers died. International pressure eventually forced the Dutch to concede independence in 1949.

The Japanese occupation of Malaya during the war had unified the Malayan people and greatly increased nationalistic feelings. Britain clamped down on protests, which led the militant wing of the Malaysian Communist Party to declare war on the British Empire in 1948. Britain responded by declaring a state of emergency and pursuing a bitter campaign against Chinese "communist terrorists." Independence was not granted to Malaya until 1957.

Unrest in Africa

In Kenya, the imposition of a state of emergency in 1952, in response to the Mau Mau (rebel) uprising, led to greater insurgency and the British rounding up of tens of thousands of Mau Mau suspects into detention camps. By 1956 the rebellion had been crushed, but the methods used by the British to regain control brought international condemnation. In central Africa, too, decolonization was born in violence. In Rhodesia, savage conflict erupted between the black majority and the fiercely racist white leadership, which had unilaterally declared independence in 1965.

The process of decolonization coincided with the new Cold War between the Soviet Union and the United States. The US became concerned that, as the European powers lost their colonies, Soviet-supported communist parties might achieve power in the new states. The US used substantial aid packages to encourage newly independent nations to adopt governments that aligned with the West. The Soviet Union deployed similar tactics in an effort to encourage new nations to join the communist bloc. Many resisted the pressure to be drawn into the Cold War and joined the "non-aligned movement." This movement began out of a 1955 meeting in Bandung, Indonesia, involving 29 African and Asian countries. Member countries decided they would not be involved in alliances or defense pacts with the main world powers, but focus on internal development instead.

Terrorism in France

France was determined to maintain its political status in Algeria. When independence was not realized after World War II, war broke out between Algerian nationalists and French settlers. In 1958, the National Liberation Front (FLN), the main nationalist group, led several terrorist attacks, first in Algeria, then in Paris. The crisis led to the return to power of Charles de Gaulle, the wartime leader of the Free French. In 1960, de Gaulle, to the horror of the French settlers, agreed to emancipate Algeria. After a long and bloody conflict in which an estimated 150,000 died, Algeria gained its independence in 1962.

Independence gained

During the 1960s and '70s, many of the countries that were once held as British colonies became independent states and joined the Commonwealth. The British Commonwealth, formed in 1931, became the successor to Britain's old empire, preserving Britain's global economic and political influence. In 1931 Britain extended dominion status to the already self-governing colonies of Canada (1867), Australia (1901), New Zealand (1907), and Newfoundland (1907). Britain and her dominions shared equal status, and they accepted the British monarch as head of the Commonwealth. In 1949 the British Commonwealth became "The Commonwealth," a free and equal association of independent states, but the end of the empire was drawing near. Britain fought a war to retain the Falkland Islands in 1982, and Hong Kong continued as a British dependency until 1997.

Gandhi had a profound influence on world politics. Other peaceful resisters—such as Martin Luther King, Jr., and Tibet's Dalai Lama—emulated his methods. Around the world, the struggle for countries to secede from nations they belong to continues, as the likes of Scotland (United Kingdom), Quebec (Canada), and Palestine fight to be seen as nations in their own right. ∎

Mau Mau suspects captured in Nairobi's Great Rift Valley, Kenya, in 1952 are led away, with their hands on their heads, to be questioned by police and possibly held in detention camps.

THE NAME OF OUR STATE SHALL BE ISRAEL
THE ESTABLISHMENT OF ISRAEL (1948)

IN CONTEXT

FOCUS
Creation of Israel

BEFORE
1897 Zionism becomes an organized movement and calls for a Jewish state in Palestine.

1917 In the Balfour Declaration, Britain promises to help the Jews establish a homeland in Palestine.

1946 As part of its campaign of terrorism against Palestine and Britain, the Jewish underground army bombs the King David Hotel, killing 91.

AFTER
1967 During the Six Day War, Arabs unite against Israel, but Israel is victorious and captures swathes of Arab territory.

1993 Oslo Peace Accords try to initiate peace between Palestinians and Israel.

2014 Sweden becomes the 135th country to recognize the state of Palestine.

Zionist theorists envisage the possibility of a **Jewish homeland**.

Jews begin **settling in and developing** Palestine.

Jews escaping Nazi control flee to **Palestine**.

The United Nations grants the land of Israel to the Jewish people.

Many Palestinians are **forcibly displaced** and become refugees.

Wars break out periodically between Arab states and Israel.

A s the sun rose on May 14, 1948, the British flag was lowered at Government House, on Jerusalem's Hill of Evil Counsel, ending the 26-year British mandate over Palestine. David Ben-Gurion, the longtime leader of the Jewish settlers, or Zionists, who had fled to Palestine from Europe, proclaimed the news of the establishment of the Jewish state in Palestine.

Israel's Muslim neighbors, united as the Arab League, rejected the state's creation and reacted with an attack. Troops moved in from Transjordan, Egypt, Lebanon, Syria, and Iraq. Hardened to fighting after years of protecting their settlements in Palestine, the Jews thwarted the Arabs.

A troubled land

Jews had immigrated to Palestine to avoid persecution in Europe since the 1880s, believing it to be the land promised to them by God. With the Balfour Declaration in 1917, the British government supported a Jewish homeland. The majority-Arab population objected to the settlers' claim on their country. Facing increasing attacks, the Jews formed local defense groups under the umbrella term the Haganah.

Escalation of violence

In 1939, the rise of anti-Semitism in Europe, particularly in Nazi Germany, forced Jews to flee to Jerusalem. Facing a much larger influx of settlers than they had anticipated, the British proposed a restriction on the free settlement of Jewish refugees in Palestine.

After World War II, violence in Palestine escalated, and in 1947 the British government said it would terminate its rule and hand the "Palestine problem" to the United Nations. The Holocaust convinced the UN that the Jewish people needed a homeland, so they resolved to partition Palestine into an area for Arabs (about 44 percent) and the rest for a Jewish state. The Jews agreed with

The flag of **Israel** was adopted in 1948, a few months after the birth of the state. It was originally designed in 1891 for use by the Zionist movement and has the Star of David at its center.

the plan, but the Arabs refused it. Despite this, on May 14, 1948, the state of Israel was born.

Israel's immediate priority was to build a credible defense force from the Haganah. After the Six Day War (1967), Israel controlled the Sinai, Gaza, the West Bank, the Golan Heights, and Jerusalem. It faced many attacks from Arab neighbors, in addition to threats from the paramilitary Palestine Liberation Army (PLO), formed in 1964.

Arab Palestinians repeatedly called for an independent state in the West Bank and Gaza. In the occupied zones, they suffer from poor living conditions, military raids, and restricted movement. ∎

David Ben-Gurion

The founder and first prime minister (1948–1963) of the state of Israel, David Ben-Gurion was born in 1886 to Jewish parents in Poland. In 1906, he immigrated to Palestine, where he became an active supporter of the struggle for an independent Jewish state. He led the Jewish campaign against the British in Palestine, authorizing acts of sabotage.

When he became the nation's leader, he established the Israeli Defense Force and guided the modern development of Israel. He promoted the use of Hebrew as the language of the country. His "Law of Return," announced in 1950, granted permission for Jews from around the world to immigrate to Israel.

He briefly retired in 1953, and in his later years in power he initiated secret talks with Arab leaders in an attempt to gain peace for the Middle East.

In 1970, Ben-Gurion retired fully from the Knesset (Israeli parliament) and devoted himself to writing his memoirs in Sde-Boker, a *kibbutz* (communal settlement) in the Negev Desert in southern Israel. He died in 1973 and is still a revered figure.

GHANA, YOUR BELOVED COUNTRY, IS FREE FOREVER

NKRUMAH WINS GHANAIAN INDEPENDENCE (1957)

IN CONTEXT

FOCUS
Postcolonial Africa

BEFORE
1946 The formation of the international Pan-African Federation promotes African independence.

1952–1960 The Mau Mau uprising in Kenya against the British marks a turning point in the struggle for independence.

1956 A humiliating defeat for France and Britain in Suez signals a further decline of the old European powers.

AFTER
1957–1975 Most African nations achieve independence from French, British, Portuguese, and Belgian rule.

1963 The Organization of African Unity is founded.

1994 South Africans are the last people on the continent to achieve majority rule.

In February 1948, at a time when the Gold Coast, a British colony in West Africa, had been demanding independence for several years, a group of unarmed African ex-servicemen marched to the British governor with a petition of grievances. Ordered to stop, they refused, and the police opened fire.

Kwame Nkrumah, Kojo Botsio, Krobo Edusei, and other Ghanaian politicians celebrate the independence of their country, which was achieved peacefully and democratically.

In response to this, in 1949, nationalist Kwame Nkrumah formed the Convention People's Party (CPP), an organization fighting for self-governance. Nkrumah initiated a campaign of positive action inspired by Gandhi's philosophy of nonviolent noncooperation in India against the British. The strikes and protests they encouraged remained peaceful but paralyzed the country, and Britain agreed to elections in early 1951. The CPP won 35 out of 38 seats, and the Gold Coast moved rapidly toward independence, which was proclaimed on March 6, 1957, with Nkrumah becoming prime minister of the nation of Ghana. It was a moment of huge hope for a new kind of Africa.

The European powers that ruled Africa had been impoverished by World War II, and attitudes to colonialism were changing. Nations that had fought against fascism found it hard to justify imperialism.

A domino effect

Events in Ghana had a significant impact in West Africa. In 1958, Guinea voted to secede from France. Determined not to be left behind, Nigeria celebrated independence from Britain on October 1, 1960. By 1964, independence had also been granted

| African nationalism **gathers pace** during the early 1900s. | The ideology of **Pan-Africanism** gains adherents worldwide. | African experiences in **World War II** spur demands for **racial equality**. |

⬇

Nkrumah wins independence for Ghana.

⬇

Nkrumah fails in his campaign for the **political unity** of Africa.

⬇

By the mid-1970s, most of Africa has gained **independence**, if not peace.

---

to Kenya, Northern Rhodesia (Zambia), Nyasaland (Malawi), and Uganda.

The French fought an eight-year war to hold on to Algeria, finally conceding independence in 1962.

The Portuguese, the first European colonial power in Africa, fought a long war to hold on to their colonies of Angola, Mozambique, and Guinea from 1961 to 1974. The collapse of Belgian authority in the Congo in 1960 led to a wave of violence across the nation and the assassination of the first prime minister, Patrice Lumumba, in 1961.

Many African countries gained independence during the Cold War. Used as pawns between the capitalist and communist superpowers, they accepted loans and military aid: in the 1970s, Ethiopia was rewarded with billions of dollars' worth of Soviet military equipment. Civil wars were also numerous, such as the ethnic civil wars in Rwanda and Zaire, as well as the clashes between warlords over food supplies in Somalia.

Dictatorial rulers

Once independence was achieved, African nationalist leaders sought to consolidate power by banning political rivals. Coups and military governments predominated—such as that of Idi Amin in Uganda. By the early 1970s, only Zimbabwe and South Africa were still ruled by the white political elite. Corruption, however, existed in most African countries. Nkrumah wanted Ghana to be a beacon of success, but his Pan-Africanism failed, and Ghana's fortunes began to slide as he became increasingly dictatorial. ∎

Kwame Nkrumah

Ambitious and well-educated, Kwame Nkrumah had big plans for both Ghana and Africa as a whole. He went to college in the US and later traveled to England, where he became involved in the West African Students' Union. In 1948, he began traveling around the Gold Coast as leader of a youth movement calling for "self-government now."

Nkrumah's calls for positive action civil disobedience as head of the Convention People's Party led to his arrest, and he was sentenced to three years in jail. While in prison, he won the general election, and five years later, in 1957, he became prime minister of the newly independent Ghana.

Nkrumah's popularity rose with the construction of new schools, roads, and health facilities, but by 1964 Ghana was a one-party state and Nkrumah its "life president." After two assassination attempts and increasing human-rights abuses, Nkrumah faced a coup in 1966 and went into exile in Guinea. He died of cancer in 1972.

WE'RE EYEBALL TO EYEBALL, AND I THINK THE OTHER FELLOW JUST BLINKED

THE CUBAN MISSILE CRISIS (1962)

IN CONTEXT

FOCUS
Nuclear arms race

BEFORE
1942–1945 The US sets up the Manhattan Project to develop the first nuclear weapon.

1945 The US drops atomic bombs on the Japanese cities of Hiroshima and Nagasaki, ending World War II.

1952–1953 Both the US and USSR develop the H-bomb, 1,000 times stronger than the atomic bomb.

AFTER
1963 The US and Russia agree to a nuclear test-ban treaty, and tensions lessen.

1969–1972 Strategic Arms Limitation Talks (SALT I) yield a superpower agreement on missile deployment.

1991 Strategic Arms Reductions Treaty I (START I) reduces the numbers of US and Soviet long-range missiles.

For 13 days, from October 15 to October 28, 1962, the world teetered on the edge of nuclear destruction. Soviet leader Nikita Khrushchev had deployed nuclear weapons in Cuba, and US president John F. Kennedy demanded he remove them. Each threatened nuclear war.

The USSR and US begin stockpiling **nuclear weapons**.

↓   ↓

The **theory of MAD** acts as a deterrent to nuclear war.

A **struggle develops** for the control of satellite states, including Cuba.

↓   ↓

Tension comes to a head in the Cuban Missile Crisis—nuclear war is only narrowly avoided.

↓

The **scale of the threat** posed by nuclear war becomes more apparent.

→

World leaders **engage in diplomacy** and reduce stockpiles; **tensions cool**.

This was no empty threat: from the 1950s, both superpowers had begun stockpiling vast nuclear arsenals. Strategists articulated the mutually assured destruction (MAD) doctrine, which held that if Russia attacked the West, the West would make sure that they retaliate. In short, there would be no winners.

When Kennedy became president in 1961, he inherited a deteriorating relationship with Cuba. The US and Cuba had a history of mutual cooperation, but this had changed with the Cuban Revolution, when, on January 1, 1959, Fidel Castro overthrew the government of President General Fulgencio Batista.

Trade embargo

The US accepted Castro as ruler of Cuba, in spite of his communist leanings, and had a large economic presence in Cuba. However, Castro began to break the American hold on the economy, nationalizing all industry without compensation. In response, the US imposed a sweeping trade embargo, so Castro turned to the Soviet Union for support. Fearing communist expansion, the US tried to topple Cuba's government with the failed Bay of Pigs invasion in April 1961, involving CIA-backed Cuban exiles.

Also in 1961, the US deployed 15 nuclear-tipped Jupiter missiles in Turkey, in readiness to strike against the USSR should the need arise. Turkey shared a border with the Soviet Union, so this was viewed as a direct threat to Soviet territory.

An ultimatum

Khrushchev came under pressure from Soviet hard-liners to take a tough stance. This, and the desire to defend his Cuban ally from American aggression, led him to install missiles in Cuba that were capable of carrying nuclear warheads. On October 14, 1962, photographs taken by a U-2 spy plane showed nuclear weapon sites being built by the Soviets. Kennedy's military advisers

Cuban president Fidel Castro and Soviet leader Nikita Khrushchev hold up their joined hands in a show of unity on an official state visit Castro made to Moscow in May 1963.

sought an immediate attack on the missile sites, but Kennedy favored a naval blockade of Cuba to prevent the installation of more missiles. He issued an ultimatum to Khrushchev to withdraw and informed the world that nuclear war was an imminent possibility. Meanwhile, Khrushchev ordered the captains of Soviet ships to hold their course for Cuban ports.

Breaking the deadlock

Frantic diplomacy behind the scenes led to a deal that broke the deadlock: Kennedy agreed to remove missiles from Turkey in secret if Khrushchev dismantled all nuclear weapons in Cuba. The Soviet leader agreed—only if America would also abort its plan to invade Cuba.

On October 28, Khrushchev ordered his ships to turn around—a defining moment of the Cold War. The superpowers became more cautious, and the threat of nuclear war began to diminish. ■

John Fitzgerald Kennedy

The 35th president of the US, John Fitzgerald Kennedy (1917–1963) was the first Roman Catholic and, at 43, the youngest man ever to be elected to that office. As president, Kennedy brought a fresh and youthful style to politics, calling his program the "New Frontier." This included a challenge to venture into outer space and to eliminate poverty. His administration quickly won popular support.

Kennedy's years in power were marked in foreign affairs by Cold War tension. His greatest test was the Cuban Missile Crisis of 1962, where his firm stance against Russia brought him even greater popularity.

His ambitious domestic reforms, however, on issues such as welfare and civil rights, were increasingly blocked by Congress.

While he was campaigning for the next presidential election, JFK was assassinated by Lee Harvey Oswald in Dallas, Texas, on November 22, 1963. Kennedy's death was a shock and a tragedy for Americans, at a time when tensions were just starting to ease between the United States and Russia.

PEOPLE OF THE WHOLE WORLD ARE POINTING TO THE SATELLITE

THE LAUNCH OF *SPUTNIK* (1957)

IN CONTEXT

FOCUS
Space race

BEFORE
1926 Robert Goddard launches the world's first liquid-fueled rocket.

1942 Germany successfully launches the first ballistic missile, the A4, or V-2.

AFTER
1961 Alan Shepard commands *Freedom 7* on the first Mercury mission, becoming the first American in space.

July 20, 1969 American Neil Armstrong becomes the first man to set foot on the moon.

1971 Russia's *Salyut 1*, the world's first space station, is launched.

1997 A US rover named Sojourner wheels on to the surface of Mars to explore the surface.

2015 *Mars Reconnaissance Orbiter* finds water on Mars.

 That's one small step for [a] man, one giant leap for mankind.
Neil Armstrong

Sputnik symbolized far more than a scientific breakthrough. It was a sensational coup for the Soviets during the Cold War with the West. No shots were fired, but the military and political ramifications were immense. Americans felt more vulnerable to a nuclear attack. The USSR was now a Superpower, stunning the US and initiating the "space race," a frantic competition between nations for technological superiority.

The US catches up

Sputnik was a mass-media event that ushered in the "Space Age," capturing the world's collective imagination. There was a boom in science-fiction books, films, and TV dramas set in space. By 1958, the US had created NASA, the National Aeronautics and Space Administration, but they could only watch in envy as the Soviets sent Yuri Gagarin into orbit in 1961, the first human to go to outer space.

The US caught up by sending John Glenn into orbit in 1962, and by 1967 they had built a rocket, *Saturn V*, that was powerful enough to reach the moon. In 1969, 12 years after the launch of *Sputnik 1*, the American astronaut Neil Armstrong left *Apollo 11* and became the first man to walk on the moon. ■

On October 4, 1957, the USSR launched the world's first artificial satellite, *Sputnik 1*. Carrying a simple radio transmitter to relay information about conditions in space, the satellite remained in orbit until January 4, 1958, when it reentered and burned up in Earth's atmosphere.

I HAVE A DREAM
THE MARCH ON WASHINGTON (1963)

IN CONTEXT

FOCUS
Civil rights movement

BEFORE
1909 National Association for the Advancement of Colored People (NAACP) is founded.

1955 Rosa Parks refuses to give up her bus seat to a white man and, in doing so, ignites the civil rights movement.

1960 Four students at a whites-only restaurant counter are refused food, leading to sit-ins across the US.

AFTER
1965 Malcolm X, founder of the Organization of Afro-American Unity, is shot dead.

1966 Stokely Carmichael introduces the idea of "Black Power," turning away from nonviolent protests.

1968 Martin Luther King, Jr., is assassinated, leading to rioting across US cities.

 There are those who say to you, we are rushing this issue of civil rights. I say we are 172 years too late!
Hubert Humphrey
Mayor of Minneapolis (1948)

One of the speakers was the Reverend Dr. Martin Luther King, Jr., who had been arrested that April during anti-segregation protests in Alabama. "I have a dream," King cried, starting his famous speech.

Calls for equality
The abolition of slavery after the American Civil War of 1861–1865 led to formerly enslaved people seeking American citizenship. However, while they were no longer enslaved, they were not equal with whites, and they endured discrimination, segregation, and violent racist attacks. In the 1950s, a number of African American groups fought back against discrimination with a policy of nonviolence. In the 1960s, civil rights marches in Birmingham, Alabama, led by King were central to the campaign. Some extremists, especially in the South, reacted with gruesome acts of violence.

After the March on Washington, US Congress passed the Civil Rights Acts of 1964, outlawing discrimination, and the Voting Rights Act of 1965. More than half a century later, however, many of the goals set on that day are still out of reach to black Americans. ∎

The March on Washington on August 28, 1963, brought roughly 250,000 people—mostly African Americans—to the nation's capital. They were calling for equality, an end to racial segregation, and for all Americans to have access to a good education, decent housing, and jobs that paid a living wage.

SCATTER THE OLD WORLD, BUILD THE NEW

THE CULTURAL REVOLUTION (1966)

IN CONTEXT

FOCUS
Maoism to capitalism

BEFORE
1943 Mao becomes Chairman of the Communist Party of China, which bolsters his image as a "strong leader."

1945–1949 A civil war between Communists and Nationalists ends with Mao's victory.

1958–1961 Millions die during Mao's Great Leap Forward, his attempt to modernize China.

AFTER
1972 US President Richard Nixon's trip to China paves the way for diplomatic relations between the two countries.

1978 Deng Xiaoping becomes new leader and starts economic reforms.

2015 The IMF ranks China as the world's largest economy, overtaking the United States.

Mao Zedong fixes on ambitious plans to **industrialize China**.

↓

In the **Great Leap Forward**, all Chinese society is **directed to this cause**.

↓

Famine strikes, and mass starvation ensues. **Tens of millions die**.

↓

Mao launches the Cultural Revolution.

↓

Mao's death marks a key turning point in China's post-war history.

↓

Deng Xiaoping's adoption of **capitalist ideas** allows China to move toward **superpower status**.

---

he Cultural Revolution was one of the darkest periods in Chinese history. Since taking power in 1949, Communist Party leader Mao Zedong had neither created his ideal China nor secured his power. To bolster his primacy and ignite revolutionary fervor, Mao decided to purge any opposition and transform capitalists and intellectuals into proletarians—ordinary workers. He ordered the Cultural Revolution, which would attack the "Four Olds": old ideas, old habits, old customs, and old culture. Squads of young communists, incited by Mao and known as the Red Guards, terrorized intellectuals, bureaucrats, and teachers.

Some 36 million people were persecuted, and up to a million died in the turmoil, which lasted until 1976.

The Great Leap Forward

After creating the Chinese People's Republic in 1949, Mao launched reforms to transform China's semi-feudal, mostly agricultural society into an industrialized socialist state. In the late 1950s, in a bid to achieve rapid economic growth, Mao ordered the Great Leap Forward. Industrial output climbed with steel and coal production, the rail network doubled, and more than half of all Chinese land was irrigated by 1961.

However, this development came at a terrible cost. Mao transformed rural China into a series of farming communes in which villagers pooled land, animals, tools, and crops. The authorities took vast amounts of grain from the communes to feed city workers, and this, along with a series of natural disasters, led to famine and starvation. The consequences were staggering: an estimated 45 million people died.

A new foreign policy

After the Cultural Revolution, Mao needed American expertise to restore China, and the US wanted an ally against the Soviet Union. In 1972, US President Richard Nixon traveled to Peking to meet with Mao. By the time Mao died in 1976, China had become a major oil producer with nuclear capabilities.

Deng Xiaoping, who led China from 1978 to 1997, was willing to use capitalist ideas to focus on economic growth. But while he initiated new and far-reaching measures, such as inviting foreign firms to invest in Chinese industry and supporting developing technologies, he also resisted pressure to make democratic reforms.

By the beginning of the new millennium, China's economic growth was spectacular. In 2001, the country was admitted to the World Trade Organization, and in 2008 it played host to the Olympic Games in Beijing. Some economists predict that by 2026 China will boast a gross domestic product (GDP) greater than Japan and Western Europe.

After Mao's death, the Chinese Communist Party condemned the Cultural Revolution as a disaster. However, as the country experienced a period of unparalleled economic growth, a sense of nostalgia for Mao's ideals, focused on the people and self-sufficiency, grew among farmers and members of the urban working class. Today, Mao's legacy continues to cast a long shadow over a modernizing China. ∎

Mao Zedong

Born in 1893 into a wealthy farming family from Hunan Province, Mao Zedong was the leader of Communist China from 1949 until his death in 1976. While working as a librarian at Peking University, he became a communist and helped found the Communist Party in 1921. Six years later, after leading an unsuccessful rebellion against nationalist leader Chiang Kai-shek, Mao was forced to retreat to the countryside, where he proclaimed the Chinese Soviet Republic in 1931. He took control of the Communist Party in 1935, after proving his leadership during the Long March, and defeated Chiang during the civil war of 1945–1949.

A devoted Leninist, Mao became disenchanted with the Soviet policy of "peaceful coexistence" toward the West and developed Maoism, a stronger form of communism. However, his radical ideas and experiments with collectivization led to the death and suffering of millions. One of his last acts, in 1972, was to hold a meeting with Richard Nixon, the first American president ever to visit China.

WE SHALL DEFEND IT WITH OUR BLOOD AND STRENGTH, AND WE SHALL MEET AGGRESSION WITH AGGRESSION AND EVIL WITH EVIL
THE SUEZ CRISIS (1956)

IN CONTEXT

FOCUS
Modern Middle East

BEFORE
1945 Egypt, Iraq, Lebanon, Syria, Saudi Arabia, northern Yemen, and Transjordan form the Arab League.

1948 Israel is established in former Palestine, dividing Arabs and Jews.

1952 A military coup removes Egypt's King Farouk from power. Colonel Gamal Nasser seizes control two years later.

AFTER
1964 The Palestine Liberation Organization calls for an end to the Jewish state.

1993 The Oslo Accords provide for mutual recognition between the PLO and Israel.

2011 Protesters across Arab states demand reforms in a series of popular uprisings.

President Nasser of Egypt announces the nationalization of the Suez Canal to a quarter-million-strong gathering in Alexandria celebrating four years since the revolution.

O n July 26, 1956, Egyptian leader, Colonel Gamal Abdel Nasser, addressed a crowd in the city of Alexandria, declaring the nationalization of the Suez Canal, the waterway through which most oil bound for Western Europe had to pass. For Egyptians, the nationalization symbolized the liberation of their country from the British imperialist dominance it had been under since the 1880s. In response to Nasser's bold move, a secret plan was hatched by Britain, France, and Israel. France was eager for Nasser's downfall because of his support for Algerian insurgents against French colonial rule in Algeria. Israel had many reasons for toppling Nasser, including Egypt's denial of passage through the canal to any Israeli-flagged ships. The three conspired that Israel would attack Egypt, and Britain and France would intervene a few days later posing as peacemakers, taking control of the canal. On October 29, 1956, the Israelis began their assault. British and French troops invaded on October 31, but faced immediate diplomatic pressure to call a ceasefire. The United States, which was trying to cultivate good relations with Arab states, was appalled by the Anglo-French invasion, believing it threatened the stability of the whole region. President Dwight Eisenhower forced through

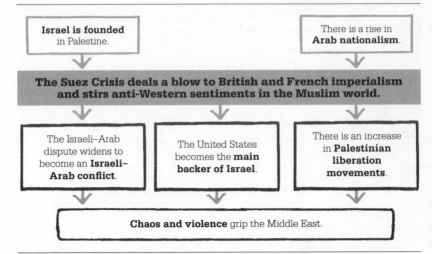

Israel is founded in Palestine.

There is a rise in **Arab nationalism**.

The Suez Crisis deals a blow to British and French imperialism and stirs anti-Western sentiments in the Muslim world.

The Israeli–Arab dispute widens to become an **Israeli–Arab conflict**.

The United States becomes the **main backer of Israel**.

There is an increase in **Palestinian liberation movements**.

Chaos and violence grip the Middle East.

a United Nations resolution imposing a ceasefire, and British and French troops had to conduct a humiliating withdrawal.

Splitting the land

The strong anti-Western sentiment in the Middle East dates back hundreds of years, fueled by the West's increased involvement in the region. Colonialism in the 1800s and the division of the Ottoman Empire after World War I were bitter humiliations for peoples who felt their religion, Islam, was the highest form of divine revelation. In 1948, the partition of Palestine to form Israel split the land into two states, one Arab and one Jewish, and was rejected vehemently by Israeli Arabs and enraged the other Arab nations. The regular armies of the Arab states—including Iraq, Lebanon, Syria, Transjordan, and Egypt—attacked Israel in the first Arab–Israeli War in May and June 1948. The conflict ended in defeat for the Arabs and disaster for the Palestinians: more than half of the country's Arabs were uprooted as refugees, and they lost any possibility of a state of their own.

Ambitious plans

Egypt continued its stance of belligerence toward Israel by closing the Suez Canal to Israeli shipping. When Nasser ousted the regime of King Farouk in 1952 and sent him into exile, he imported arms from the Soviet Union to build his arsenal for future confrontations with Israel. Britain had agreed to withdraw its troops from the Suez area by June 1856, but as the last troops left Egypt, Nasser relied on funds from Britain and the US to fund ambitious plans to develop Egypt. This included the Aswan Dam project on the Nile. Nasser was angered when Britain and the United States withdrew their offer of loans to help him pay for the dam. The US and Britain backed out because of Nasser's association with the Soviets and his unceasing diatribes against the West. Nasser felt insulted and immediately nationalized the Suez Canal. The move was popular in Egypt, as the canal was a source of Arab pride.

Nasser was a secular modernizer who advocated the separation of religion from political life, believing it the hallmark of Arab modernity, but this was not universally welcomed. The Muslim Brotherhood, founded in Egypt in 1928, argued for Islam to have a central role in government. After repeated calls for the application of Sharia law—a legal system based on Islam—and an assassination attempt against Nasser, the organization was finally banned in 1954.

In 1967, Arab countries suffered a crushing defeat at the hands of Israel in the Six Day War, in which Israel took the Sinai from Egypt, the Golan Heights from Syria, and the West Bank and East Jerusalem »

US President Jimmy Carter (center) looks on as President Anwar Sadat of Egypt shakes hands with Menachem Begin, Israel's premier, after signing a peace treaty at the White House in 1979.

from Jordan, meaning Israel was now an occupier. In the 1970s and '80s, the Arab–Israeli conflict largely moved in the direction of peace: in 1979 the Israeli–Egypt peace deal ended 30 years of war. The rise of the Palestine Liberation Army (PLO) and of other Palestinian groups attacking Israel, however, as well as Israel's invasion of Lebanon in 1982, where many of the PLO were grouped, destabilized the fragile peace continuously.

The Iran–Iraq War

Like many countries in the Middle East, modern Iraq was carved out of the ruins of the Ottoman Empire in the aftermath of World War I. Iraq was a land divided along ethnic lines between Arabs and Kurds, as well as sectarian lines between Sunni and Shia Muslims, the latter being the majority group. Saddam Hussein, a Sunni, became leader in 1979, and suppressed ethnic Kurds and Shias alike using immense brutality. He, like Nasser in Egypt, espoused Arab nationalism and ruled Iraq as a secular state.

In 1979, events in Iran inspired Islamists throughout the Middle East. The secular, Western way of life was swept away in an Islamic revolution in which the US-backed Shah was ousted. The new regime, under Ayatollah Khomeini, a Shia Muslim, based its laws and ideology on the strict teachings of the Quran. Saddam felt threatened by the Islamic revolution and a possible Shia uprising in his own country, so he invaded Iran on September 22, 1980, under the pretext of a territorial dispute over the Shatt al-Arab, a waterway that lies between the two countries.

The invasion triggered a bruising eight-year war that devastated both countries and increased tensions in the Middle East. Iran's principal ally was Syria, but Libya, China, and North Korea all also sent it weapons. Iraq's support came mostly from the Arab Gulf states, which viewed Iran as the greater danger to their security; Saudi Arabia and Kuwait provided billions of dollars in loans. Ultimately, there were no victors; and Iraq, now awash with armaments supplied by several Western nations, including Britain, France, and the United States, invaded the oil-rich state of Kuwait in 1990. The UN demanded their withdrawal, but Saddam announced that Kuwait had been annexed by Iraq. The United States, with support from coalition forces, sent in troops during the First Gulf War (1990–1991) and freed Kuwait.

The 9/11 attacks

The continued US support of Israel led to profound grievances among Islamists. To them, the capitalist, secular US, with its greed for oil, symbolized all that was wrong with the West, and terrorist strikes on US targets grew. Al-Qaeda carried out the most shocking on September 11, 2001, against four targets in the United States, including the World Trade Center in New York City.

In response to the 9/11 attacks, a successful US-led international intervention brought down the Taliban regime in Afghanistan, which the US believed had given sanctuary to Osama bin Laden and al-Qaeda. After September 11, President Bush declared a "War on Terror" and, in 2002, with help from the British government, attacked Iraq on the premise of destroying "weapons of mass destruction" (WMDs) deemed a threat to national security.

During the First Gulf War, Iraqi forces set fire to more than 600 Kuwaiti oil wells. Saddam Hussein's desire to control Kuwaiti oilfields had initially led to Iraq invading Kuwait in 1990.

Western intervention in the Muslim world heightened the belief among Islamists that the West was the enemy of Islam.

The Arab Spring

The 9/11 attacks were inspired by a radical ideology and belief that the fundamental problems plaguing Arab and Muslim people could be resolved by attacking foreign powers that were seen to oppress Islam. In 2011, young Arabs—looking inward to promote change and blaming their own leaders for decades of political, economic, and cultural decline—were at the heart of uprisings across the Arab world. At its core, what became known as the Arab Spring was a new generation's attempt to change the state order. An extraordinary series of pro-democracy uprisings, the Arab Spring caused huge upheavals in the Middle East and North Africa. It started in Tunisia on December 17, 2010, when a street vendor set himself on fire in a protest against police brutality. Protesters throughout Tunisia demanded democracy, and President Zine el Abidine fled the country on January 14. Disorder spread from Tunisia to Algeria, where there was unrest over lack of jobs.

On January 25, thousands of protesters took to the streets in Egypt, and after 18 days of protests there, President Hosni Mubarak resigned. By mid-February, civil unrest had swept through Bahrain, where it was brutally suppressed, and into Libya. Muammar Gaddhafi's violent response to the dissidents led to civil war. An international coalition led by NATO launched a campaign of air strikes targeting Gaddhafi's forces, and he was killed in October 2011.

Further uprisings occurred in Jordan, Yemen, and Saudi Arabia, but the worst violence against civilians was seen in Syria, where President Bashar Assad promised reforms but used force to crush the dissent—a move that merely hardened the protesters' resolve. In July 2011, hundreds of thousands of people took to the streets, and the country descended into civil war. By August 2015, the United Nations reported that more than 210,000 people had been killed in the conflict. Capitalizing on the chaos in the region, so-called Islamic State (also referred to as IS, ISIS, or ISIL), the extremist Muslim group born from a fringe of al-Qaeda, took control of huge swathes of territory across northern and eastern Syria, as well as neighboring Iraq.

Middle East instability

The Suez Crisis was the end of one era in the politics of the Middle East and the start of another. It marked the humiliating end of imperial influence for two European countries, Britain and France, whose role was soon taken over by the US. It stimulated Arab nationalism and opened an era of Arab-Israeli wars and Palestinian terrorism.

In modern times, the Middle East has never seemed so unstable. Wars are being fought over religion, ethnicity, territory, politics, and commerce, and these conflicts have led to the worst refugee crisis since World War II, with millions fleeing anarchy and fanaticism. ∎

Terrorism in the Middle East

Since the mid-20th century, terrorism has been synonymous with the Middle East. The Israel–Palestine conflict is one of the world's most challenging.

In 1964, Arab leaders formed the Palestine Liberation Organization (PLO), declaring Israel's establishment illegal. The PLO used terrorism to attack Israel and Western targets for their support of Israel. In 1970, Palestinian militants blew up three hijacked planes in the Jordanian desert, and in 1972 a group linked to the PLO hit the Israeli Olympic team during the games in Munich, Germany.

In 1983, Hezbollah, an Iran-backed fundamentalist Shiite Muslim group in Lebanon, blew up the Beirut barracks of both US Marine and French forces, killing 298 people. Hezbollah pioneered the use of suicide bombers in the Middle East.

Both Jews and Muslims have employed terrorism to derail the many attempts that have been made at peace in the region.

THE IRON CURTAIN IS SWEPT ASIDE

THE FALL OF THE BERLIN WALL (1989)

IN CONTEXT

FOCUS
Collapse of communism

BEFORE
August 1989 After 45 years, Poland sees the end of communist rule. Solidarity, a trade union, forms a new non-communist government.

August 23, 1989 Two million people form a human chain across Estonia, Lithuania, and Latvia in protest at Soviet rule.

September 11, 1989 Hungary opens its border with Austria to allow the departure of East German refugees.

AFTER
December 3, 1989 The US and USSR jointly declare that the Cold War has ended.

October 3, 1990 Germany is reunified.

December 1991 The Soviet Union disintegrates into 15 separate states.

For decades, the Berlin Wall, which separated East and West Berlin, stood as a reminder of the Cold War, the bitter division between Soviet communism and Western capitalism. On November 9, 1989, the East German government lifted travel restrictions, and thousands of people began converging at the wall. East German border guards yielded in the face of ecstatic crowds. On November 10, in extraordinary scenes, soldiers from both sides helped Berliners break through the wall. Over the next two days, more than 3 million people crossed the border.

Ruling the Eastern Bloc
At the end of World War II, the USSR had banned anti-communist parties in every Eastern European country, and created a bloc of satellite states under Soviet leadership, ruthlessly suppressing any opposition. In the fall of 1956, Hungary rose against its communist government, only to be crushed by Soviet tanks, and in 1968, the USSR invaded Czechoslovakia to remove a government it found too liberal.

In the 1960s, Germany was still divided between East and West, and its former capital Berlin split into the Allied-operated West and the Soviet-controlled East. Each had its own German administration: democratic in the West, communist in the East. Thousands of East Germans escaped to the West, and the country hemorrhaged its skilled workers. On August 13, 1961, the government sealed off East from West Berlin with a fence, which, over time, became a heavily fortified barrier dividing the city, the nation, and family and friends.

In 1985, Mikhail Gorbachev was appointed as General Secretary of the Soviet Communist Party. Aiming for warmer relations with the West, he set out new reforms: *glasnost* (political "openness") and *perestroika* (liberal

Gorbachev is elected president of the USSR. He introduces **radical political and economic reforms**.

This process of democratization **reduces Cold War tensions**.

Gorbachev has no intention of using **military force** to prop up satellite communist regimes.

Uprisings take place across Eastern Europe, and **communist regimes** are ousted.

The Berlin Wall is dismantled, followed soon after by the collapse of the Soviet Union.

economic "restructuring"). Critically, he lifted the ban on Eastern Bloc countries reforming their political systems.

Collapse of communism

With the threat of Soviet military intervention removed, citizens in all Eastern Bloc countries protested to end communist rule. In June 1989, Poland's Solidarity, originally a banned trade union, was elected to lead a coalition government. As the push for reform gathered pace, the East German government declared that its citizens would be able to visit West Berlin through any border crossing, including the Berlin Wall.

The fall of the Berlin Wall was a momentous event. It marked an era that saw the end of the Cold War and the dissolution of the Soviet Union. It allowed millions to travel more freely, and previously stifled economies across Eastern Europe and the Former Soviet Union opened up to the world. Many former communist countries were welcomed into NATO and joined the European Union.

The world changed course in 1989. Communism was dead in the East, and a reunified Germany was about to take its place at the heart of Europe. ■

The breakup of the Soviet Union

In 1985, Mikhail Gorbachev became leader of a stagnating Soviet Union. He laid out radical reforms—*glasnost* and *perestroika*—and in July 1989 he announced that countries within the Warsaw Pact could hold openly contested elections. Poles, Czechs, Hungarians, and others opted for democratic governments, destabilizing the Soviet Union itself.

In July 1991, the anti-communist Boris Yeltsin was elected president of Russia. A month later, with Gorbachev weakened by an attempted coup by hard-line communists, Yeltsin took advantage. He banned the Communist Party in Russia and met secretly with the leaders of Ukraine and Belarus, who agreed to secede from the Soviet Union. On Christmas Day 1991, Gorbachev resigned, leaving Yeltsin as president of the new Russian state. The former empire split into 15 new independent states, and the USSR was no more.

CREATE AN UNBEARABLE SITUATION OF TOTAL INSECURITY WITH NO HOPE OF FURTHER SURVIVAL OR LIFE
THE SIEGE OF SARAJEVO (1992–1996)

IN CONTEXT

FOCUS
Conflicts since the collapse of the USSR

BEFORE
November 9, 1989 The Berlin Wall collapses, leading to the reunification of Germany.

1989 Romania overthrows the ruthless regime of Nicolae Ceaușescu.

1990 In Poland, Hungary, and Czechoslovakia, newly formed center-right parties take power.

1992–1995 The war in Bosnia-Herzegovina results in the death of some 100,000 people.

AFTER
1998–1999 War breaks out in Kosovo between ethnic Albanians and ethnic Serbs. NATO troops intervene.

2014 Fighting erupts between Russians and Ukrainians in eastern Ukraine.

T he Siege of Sarajevo, Bosnia, was one of the most appalling tragedies in Yugoslavia's civil war (1991–2002). During the 44-month siege, the city's food and electricity supplies were cut off, and the civilian population was bombarded by nationalist Bosnian Serbs. Thousands of Bosnian Muslims were targeted and murdered.

A new wave of nationalism
Yugoslavia was comprised of six socialist republics: Croatia, Montenegro, Slovenia, Bosnia and Herzegovina, Macedonia, and Serbia, each with its own prime minister and constitution. Overall power in Yugoslavia was held by a president, notably communist leader Josip Broz Tito from 1953 to 1980.

After the 1991 breakup of the Soviet Union, a nationalist revival swept Eastern Europe. Croatia and Slovenia's call for independence was opposed by Serbia, and Vukovar, in eastern Croatia, was destroyed by the Yugoslav army under Serbian leader Slobodan Milosevic. When Bosnia also declared independence in 1992, the violence intensified. Bosnian Serbs aimed to create a separate, ethnically pure Serbian state, the Republika Srpska, carving it from the new Republic of Bosnia-Herzegovina. Nationalist Bosnian Serbs, supported by neighboring Serbia, launched a campaign to expel non-Serbs, and during the Siege of Sarajevo, they targeted the majority Bosnian Muslim population.

The Bosnian War ended in 1995, but fighting continued in Kosovo, where ethnic Albanians began a separatist movement against the Serbs. Ethnically based nationalism also led to bloody anti-Armenian pogroms in the Nagorno-Karabakh region and in Baku, the capital of Azerbaijan. In Georgia, violence erupted between the Georgian and Abkhazian population.

The wars in Yugoslavia forced the issue of the global community's responsibility to resolve disputes that threaten wider instability or cause unacceptable human suffering or rights violations. ■

TODAY, OUR FELLOW CITIZENS, OUR WAY OF LIFE, OUR VERY FREEDOM CAME UNDER ATTACK
THE 9/11 ATTACKS (2001)

IN CONTEXT

FOCUS
Rise of Islamic radicalism

BEFORE
1979 The Islamic Revolution of Iran replaces the pro-Western shah with Shia Muslim cleric Ayatollah Khomeini.

1989 As Soviet troops leave Afghanistan, Saudi millionaire Osama bin Laden forms al-Qaeda to fight a new *jihad* (struggle).

February 26, 1993 Al-Qaeda makes its ambitions clear with an audacious attack on the World Trade Center, New York.

AFTER
2004 Al-Qaeda urges Sunni Muslims to rise up against US forces in Iraq. Bombings by Islamic extremists in Madrid, Spain, kill 190 people.

February 2014 Terrorist group ISIS aims to create an Islamic caliphate that covers Iraq and Syria and spreads its influence worldwide.

On September 11, 2001, a group of Islamic extremists launched a devastating attack against the US. Two hijacked airliners crashed into the World Trade Center in New York; another hit the Pentagon, in Washington, D.C.; and a fourth plane crashed in Pennsylvania. Almost 3,000 people were killed.

 We love death more than you love life.
al-Qaeda motto

The seeds of extremism

September 11 was not the first terror attack on American soil by Islamic extremists. On February 26, 1993, a bomb was detonated at the World Trade Center by men thought to have links to al-Qaeda, a militant Islamist organization. Some Muslims had been radicalized and adopted international terrorism during the struggles over Israel. In 1979, the Soviet invasion of Afghanistan led to the worldwide mobilization of Muslim militants to fight the invaders. Around that time, Osama Bin Laden formed al-Qaeda. Intelligence reports suggested that he was the mastermind behind September 11. He was killed in 2011.

The civil war in Syria since 2011 and the power vacuum left by the departure of US forces in Iraq has led to the emergence of ISIS, the so-called Islamic State of Iraq and Syria, which has taken control of several towns in the region.

The events of September 11 mark the largest terrorist attack ever on US soil. Subsequent attacks in London, Madrid, and Paris, carried out by a diffuse network of regional terrorist groups, have added a chilling dimension to the threat of Islamic terrorism. ∎

YOU AFFECT THE WORLD BY WHAT YOU BROWSE
THE LAUNCH OF THE FIRST WEBSITE (1991)

IN CONTEXT

FOCUS
Communication and computing

BEFORE
1943–1944 John Mauchly and
J. Presper Eckert build the
Electronic Numerical Integrator
and Calculator (ENIAC), the forebear
of digital computers.

1947 The transistor allows for small,
powerful electronics, enabling later
developments such as home computers.

1962 The Telstar 1 satellite is
launched, sending TV signals,
telephone calls, and fax images
through space.

1980s The first mobile phones
come onto the market.

AFTER
2000s The boom in wireless
communication connects nearly
all of humankind.

2003 The invention of Skype allows for
free communication over the Internet.

The US military sets up
the **Advanced Research Projects
Agency Network** (ARPANET).

↓

The **ARPANET** grows
and develops to become
the Internet.

↓

**The first website is launched to
help users navigate the Internet.**

↓

The Web becomes a **global
telecommunications
tool** used by millions.

↓

The Internet radically changes how
the world **shares information
and conducts business**.

T
he first website was titled
"World Wide Web" and gave
basic information about the World
Wide Web project and how to create Web
pages. It was built by Tim Berners-Lee, a
British computer scientist at the European
Organization for Nuclear Research
(CERN) in Geneva, Switzerland.

Berners-Lee was interested in facilitating
the exchange of ideas between scientists
in universities and research institutes, and
he first proposed his idea for a worldwide
network of computers sharing information
in 1989. His site went live in 1991 and was
accessed by a small group of fellow CERN
researchers. Crucially, Berners-Lee persuaded
CERN that the World Wide Web should be
given to the world as a free resource.

Although it revolutionized the computer and communications world like nothing before, the World Wide Web was only possible by bringing together several existing technologies: the telephone, television, radio, and Internet.

The Internet

The Soviet Union's launch of the *Sputnik 1* satellite in 1957 spurred the US Defense Department to consider means of communication after a nuclear attack. This led to the formation of the ARPANET (Advanced Research Projects Agency Network) in 1969, a system initially of four computers. In the mid-1980s, this growing network of interconnected computers became known as the Internet. Both the Internet and the World Wide Web were limited to academic and research organizations.

It wasn't until the 1993 launch of a user-friendly Web browser called Mosaic that the Web took off for more general use. Mosaic could show pictures as well as text, and users could follow Web links simply by clicking on them with a mouse. The Web became synonymous with the Internet, but they are distinct from one another. The World Wide Web facilitated navigation of the Internet and helped make the Internet such an effective mode of communication.

The computing revolution

The introduction in 1981 of IBM's 5150 personal computer drove a revolution in home and office computing. Smaller and cheaper than the large office computers, it and its successors had access to the Internet and email. With personal computers, the Internet saw huge growth. The first search engines began to appear in the early 1990s; Google, which is now almost synonymous with Web searches, arrived a little later, in 1997. The launch of online marketplace Amazon in 1994 revolutionized the way people shopped, allowing the purchase of everything from books and CDs to hotel rooms and airline tickets from the comfort of home.

The Internet brought about significant changes to the way businesses operated; globalization escalated, and the world

Sir Tim Berners-Lee, creator of the World Wide Web, was fascinated by computers from a young age. Today, he is an advocate for an open and free Internet.

seemed to become a much smaller place, with communication improved by the speed and efficiency of the Internet. Jobs were outsourced, and companies effectively became "nationless," since it was easier to operate from anywhere in the world.

The next wave of technological advances saw devices become smaller and more mobile due to electronic components on tiny integrated circuits, or "chips."

The future is now

Nowhere has the introduction of microchip technology had more impact than the introduction of the Apple iPhone in 2007. So-called smartphones have made the Internet a mobile resource, with wireless connectivity offering on-the-go access to news and satellite navigation, for example. Information and ideas can be shared from anywhere at the touch of a button via social-networking sites such as Facebook and Twitter. Smartphones have also had an impact on education, health care, and culture, and have changed the political landscape through use by protesters organizing rallies via social media to undermine regimes. Uprisings such as the Arab Spring, which began in 2010, were partly powered by activists who communicated across the Internet. Internet activism, or "clicktivism," has since become a powerful way to share ideas, raise awareness, or support a cause. With more than 3 billion users, the World Wide Web has transformed every aspect of modern daily life. ∎

194

A CRISIS WHICH BEGAN IN THE MORTGAGE MARKETS OF AMERICA HAS BROUGHT THE WORLD'S FINANCIAL SYSTEM CLOSE TO COLLAPSE
THE GLOBAL FINANCIAL CRISIS (2008)

IN CONTEXT

FOCUS
Globalization and inequality

BEFORE
1929 The Wall Street Crash leads to the Great Depression, the worst economic crisis of the 20th century.

1944 Delegates of 44 countries meet at Bretton Woods, New Hampshire, to reshape the global financial system.

1975 France, Italy, Germany, Japan, Britain, and the US form the Group of Six (G6) to foster international trade.

1997–1998 The Asian financial crisis, starting in Indonesia and spreading around the world, is a precursor to events in 2008.

AFTER
2015 World leaders pledge to eradicate world poverty by 2030.

Many countries enjoy historically **low interest rates**.

↓

Subprime mortgages in the US are considered a **safe investment**.

↓

Complex financial instruments mask **debt levels** incurred by banks.

↓

Mortgage defaults soar. Banks and financial institutions risk **collapse**.

↓

The interlinking of financial markets leads to a global crisis.

↓

The world is plunged into the **worst recession** since the **Great Depression**.

The turn of the 21st century brought troubling signs of a worldwide recession. Low interest rates and unregulated credit had induced more and more people to get into unsustainable debts. Bankers, particularly in the US, offered mortgages to customers with a poor credit history. These mortgages were called "subprime mortgages." It was hoped that if people could not keep up with their mortgage payments, their houses could be repossessed and sold at a profit, but this depended on house prices rising. In 2007, interest rates crept up, and house prices fell. People began defaulting on their monthly repayments. Across the US, houses were repossessed at a great loss, with bankers fearing they would not get their money back.

The crisis spreads to Europe
In August 2007, the French bank Paribas revealed that it was at risk from the subprime mortgage market.

Bankers had gambled with trillions of dollars of investment on risky mortgages that might now be worthless. Panic set in, and banks stopped lending to one another. British bank Northern Rock faced a shortage of readily available cash, and was forced to ask the British government for an emergency loan.

Around the world, shares began to plummet. In September 2008, US mortgage lenders Fannie Mae and Freddie Mac were rescued by the American government, while Lehman Brothers, a powerful investment bank heavily involved in the subprime mortgages market, was forced to file for bankruptcy. The US government considered Lehman Brothers too insolvent and did not bail it out.

The turmoil in financial markets led to a severe economic downturn in most Western economies. Share prices plummeted, and world trade decreased because governments spent less. Ireland became the first European country to fall into recession, a period of economic decline. Iceland's government resigned in October 2008 after the country became almost bankrupt. Some governments—such as those in the US, China, Brazil, and Argentina—planned stimulus packages to boost their economies. They increased government spending and decreased taxes. Others, especially in Europe, opted for austerity, freezing public spending, and increasing taxes. Protests and strikes swept through Europe in response to these measures. Portugal, Spain, and Greece came under pressure from the European Union (EU) to lower their debts. The EU spent billions propping up weak economies in an attempt to keep the Eurozone, and the euro, viable. But the effect of the economic crisis was devastating, and many people lost their homes and jobs. It was the worst economic downturn since World War II.

Post-war economy

After World War II, most of Europe, Japan, China, and the Soviet Union, all devastated by war, needed time to recover. The US, which had experienced a huge rise in manufacturing for the war effort and was spared destruction, continued manufacturing at higher levels than ever before and dominated the world economy. »

Lehman Brothers, an investment bank with a long history of trading, filed for bankruptcy on September 15, 2008, after getting involved in the failing subprime mortgage market.

The oil crisis that struck Western countries in 1973–1974 was the result of the Yom Kippur War. Fuel rationing in the US led to scenes such as this, with motorists getting stranded.

The post-war economic planners sought a new economic order based on industrial strength and a stable dollar. In 1944, the International Monetary Fund (IMF) was formed to foster the revival of global trade. The US's strong post-war economy and the Marshall Plan of 1947, a US-led initiative to aid Western countries, invigorated world trade through encouraging capitalism and the free exchange of goods between nations. Signed in 1947, the General Agreement on Tariffs and Trade (GATT) dictated that tariffs be removed to open up markets around the world.

The Asian tiger

Japan, meanwhile, saw massive economic growth. The Japanese government implemented reforms based on efficiency and restricted foreign imports. They did not sign up to the GATT agreement until 1955. Japan invested in its coal and steel industries, as well as shipbuilding and car manufacturing. In the 1960s, Japan specialized in high-tech products such as cameras and computer chips. Countries such as South Korea, Taiwan, Singapore, and Malaysia experienced similar growth with an emphasis on electronics and technology. These successes became collectively known as "Asian tiger economics."

The role of oil

By the 1970s, the world was divided between rich industrial countries and poor developing nations, and oil had become increasingly important. In 1960, the Organization of Arab Petroleum Exporting Countries (OAPEC), including Saudi Arabia, Egypt, Iraq, and Iran, was founded. As oil reserves in other countries dwindled, the states around the Persian Gulf, where this resource had remained plentiful, became dominant. In October 1973, when Egypt and Syria invaded Israel during the Yom Kippur War, OAPEC embargoed oil to any country helping Israel, and prices tripled. Without oil, industrial output dropped. The United States introduced strict fuel rationing, which ended in March 1974, when the oil embargo was lifted.

A new economic model

The oil crisis in the mid-1970s led to a deep global recession, soaring inflation, and high unemployment. In response, a new "neo-liberal" economic policy was adopted, transferring control of economic factors from the public to the private sector. Welfare programs were perceived to be one cause of economic failures, and there were drastic cutbacks. Deregulation became the driving force behind world economics, sweeping away many governmental controls and freeing up organizations to trade across a wider range of territories. The need for this was particularly felt in the United States, which faced stiff competition from a world now fully rebuilt from the destruction of World War II. Some of the rigid laws and regulations that had been put in place to protect consumers were now considered to be interfering with free enterprise.

The global push for deregulation resulted in the adoption of new markets, greater competition, and openness, especially as the world adapted to the end of the Cold War and the collapse of the Soviet Union. The example set in east Asia influenced policy makers in other Asian countries, such as India and China. Mexico and Brazil lowered their barriers to trade and embarked on economic reform, leading to a dramatic improvement in living standards. As East and West Germany reunited in 1989, after the fall of the Berlin Wall, the European Union (EU), an economic union of 28 European countries, emerged as a major force in the world economy. Also in the 1980s, China opened up to foreign trade, and huge sums of foreign investment poured in, leading to extraordinary growth.

Global economy

The world economy is now far more open. Internet use allows people to order goods in one part of the world and have them delivered elsewhere within a matter of days. World trade is made up of global partnerships, with multinational companies that boast huge turnovers. Across the globe, people tend to migrate to cities to find work, resulting in an increase in urbanization.

One complaint that is often aimed at globalization is that some companies exploit cheap labor and behave unethically in their bid for profit. Another is that globalization has contributed to the extraordinary accumulation of wealth by a few individuals and, thus, increased inequality. Some countries have also remained extremely poor—areas of sub-Saharan Africa, for example have fared badly and been left behind, in debt to wealthier nations.

Economic recessions have occurred throughout history, but the financial crisis of 2008–2011 was the worst—at least since

 September and October of 2008 was the worst financial crisis in global history, including the Great Depression.
Ben Bernanke
Former head of the Federal Reserve

the Great Depression of 1929—and maybe the worst ever. Many felt it was an avoidable disaster caused by widespread failures in government regulation and heedless risk-taking by investment bankers. Only massive monetary and fiscal stimuli prevented catastrophe. Household and business debts remained high, and there was widespread fury directed at bankers, whom many felt had survived relatively unscathed. Austerity measures provoked civil unrest. Demonstrations were held against capitalism; the Occupy Movement spread, with tens of thousands marching in New York, London, Frankfurt, Madrid, Rome, Sydney, and Hong Kong. While financiers argued over the causes of the Global Recession, the impact on the lives of ordinary people had profound, lasting consequences. ∎

An era of protest

The global economic crisis that began in 2008 generated much anger at institutional symbols of power and greed, and there was an upsurge of popular protest. Demonstrations united those venting at bankers and capitalists, anti-globalization protesters, and environmentalists. There was growing anger at the level of inequality, corporate greed, and the lack of jobs.

When the G20, an international forum for finance ministers, met in the financial heart of London in 2009, they were faced with thousands of angry protesters. Social media became critical in the organization of large gatherings and the occupation of physical spaces. As protests spread throughout Europe, they used the banner of "Occupy," a movement set up in New York to protest against social and economic inequality. There were riots in Rome, strikes in Greece, demonstrations in Portugal, and occupations in the public squares of

Barcelona, Moscow, Madrid, New York, Chicago, and Istanbul.

People took to the streets to protest against the actions of banks and multinationals, which were seen as the trigger of the financial crisis.

INDEX

Numbers in **bold** refer to main entries, those in *italics* refer to the captions to illustrations.

H

I

N